International Series on Consumer Science

Series Editor:
Jing Jian Xiao
University of Rhode Island

More information about this series at http://www.springer.com/series/8358

Jing Jian Xiao

Consumer Economic Wellbeing

Springer

Jing Jian Xiao
University of Rhode Island
Kingston, RI, USA

ISSN 2191-5660 ISSN 2191-5679 (electronic)
International Series on Consumer Science
ISBN 978-1-4939-2820-0 ISBN 978-1-4939-2821-7 (eBook)
DOI 10.1007/978-1-4939-2821-7

Library of Congress Control Number: 2015939893

Springer New York Heidelberg Dordrecht London

Printed on acid-free paper

Springer Science+Business Media LLC New York is part of Springer Science+Business Media (www.springer.com)

Preface

This book is about important issues relevant to consumer economics, specifically about how to help consumers improve economic wellbeing. Motivations for writing this book are from my teaching. I have been teaching consumer economics courses at the University of Rhode Island for many years. I used several consumer economics textbooks before. These books are rich in contents about current consumer issues but lack theoretical depths. I was looking for a book with more specific details on relevant consumer economic theories and research findings. In May 2008, I was invited to teach a Ph.D. seminar course on consumer economics at Renmin University of China in Beijing. Since then, I returned to teach the course once a year for several times. I used journal papers as teaching materials. Many Ph.D. students asked if there is a book that systematically presents the content of consumer economics. I searched the textbook market and could not find a satisfying one. Then I thought maybe I could write one.

The book in my mind is a textbook that focuses on the development of theories and concepts relevant to important consumer economic issues that are relevant to consumer economic wellbeing. Many important consumer issues discussed in my classes will be described in the book but they will have theoretical explanations and research findings instead of just fact compilations. I will use an interdisciplinary approach to select material to be included in the book. I will use concepts and theories that are developed not only in the field of consumer economics but also in any relevant fields, such as economics, marketing, finance, psychology, sociology, and political science. I expect to draw material heavily from the literature of behavior economics and finance, an emerging field that integrates advances of psychology and economics to address critical consumer economic issues. I started to plan this book in fall 2009 and continued working on it until now (end of 2014). During the process, I realized the work of synthesizing research theories and findings from multiple disciplines is much more than I expected. I am not sure if I have achieved my goal after 5 years of work but at least I tried my best. Originally I thought I could develop a theoretical framework to incorporate all relevant topics and later I found my plan is too ambitious to accomplish. A realistic way for now is to identify important concepts relevant to consumer economic wellbeing and then use brief charts to link them. Also, it is no way to fully evaluate research theories and findings from multiple fields by myself. In many sections, I just presented current research with minimum evaluations. I hope this is the first step toward building a systematic theory for consumer economics.

My interests in consumer economics, a field addressing critical consumer economic issues from a consumer's perspective, resulted from my backgrounds and training. I received my BS and MS in economics from Zhongnan University of Economics and Law in China in the early and mid-1980s. When I was a master student, I was interested in consumer protection issues. My thesis topic was on the consumer movement in China, under the guidance of Professor Peng Xinyu, who was among the first in China to introduce marketing as a field to the country. I also taught marketing courses before and after I received the master's degree. In 1987, I went to Oregon State University to pursue my Ph.D. in consumer economics under the guidance of Professor Geraldine Olson. Since then, I started my career as a consumer economist. Besides being the director for a consumer financial education research institute at the University of Arizona for two and half years (January 2005–June 2007), I have been teaching consumer economics and finance courses at the University of Rhode Island since 1991. I have grown from a young consumer economist to a measure one mainly benefited by three professional organizations, American Council on Consumer Interests (ACCI) that publishes *Journal of Consumer Affairs* (*JCA*), Association for Financial Counseling and Planning Education (AFCPE) that publishes *Journal of Financial Counseling and Planning* (*JFCP*), and Asian Consumer and Family Economics Association (ACFEA) that published its selected conference papers in several special issues in *Journal of Family and Economic Issues* (*JFEI*). During these years, I presented papers and extended my networks there. I also provided my services for these organizations and journals. I served as the editor of JFEI for 11 years (2000–2011) and have been on the editorial board of JCA for many years. I am currently serving as the editor of JFCP. I also served on and chaired several committees of these organizations including being the president of ACCI and ACFEA. I also worked with scholars at several universities in China and Japan (Renmin University, Tsinghua University, Central University of Finance and Economics, Yamaguchi University, etc.) on research projects on consumer financial literacy, capability, and wellbeing. My interest in and commitment to consumer economics is even reflected in my name. In Chinese, my name is pronounced in a way that sounds like "consumer economics construction," which was originally by accident but later I felt it may be my fate to devote my life working in this important field.

The book has three parts. Part I discusses the concept of consumer economic wellbeing (Chap. 1) and two important concepts relevant to consumer economic wellbeing, which are consumer rights (Chap. 2) and consumer financial capability (Chap. 3). Part II includes four chapters discussing consumer economic environments, such as government (Chap. 4), business (Chap. 5), media (Chap. 6), and Internet (Chap. 7). In these chapters, the research literature on how government and business organizations (news media, advertisement, and Internet companies are also businesses in the USA) behave that affect consumer economic wellbeing is examined. Part III includes four components of consumer economic wellbeing: consumer income (Chap. 8), spending (Chap. 9), borrowing (Chap. 10), and saving (Chap. 11). In these chapters, relevant research theories and findings on the title topics are described and summarized.

I tried to write the book with less technical language so that college educated readers who are not experts in consumer economics can understand. I hope the book can be used for both undergraduate and graduate courses dependent on instructors' needs. Instructors may also assign the book to college students taking courses with a focus on consumer economic issues in consumer science departments, business schools, and economics departments. Law school faculty teaching a course in consumer services law would find the material useful. Similarly, instructors of "special topics" courses with a focus on consumer economic issues outside of the disciplines listed above (e.g., psychology, political science, public policy, social work, sociology) may also assign the book to their students. Also, high school teachers in business, social studies, and family and consumer science may find the book of interest.

The book can be used as a reference book for business researchers and practitioners who are working to solve critical consumer issues and improve consumer wellbeing. The book is also of interest to practitioners in the field of consumer education. In particular, those who are concerned about critical consumer economic issues and actively involved in consumer advocacy activities may find the book of interest. Finally, public policy makers at all levels of government are likely to encounter legislation dealing with consumer economic issues and therefore would find the book a useful reference on many of the topic areas covered.

I hope this book will inspire more research studies on important consumer economic issues that inform relevant public policies and business practices to help improve consumer economic wellbeing. More rigid theories relevant to consumer economics will also be inspired and developed based on information provided in this book.

Kingston, RI, USA Jing Jian Xiao

Acknowledgements

Professor Peng Xinyu is my master's degree advisor and Professor Geraldine Olson is my doctoral degree advisor. Under their competent and patient guidance, I started my professional career as a consumer researcher. They taught me not only professional knowledge but also many other qualities that are needed to be successful in my professional development. They are my role models forever.

During my over 20-year career, I worked with dozens of colleagues and many of our collaborated products are reflected in this book. Without working with them, I would have not accomplished what I have now. They are Mohamed Abdel-Ghany, Sunyoung Ahn, M. J. Alhabeeb, Joan Gray Anderson, Dottie Bagwell, William Bailey, Bonnie Barber, Robert Bassett, Linda Block, Patricia Brennan, Barbara Bristow, Bruce Brunson, Noel Card, Swarne Chatterjee, Cheng Chen, Fuzhong Chen, Dongyao Cheng, Bie-shuein Chu, Michael Collins, June Cotte, Stuart Cohen, Brenda Cude, Sharon DeVaney, Jeffery Dew, Nik Dholakia, Ruby Dholakia, Jessie X. Fan, Matthew Ford, Alyssa Francis, Tom Garman, Ronald Gibbs, John Grable, Lin Guo, Sherman Hanna, Celia Hayhoe, George Haynes, Misako Higa, Tahira Hira, Arlene Holyoak, Gong-soog Hong, Kenneth Huggins, Janet Johnson, Punam Keller, Claudia Kerbel, Jinhee Kim, Larry Kirsch, Masayuki Kometani, Weida Kuang, Christine Lai, Fran Lawrence, Irene Leech, Berta Leon, Chunming Li, Haifeng Li, Tao Li, Li Liao, Suzanne Lindamood, Jean Lown, Angela Lyons, Lakshmi Malroutu, Robert Mayer, Jane Meiners, Xiangyi Meng, Carole Miller, Norbert Mundorf, Barbara Newman, Fran Noring, Barbara O'Neill, Geraldine Olson, Lance Palmer, Linda Price, Janice Prochaska, Lee Richardson, Barbara Robles, Jane Schuchardt, Joyce Serido, Deanna Sharpe, Soyeon Shim, Shunfeng Song, Benoit Sorhaindo, Feng Sun, Jing Sun, Lei Sun, Yunxiao Sun, Chuanyi Tang, Shayna Thums, Hilary Tso, Yongshi Tu, Radovan Vadovic, Houfen Wuan, Jeff Wang, Richard Widdows, Jiayun Wu, Jieying Xi, Yinzhou Xu, Xuejun Yan, Rui Yao, Zhihong Yi, Qingfei Yin, Shijie Yin, Bing Ying, Yoonkyung Yuh, Jinbao Zhang, Yixiao Zhang, Lucy Zhong, Pengrong Zhong, and Yi Zhou.

I would like to thank the following scholars, who are my long-term colleagues and mentors, for carefully reviewing the chapters and providing many helpful suggestions. They are Tom Cai, Richard Caputo, Jessie Fan, John Grable, Sherman

Hanna, Robert Mayer, Barbara O'Neill, Marla Royne Stafford, Jeffrey Sovern, Richard Widdows, and Rui Yao.

The University of Rhode Island granted me a sabbatical leave in fall 2010 to work on this project. My then department chair, Jerome Adams, and current chair, Karen McCurdy, provided needed moral and administrative support for my research on this book and other projects during these years. Their support is highly appreciated.

I thank Alyssa Francis for providing able assistance in copy editing.

Jennifer Hadley at Springer provided prompt and helpful guidance and assistance from the beginning of the book project, which is greatly appreciated.

Finally, I thank my wife for providing much needed moral and other supports during my working on this book. Without her encouragement and support, I would have not finished this important project.

Contents

About the Author

Dr. Jing Jian Xiao is a professor of consumer economics and finance at the University of Rhode Island. He teaches courses and conducts research on consumer economic and financial issues. He is the editor-in-chief of *Journal of Financial Counseling and Planning* and a book series, *International Series on Consumer Science*. For 11 years, he served as the editor-in-chief of *Journal of Family and Economic Issues* (2001–2011). In addition, he serves on editorial boards of several journals in consumer economics and finance such as *Journal of Consumer Affairs*, *Journal of Personal Finance*, *Journal of Consumer Education*, and *International Journal of Bank Marketing*. He has published extensively in areas of consumer economics and finance. He edited and contributed to books such as *Mathematics of Personal Finance* and *Handbook in Consumer Finance Research*. He has played active roles in professional organizations in consumer economics and finance and has served as the president of American Council on Consumer Interests, the president of Asian Consumer and Family Economics Association, among others. He received research grants and provided consulting services for government and nongovernment organizations including the U.S. Department of Agriculture, Department of Treasury, Department of Transportation, National Endowment on Financial Education, and Certified Financial Planner Standard Boards. He was invited to speak on national and international professional conferences on consumer economic wellbeing. He received his BS and MS in economics from Zhongnan University of Economics and Law and Ph.D. in consumer economics from Oregon State University. He was the inaugural Take Charge American Endowed Chair Professor and Director of Take Charge America Institute for Consumer Financial Education and Research at the University of Arizona in 2005–2007.

About the Author

Part I
Basic Concepts of Consumer Economic Wellbeing

Chapter 1
Consumer Economic Wellbeing

Abstract Consumers in this book refer to individuals and families. The term consumer can be defined in broad and narrow ways. Broadly, consumers are those who acquire and use natural, market, and other goods. Natural goods are air and natural resources that are not privately owned and priced. Market goods are priced products and services provided by commercial companies. Other goods refer to products and services provided by nonprofit organizations. Narrowly, consumers are those who purchase and use market goods. In this book the narrow definition of consumer is used in most discussions. This introductory chapter first discusses several definitions relevant to consumer economic wellbeing, such as wellbeing, subjective wellbeing, economic wellbeing, and consumer wellbeing. Then, the key term of this book, consumer economic wellbeing, is defined and introduced. The organization of the book is presented at the end of this chapter.

1.1 Wellbeing

In the literature, the spelling of wellbeing has two alternative forms, well being and well-being. In this book, "wellbeing" is used. Wellbeing can be defined in many ways. For example, wellbeing is the state of being healthy, happy, and free of want (Zimmerman 1995). For this book, a slightly revised definition is used: Wellbeing is the state of being healthy, happy, and wealthy. This definition suggests that wellbeing means doing well physically, mentally, and financially, which is an appropriate definition for the purpose of this book, to identify academic theories and research that enhance consumer economic wellbeing. In psychological literature, wellbeing often refers to happiness that emphasizes the subjective measure of welfare. In this book, wellbeing can be measured by both subjective and objective indicators.

Throughout the literature wellbeing is used as a synonym for quality of life (QOL). In this book, wellbeing and QOL are used interchangeably. Contemporary QOL or wellbeing research can be traced back to 1970s (Campbell et al. 1976). As indicated by Alex Michalos (2008), a leading scholar of QOL, because human beings are complex organisms and an adequate construction of the idea of human wellbeing is complex, an interdisciplinary perspective is needed to study this important topic. In a comprehensive review, several leading scholars from multidisciplinary

J.J. Xiao, *Consumer Economic Wellbeing*, International Series on Consumer Science, DOI 10.1007/978-1-4939-2821-7_1

fields provide historical overviews of QOL research (Sirgy et al. 2006b). Coauthors of this overview are scholars from diverse fields such as Joseph Sirgy from marketing, Alex Michalos from philosophy, Abbott Ferriss from sociology, Richard Easterlin from economics, William Pavot from psychology, and Donald Patrick from health. According to Michalos, QOL can be a descriptive measure, quantity of things, or an evaluative measure, the value or worth of things. For example, weight is descriptive and desirable weight is evaluative. Indicators of QOL can be both objective and subjective.

Wellbeing can be measured at both individual and collective levels. Most social indicators are measured at collective levels such as at city, state, regional, country, or global levels. At the global level, the United Nations Development Program (UNDP)'s annual human development reports provide indicators on the wellbeing of world populations and comparisons between countries. This report presents several internationally comparable indicators including the Human Development Index (HDI). HDI includes three components: life expectancy index, education index, and GDP index, covering wellbeing indicators from physical, psychological, and economic perspectives. These measures are considered as objective measures. For example, the 2013 report lists HDI and other indicators for 186 countries and areas in four categories: very high human development, high human development, medium human development, and low human development. Based on data from 2013, the top five countries that have the highest HDIs are Norway, Australia, Switzerland, the Netherlands, and the USA. China is listed as the 91st in the category of high human development (UNDP 2013).

In the USA, with assistance of a team of top researchers, Gallup and Healthyways have developed wellbeing indexes for American cities and states since 2008. With the goal of providing the world's most up-to-date measure of individual and collective health and wellbeing, this index tracks the wellbeing of US residents 350 days out of the year, interviewing no fewer than 1,000 US adults nationwide each day. The index includes components of life evaluation, emotional health, physical health, healthy behavior, work environment, and basic access (http://www.well-beingindex.com/). This database has been used by researchers to produce some interesting research findings (e.g., Diener et al. 2010; Kahneman and Deaton 2010).

1.2 Subjective Wellbeing or Happiness

1.2.1 The Concept of Subjective Wellbeing

In the literature, subjective wellbeing (SWB) research is also called happiness research (Sirgy et al. 2006b). As discussed by psychologist, William Pavot, this line of research can be traced back to the 1960s. A comprehensive review by Diener (1984) serves as a focal point for investigators working within the growing area of SWB research. Diener himself is a leading researcher in the SWB research and published numerous influential studies on this topic.

SWB can be defined in many ways. Diener et al. (1999) offer the following definition: "Subjective well-being is a broad category of phenomena that includes people's emotional responses, domain satisfactions, and global judgments of life satisfaction" (p. 277). Such a definition casts SWB as representing a broad area of research activity and interest, rather than as a specific construct (Sirgy et al. 2006b).

The measure of SWB has three components, positive affect, negative affect, and life satisfaction. The labels "life satisfaction" or "satisfaction with life" are usually associated with a very broad conceptual level, involving summary judgments of one's life as a whole (Pavot and Diener 1993). Multi-method longitudinal research has demonstrated that all three components are separable constructs (Lucas et al. 1996).

Diener (1984) identifies several characteristics of SWB. First, it is subjective, residing within the individual and based on one's unique experience of the world. Second, SWB includes positive experience, rather than just the absence of negative factors. Third, SWB is usually considered from a broad level, as an overall assessment, rather than according to specific experiences or aspects of the individual's life.

Measures of SWB can be categorized in a variety of ways. From a public policy perspective, these measures are divided into three broad categories: evaluation, experience, and eudaimonic (Dolan et al. 2011). The evaluation measure refers to life satisfaction and satisfaction of specific life domains. The experience measurement equates to past happiness and positive or negative affect ("worried, energetic, or relaxed yesterday"). The eudaimonic measure refers to purpose in life. The measure asks people to identify the purpose of life in general, and purposes and meanings of specific activities. The three types can be considered daily happiness, life satisfaction, and living a meaningful life. Most existent studies focus on daily happiness and life satisfaction. More research is needed to study living a meaningful life.

1.2.2 Money and Happiness

Many studies have examined the relationship between income and SWB and generated many interesting findings (Xiao 2013). For instance, data from Russian consumers show that the relationship between income and life satisfaction is complex (Schyns 2001). Furthermore, data collected from five countries indicate the effects of wealth and non-durable consumptions on life satisfaction (Heady et al. 2008). Money buys happiness and people care about relative income (Blanchflower and Oswald 2004). Cummins (2000) find that income is associated with happiness through mediating variables. Subsequently, Diener and Biswas-Diener (2002) review studies on the relationship between income and SWB and conclude that there are, at most, small correlations between income and SWB within nations. In addition, unless they are rich, people who value material goals are less happy than those who do not. Another review study has similar conclusions in a more focused review of the relationship between income and happiness within nations and across nations (Arthaud-Day and Near 2005).

One limitation throughout the literature is the various measures of happiness employed throughout research; depending on the measure used, income effects may vary. Kahneman and Deaton (2010) have analyzed more than 450,000 responses to a daily survey of 1,000 US residents conducted by the Gallup Organization and find that emotional wellbeing and life evaluation have different correlates. Income and education are more closely related to life evaluation, but health, care giving, loneliness, and smoking are relatively stronger predictors of daily emotions. When plotted against log income, life evaluation rises steadily. Emotional well-being also rises with log income, but does not progress beyond an annual income of $75,000.

Happiness researchers also observe the *adaptation effect* of personal income on happiness over time. People are happy when their incomes increase. The effect decreases over time but lasts for several years. Based on panel data, researchers find that German homeowners, who are presumably wealthier than tenants, adapt fully to the effects of higher levels of log income after approximately 7 years. With panel data from Europe, researchers find that in wealthy European countries, full adaptation may take at least 5 years (Di Tella and MacCulloch 2010). In another study with a panel of German data, researchers examine happiness adaptation to income and to status. They find that in the short term, one standard deviation increase in status and 52 % of one standard deviation increase in income are associated with similar increases in happiness. However in the long run, 65 % of the current year's impact of income on happiness is lost over the following 4 years whereas the impact of status remains intact (Di Tella et al. 2010).

Income inequality may cause unhappiness. Research indicates that individuals have a lower tendency to report being happy when inequality is high. The effect, however, appears to be stronger in Europe than in the USA (Alesina et al. 2004). Decreased happiness associated with inequality may be related to perceived fairness and trust. Data from the General Social Survey from 1972 to 2008 show that Americans are, on average, happier in the years with less income inequality than in the years with more income inequality. The researchers demonstrate that the inverse relation between income inequality and happiness is explained by perceived fairness and general trust. The negative association between income inequality and happiness held for lower income respondents, but not for upper-middle and highest income groups. Most importantly, the negative link between income inequality and the happiness of lower income respondents is explained not by lower household income, but by perceived unfairness and lack of trust (Oishi et al. 2011).

1.2.3 Can Happiness Buy Money?

Many happiness studies attempt to examine whether higher income contributes to happiness. However, some researchers explore if happiness can increase one's income. If they find causality, SWB may be a factor to be promoted to increase productivity for society. Oishi (2012) considers happiness as psychological wealth and contends that a nation's psychological wealth is important for a good society.

Researchers document the causal relationship between happiness and positive life outcomes including economic outcomes. Happiness may result in positive life outcomes. Researchers propose a conceptual model arguing that the happiness–success link exists not only because success makes people happy, but also because positive affect engenders success. Their results reveal that happiness is associated with and precedes numerous successful outcomes, as well as behaviors paralleling success (Lyubomirsky et al. 2005).

Happiness may raise productivity. Experimental research shows that happiness raises productivity in research experiments (Oswald et al. 2009). Happiness may contribute to job satisfaction and high income by examining the relationship between dispositional affect and job outcomes. Research shows that individuals with a higher cheerfulness rating at college entry have higher current income and a higher job satisfaction rating 19 years later and are less likely to have been unemployed than individuals with a lower cheerfulness rating. Although cheerfulness generally has a positive effect on current income, this effect is curvilinear, with current income increasing more rapidly at lower than at higher cheerfulness ratings (Diener et al. 2002). Panel data from Russia show that happiness itself affects income, health, and other factors. For instance, people who have higher "residual happiness" in 1995 (i.e., people who are happier after correcting for the usual determinants of well-being) make more money and are in better health in a survey 5 years later (Graham et al. 2004).

Adolescents and young adults who report higher life satisfaction or positive affect grow up to earn significantly higher levels of income later in life, based on data from a large US representative panel of more than 10,000 individuals (De Neve and Oswald 2012). The study's results are robust to the inclusion of controls such as education, intelligence quotient, physical health, height, self-esteem, and later happiness. To explore how psychological wellbeing may influence income, the authors identify several mediating factors: being happy may be associated with a higher probability of obtaining a college degree, getting hired and promoted, and having higher degrees of optimism and extraversion and less neuroticism. The study authors contend that the relationship between income and happiness is dynamic and the effects may run in both directions. The literature of happiness research shows that happiness has various correlates such as health (Frey 2011), social networks (Fowler and Christakis 2008), and self-esteem (Lyubomirsky et al. 2006) that, in turn, are known to positively influence labor market outcomes and thus may play a mediating role. More recent neuroscientific research provides clues that greater SWB is associated with particular neurological variation, which in turn is associated with improved cognitive skills and economic outcomes (De Neve and Oswald 2012).

Happier people make more money but the association may be nonlinear. Different life outcomes may occur between moderately and extremely happy people. Researchers find that people who experience the highest levels of happiness are the most successful in terms of close relationships and volunteer work, but that those who experience slightly lower levels of happiness are the most successful in terms of income, education, and political participation. Once people are moderately happy, the most effective level of happiness appears to depend on the specific outcomes used to define success as well as the available resources (Oishi et al. 2007).

Happiness contributes to consumption and saving behavior. Using the number of unexpected sunny days as a proxy measure of happiness, data from the Netherlands and Germany show that happier people save more, spend less, and have a lower marginal propensity to consume. Happier people take more time for making decisions and have more control over expenditures; they expect a longer life and seem more concerned about the future than the present; they also expect less inflation in the future (Guven 2012).

Happiness and life outcomes may interact with each other. Researchers examine the coevolution of changes in happiness and changes in income, health, marital status, and employment status with the British Household Panel Survey (BHPS) data set. They find that increases in happiness are associated with subsequent increases in income, marriage, employment, and health variables, while increases in these life-domain variables (except health) tend to be followed by decreases in happiness in subsequent periods, suggesting adaptation dynamics in all domains (Binder and Coad 2010).

If happiness is a resource for a better life, people should mobilize and use it. Based on his research of college students at Harvard, Achor (2010) developed principles to fully take the "happiness advantage." The principles include the happiness advantage (to retrain the brain to capture on positivity), the fulcrum and the lever (to adjust the mindset in a way to gain power to be more fulfilled and successful), the Tetris effect (to retrain the brain to spot patterns of possibilities and seize opportunities), falling up (to map the brain to be happier and more successful in front of adversities), the Zorro circle (to regain control by focusing on small and manageable goals first), the 20-s rule (to reroute the path of the least resistance and replace bad habits with good ones), and social investment (to invest more in the social support network).

1.3 Economic Wellbeing

1.3.1 The Historical Perspective of Economic Wellbeing

Economists started research on economic wellbeing for the purpose of informing public policies. Richard Easterlin provided a historic review of the development of economic wellbeing contributed by economists (Sirgy et al. 2006b). In the last half of the twentieth century, economic wellbeing research was done through three strains: to develop and adjust GDP and related measures for economic welfare; develop measures directly related to specific aspects of QOL such as food and housing; and develop more comprehensive indicators of wellbeing by synthesizing indicators related to material living conditions, length of life, education, and the like. All these measures were objective indicators since most economists then did not trust subjective measures.

National income or GDP is considered the primary measure of economic wellbeing. Pigou (1929) proposed the measure of national income and discussed the relationship between economic welfare and social welfare. He believed that economic wellbeing is a part of social wellbeing and both should increase in the same direction.

The foundation work in the measurement of national income was done by Simon Kuznets (1933, 1946), the fourth Nobel laureate in economics. Starting in the late 1920s, he established a comprehensive research program on national income under the sponsorship of the National Bureau of Economic Research (NBER), which was at the time, and still is, the USA's leading organization in empirical economic research. Empirical implementation of this concept raises three types of questions—scope, netness, and valuation. A common system of national economic accounts was adopted by the USA, the UK, and other countries, as well as the Statistical Office of the United Nations; it was due particularly to the pioneering work of 1984 Nobel laureate Richard Stone (1986).

Adjusting GDP has been a research interest for economists. The best known attempt within the economics profession to adjust GNP to obtain a more meaningful measure of economic wellbeing is a study by Nordhaus and Tobin (1973), which is the first of contemporary measures such as the Index of Sustainable Economic Welfare.

In contrast, the proposed Index of Sustainable Economic Welfare grew hardly at all in the UK between 1950 and 1996 (Jackson et al. 1998). Among other differences from the Nordhaus–Tobin measure, this index includes sizeable adjustments for income inequality, costs of climate change, and the cost of ozone depletion, and does not include an imputation for leisure.

Among the leaders of those motivated by the desire to get meaningful empirical measures for less developed areas were scholars at Stanford University's Food Research Institute. Bennett (1951) sought to compare international differences in consumption levels in 1934–1938 by developing 16 non-monetary indicators ranging across five categories of consumption: food and tobacco; medical and sanitary services; housing; education and recreation; and transportation and communications. Jones and Merat (1962) tried to study material living levels in sub-Saharan Africa by drawing on the data most widely available, statistics of international trade (Jones and Merat 1962). This work foreshadowed, in a modest way, current efforts to develop alternative indexes of economic welfare that build out from measures of personal consumption: for example, the Index of Economic Well-Being, which incorporates, in addition to consumption, allowances for wealth accumulation, inequality, and, an especially novel element, economic insecurity (Osberg 2001; Osberg and Sharpe 1998).

Among early reactions against primarily economic measures of wellbeing were the reports of the United Nations Department of Social Affairs, which assembled data on the world's social situation and pointed out that international disparities in conditions such as length of life did not simply parallel those in the economic condition (United Nations, 1952, 1961). A valuable study in this vein was published in 1970 by four economists at the United Nations Research Institute for Social Development (McGranahan et al. 1970). This body of work has counterparts today in such measures as the Weighted Index of Social Progress (Estes 1995).

An economic historian proposed a physical QOL index (Morris 1979), combining measures of economic output, life expectancy, and education. This measure is a direct forerunner of today's Human Development Index published annually in the United Nations Human Development Report (UNDP 2002). Currently, economic historians, following the lead of Fogel (1986, 1993), are focusing on measures of stature, taken to be indicative of an undefined "biological" standard of living (Komlos 1995; Steckel and Floud 1997).

1.3.2 Economic Growth and Happiness

The first attempt in economics to assess the trend of wellbeing in terms of personal reports on happiness or life satisfaction was done by Easterlin (1974), who found that over the period 1946–1970, average happiness in the USA rose through the late 1950s, and then fell, returning to near its 1946 level. Ever since, many studies tested this hypothesis and uncovered controversial findings (for a comprehensive review on this topic, see Clark et al. 2008). Recent papers by Easterlin et al. (2010, 2012) using data from Southern American countries and China confirmed this hypothesis repeatedly. Globally, Easterlin's paradox poses a challenge for economic development policy makers when considering how to please the public when creating policies. A few other economists also conduct economic research in this line of research such as the analysis of subjective data on the adequacy of income (Van Praag and Frijters 1999). Since around 1990 there has been a small upsurge in economic research on SWB. Considerable credit for this is due to the work of British economist Andrew Oswald and his collaborators, as well as to Bruno Frey, a long-time scholar in economic psychology (Frey and Stutzer 2002; Oswald 1997).

The Easterlin Paradox is the most controversial part of income and happiness research. Easterlin (1974) shows no association between life satisfaction and economic growth. In the past 40 decades, Easterlin and many other researchers repeatedly confirm this fact with data from both developed and developing countries and using both cross-sectional and longitudinal data (Easterlin and Sawangfa 2010). Some researchers even document a negative association between per capita income growth rate and life satisfaction, which is labeled the *paradox of unhappy growth* (Graham et al. 2010). Other researchers also provide evidence to support this paradox. For example, Blanchflower and Oswald (2004) find that reported levels of well-being have declined over the last quarter of a century in the USA and life satisfaction has run approximately flat through time in the UK. The happiness of African Americans, however, has risen. White women in the USA have decreased the most in happiness since the 1970s. These findings are consistent with the Easterlin hypothesis.

Some researchers claim that their evidence does not support the Easterlin Paradox (Deaton 2008; Stevenson and Wolfers 2008). However, several major researchers believe that the evidence is too weak to solve the paradox (Easterlin and Sawangfa 2010; Layard et al. 2010). The general consensus now is that the relationship between economic growth and happiness is complicated and requires more systematic data collection in a broader scale and longer time frame to clarify the issue (Diener et al. 2010).

Many researchers attempt to explain the paradox. For example, using data from almost 400,000 people living in the OECD countries during 1975 and 1997, researchers find a positive correlation between the happiness responses and absolute income, generosity of the welfare state, and life expectancy but a negative correlation with the average number of hours worked, measures of environmental degradation, crime, openness to trade, inflation, and unemployment (Di Tella and MacCulloch 2008). The researchers claim that the unexplained trend in happiness would be even larger than would be predicted if income were the only argument in the utility function. In other words, introducing omitted variables worsens the income-without-happiness paradox. Using data from the Gallup international study of happiness, researchers find that the economic growth rate increases life satisfaction among poorer countries but not among richer countries. The difference is attributed to the *adaptation effect* (i.e., happiness fades after several years of income increase) (Di Tella and MacCulloch 2010).

Researchers in a comprehensive review of happiness research emphasized the importance of social comparison and self-comparison under the framework of a utility function (Clark et al. 2008). Other researchers speculate that several factors such as the choice of micro or macro data, framing of happiness questions, countries included in the sample, and possible mediating factors affected the relationship between economic growth measured by per capital income growth and happiness (Graham et al. 2010).

1.3.3 Microeconomic Indicators and Happiness

In recent years, more economists pay attention to happiness data and attempt to relate it to important macroeconomic indicators. They believe that using happiness data in economic research is natural because many questions in economics are fundamentally about happiness. Using happiness data, economists simply compare measures of welfare and what causes changes in welfare under different scenarios (Di Tella and MacCulloch 2006).

Macroeconomic movements may affect the happiness of nations. Using data from a quarter of a million randomly sampled Europeans and Americans from the 1970s to 1990s, researchers showed a correlation between movements in reported well-being and changes in macroeconomic variables such as GDP. Recessions create large psychic losses that extend beyond the fall in GDP and rise in unemployment. The welfare state appears to be a compensating force: higher unemployment benefits are associated with higher national wellbeing (Di Tella et al. 2003).

Undesirable macroeconomic indicators may have differential negative effects on happiness. Researchers find that people appear to be happier when inflation and unemployment are low. At the margin, unemployment depresses happiness more than inflation does. Their estimates suggest that people would trade off a 1 percentage point increase in the unemployment rate for a 1.7 percentage point increase in the inflation rate. In other words, unemployment seems more painful than inflation for consumers (Di Tella et al. 2001).

1.3.4 Economic Policy and Happiness

Researchers in economics and psychology consider plans to use happiness data for economic policy making. They propose a National Time Accounting approach using a U-index to introduce happiness data into the economic policy-making process (Kahneman and Krueger 2006; Krueger 2009). They believe that both National Income Account and National Time Account represent the true welfare of people in an economy. The authors propose a summary measure of SWB called the U-index, or percentage of time that an individual or group of individuals spends in an unpleasant emotional state. An *unpleasant emotional state* is an interval in which the strongest negative emotion is coded as 1 under the economic utility framework.

Public perceptions of social policies contribute to SWB. Progressive policy makers also need to hear people's perceptions and evaluations of existent and new social policies in addition to information from objective measures (Veenhoven 2002). Using data from Hong Kong, researchers find positive associations between perceptions and evaluations of social programs on SWB (Wong et al. 2006). Consumer perceptions on different economic policies may have different effects on happiness. Using data from a random telephone survey conducted in Beijing, China, researchers find that perceived fairness of social security is four times more positively associated with life satisfaction than that of income distribution policies (Sun and Xiao 2012).

1.3.5 Financial Satisfaction

Financial satisfaction is a subjective measure of economic wellbeing. Previous studies have examined factors associated with financial satisfaction. Income is identified as an important determinant of financial satisfaction. For instance, data from General Social Surveys in the USA is used to examine the association between income and financial satisfaction of American elders and results show that different definitions of incomes have different effects on financial satisfaction (Hsieh 2004). Research based on data from a national survey in Spain indicates that not only income but also income expectation affected financial satisfaction (Vera-Toscano et al. 2006). A study based on a sample of American consumers finds that perceived income adequacy is positively associated with financial satisfaction (Grable et al. 2013).

Research also identifies other factors associated with financial satisfaction. Financial satisfaction may be associated with financial behavior-, financial knowledge-, and risk tolerance-based data from a sample of American clerical workers

(Joo and Grable 2004). A Norwegian study of older consumers finds that financial circumstances such as levels of assets and debts affect financial satisfaction (Hansen et al. 2008). A study conducted in a transitional economy, Albania, reveals that workers in informal sectors are less financially satisfied than their counterparts in formal sectors (Ferrer-i-Carbonell and Gërxhani 2011). Data from nine European countries show that the relationship between income and financial satisfaction is positive up to a point and other variables, such as differing household characteristics, explained 30 % of the variances regarding financial satisfaction (Seghieri et al. 2006). Research using American data shows that consumer financial satisfaction is associated with consumer financial capability variables (Xiao et al. 2014).

1.4 Consumer Wellbeing

1.4.1 The Concept of Consumer Wellbeing

Consumer wellbeing (CWB) is considered an emerging field conducted by marketing researchers (see Pancer 2009 for an informative historical analysis on this topic). As a leading researcher of CWB, Sirgy (2008) groups CWB research programs into five ethic perspectives: (1) ethics of consumer sovereignty, (2) duty ethics of non-maleficence, (3) ethics of stakeholder theory, (4) ethics of social justice, and (5) ethics of human development and QOL. These ethics are considered motivations to conduct CWB research by these researchers.

After reviewing 14 conceptualizations and measures of CWB, Sirgy et al. (2007) conclude that all the conceptualizations and measures of CWB are grounded on the implicit or explicit assumption that high levels of CWB lead to higher levels of consumers' QOL—higher levels of life, implying that CWB is a subdomain of QOL.

Sirgy and Lee (2006) propose that the ideal definition of CWB should (1) capture the varied experiences that consumers have with the marketplace; (2) capture CWB to reflect both individual and societal welfare; and (3) be highly diagnostic and practical to help decision makers identify causes and therefore take remedial action.

After reviewing ten measures of CWB, Sirgy and Lee (2006) propose their definition of CWB: "a state in which consumers' experiences with goods and services—experiences related to acquisition, preparation, consumption, ownership, maintenance, and disposal of specific categories of goods and services in the context of their local environment—are judged to be beneficial to both consumers and society at large (p. 43)." They also emphasize that the consumer population can be segmented by demographic and geographic characteristics so that policy makers can easily use the measure. Compared to measures of other CWB reviewed, this definition is more comprehensive, macro, and practical. However, this definition is too narrow at the macro level, according to the authors; it leaves out important aspects such as consumer socialization, involvement with the society, social causes, and so on. Furthermore, it has a very heavy emphasis on materialism (Malhotra 2006). In addition, it does not address the issue of consumer representation in public and private policy making. Sirgy and colleagues also develop several specific CWB concepts such as process-based, community-based, product-based, and consumption-based CWB.

1.4.2 Process-Based CWB

Process-based CWB is to capture satisfaction with the entire consumption process (Lee et al. 2002). The measure taps into five major dimensions of satisfaction with consumer goods and services: (1) acquisition, (2) possession, (3) consumption, (4) maintenance, and (5) disposition. This measure is based on the concept of bottom-up spillover. *Bottom-up spillover* between CWB and life satisfaction is conceptualized using a satisfaction hierarchy model. The basic premise is that overall life satisfaction is functionally related to satisfaction with all of life's domains and subdomains. Based on data from a survey of university students, the proposed measure is found to have predictive validity in relation to life satisfaction for three out of its five dimensions—acquisition, possession, and consumption.

1.4.3 Community-Based CWB

The measure for community-based CWB is based on the notion that consumers experience wellbeing to the extent that they are satisfied with local marketplace experiences related to (1) shopping for desired consumer goods and services in the local area, (2) preparing locally purchased consumer durables for personal use, (3) consuming locally purchased goods and services, (4) owning consumer durables purchased in the local area, (5) using repair and maintenance services in the local area, and (6) using selling, trading-in, and disposal services in the local area. Data were collected from ten localities in nine countries using the mall intercept method. The data support the predictive validity of the measure by verifying the relationship between the CWB construct and other wellbeing constructs such as life satisfaction (Sirgy et al. 2008).

1.4.4 Product-Based CWB

Cell phone use is used as a case to develop a measure for product-based CWB. The measure is based on the theoretical notion that the perception of the overall QOL impact of cell phone use is determined by users' perceptions of the impact of their cell phone in various life domains such as social life, leisure life, family life, educational life, health and safety, love life, work life, and financial life. In turn, the perception of the impact of the cell phone in a given life domain (e.g., social life, leisure life) is determined by perceptions of benefits and costs of the cell phone within that domain. Researchers have conducted two studies using college students and adults to select items capturing perceived benefits and costs that are predictive of the perceived QOL impact of the cell phone (Sirgy et al. 2007).

1.4.5 Consumption-Based CWB

Personal transportation is used as a case to develop a measure for consumption-based CWB. The measure is developed under the theoretical notion that the CWB in relation to personal transportation vehicles is significantly enhanced when the consumption of the vehicle meets the full spectrum of human developmental needs (i.e., safety, economic, family, social, esteem, actualization, knowledge, and aesthetics needs). The validity of the CWB measure is tested through exploration of the various antecedents and consequences of the construct within three studies (Sirgy et al. 2006a).

1.5 Consumer Economic Wellbeing

Consumer economic wellbeing refers to a state in which consumers have adequate economic resources to live a comfortable life. This definition is similar to family economic wellbeing in the family setting (Xiao 2012) and financial wellness in the setting of personal financial planning (Joo 2008). Consumer economic wellbeing can be measured with both objective and subjective indicators. For objective measures, four sets of indicators are used to measure consumer economic wellbeing, which are income, expenditure, debt, and asset. These indicators are also called earning, spending, borrowing, and saving. These indicators can be used to form more indicators. For example, net worth is the difference between asset and debt. The most obvious indicator of economic wellbeing is income. Because of taxes and required savings, there are significant differences between nominal income and take-home income. Consumer spending is a better measure for economic wellbeing because it is a measure of current consumption. Consumer debt indicates consumers borrowing future income for current consumption, whereas consumer saving means consumers forgoing current consumption to finance consumption in future. In sum, spending or consumption is the key among these four sets of indicators. Consumers are considered doing well if they maintain a certain level of consumption compared to their peers and to the past. Consumer economic wellbeing can also be measured by subjective measures such as financial satisfaction, income satisfaction, and satisfaction with retirement savings. Examples of direct measures of consumer economic wellbeing are presented in Table 1.1.

In marketplace, individual consumers are vulnerable regarding monetary and nonmonetary resources comparing with businesses. To gain bargaining powers in

Table 1.1 Indicators of consumer economic wellbeing

	Objective measures	Subjective measures
Direct measures	Income	Income satisfaction
	Debt	Financial satisfaction
	Expenditure	Consumer satisfaction
	Asset	
	Net worth	
	Consumer right	
Instrumental measures	Financial capability	Money attitude
	Financial behavior	Risk tolerance
	Financial knowledge	

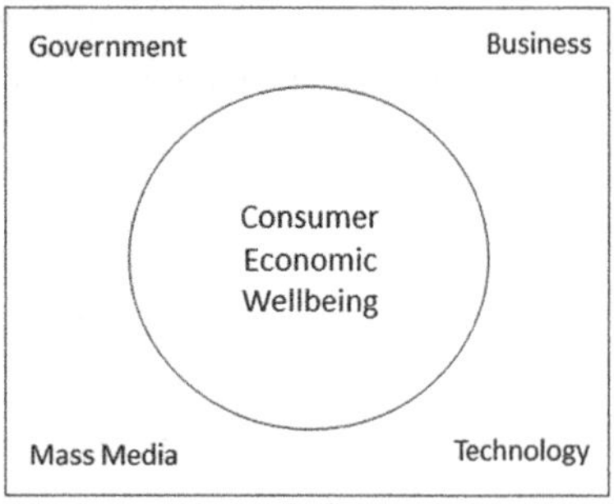

Fig. 1.1 Consumer economic wellbeing

marketplace, consumers need to be active in public policy-making processes to seek and preserve consumer rights. Consumer rights are indicators of consumer economic wellbeing in political terms.

Consumer economic wellbeing is also influenced by instrumental measures. To achieve economic wellbeing, consumers need to be able to manage their money effectively, possess a certain level of financial knowledge, and perform desirable financial behaviors. In addition, they should have appropriate attitudes towards money and risk when living their financial life and planning their financial future (Table 1.1).

Consumer economic wellbeing is influenced by many surrounding factors. The key components of consumer environments are governments, businesses, mass media, and technology (Fig. 1.1). Governments through economic policies affect consumer income, expenditure, debt, and asset. Businesses provide consumers opportunities to earn and spend money. Businesses or governments in different countries control mass media to frame and influence consumer spending and other economic behaviors. Advances in technologies, especially information technologies, change the world on the daily basis and provide consumers novel products and services that increase the comfort level of consumer life in many ways.

1.6 Focus and Organization of the Book

The focus of this book is to review research literature on consumer economic wellbeing through economic indicators such as consumer earning, spending, borrowing, and saving. The book also discusses how these indicators of consumer economic wellbeing are influenced by consumer environments. Research literature from multidisciplinary fields such as consumer science, economics, business, and other social science fields is drawn to address these issues.

This book includes three parts. Part I discusses basic concepts related to consumer economic wellbeing. Besides this chapter, the other two chapters discuss consumer right and consumer capability. Part II discusses environments around consumers such as governments, businesses, mass media, and the Internet that influence consumer economic wellbeing. Part III discusses major components of consumer economic wellbeing such as consumer earning, spending, borrowing, and saving.

This book attempts to view consumer economic wellbeing from the consumer perspective, which is different from the psychological perspective, economic perspective, or marketing perspective. The consumer perspective tends to use integrated information from all related disciplines for the interest of consumers. In addition, it attempts to provide helpful information for public policy makers, business professionals, and consumer leaders on how to help consumers improve their economic wellbeing. Individual consumers can also benefit from reading this book by understanding research theories and findings that may be helpful in enhancing their economic wellbeing.

References

Achor, S. (2010). *The happiness advantage*. New York: Random House.

Alesina, A., Di Tella, R., & MacCulloch, R. (2004). Inequality and happiness: Are Europeans and Americans different? *Journal of Public Economics, 88*(9), 2009–2042.

Arthaud-Day, M. L., & Near, J. P. (2005). The wealth of nations and the happiness of nations: Why "accounting" matters. *Social Indicators Research, 74*, 511–548.

Bennett, M. K. (1951). International disparities in consumption levels. *American Economic Review, XLI*, 632–649.

Binder, M., & Coad, A. (2010). An examination of the dynamics of well-being and life events using vector autoregressions. *Journal of Economic Behavior & Organization, 76*(2), 352–371.

Blanchflower, D. G., & Oswald, A. J. (2004). Well-being over time in Britain and the USA. *Journal of Public Economics, 88*(7), 1359–1386.

Campbell, A. C., Converse, P. E., & Rodgers, W. L. (1976). *The quality of American life*. New York: Russell Sage.

Clark, A. E., Frijters, P., & Shields, M. A. (2008). Relative income, happiness, and utility: An explanation for the Easterlin paradox and other puzzles. *Journal of Economic Literature, 46*(1), 95–144.

Cummins, R. A. (2000). Personal income and subjective well-being: A review. *Journal of Happiness Studies, 1*, 133–158.

De Neve, J. E., & Oswald, A. J. (2012). Estimating the influence of life satisfaction and positive affect on later income using sibling fixed effects. *Proceedings of the National Academy of Sciences, 109*(49), 19953–19958.

Deaton, A. (2008). Income, health and wellbeing around the world: Evidence from the Gallup World Poll. *The Journal of Economic Perspectives, 22*(2), 53–72.

Di Tella, R., Haisken-De New, J., & MacCulloch, R. (2010). Happiness adaptation to income and to status in an individual panel. *Journal of Economic Behavior & Organization, 76*(3), 834–852.

Di Tella, R., & MacCulloch, R. (2006). Some uses of happiness data in economics. *The Journal of Economic Perspectives, 20*(1), 25–46.

Di Tella, R., & MacCulloch, R. (2008). Gross national happiness as an answer to the Easterlin Paradox? *Journal of Development Economics, 86*(1), 22–42.

Di Tella, R., & MacCulloch, R. (2010). Happiness adaptation to income beyond "Basic Needs". In E. Diener, J. F. Helliwell, & D. Kahneman (Eds.), *International differences in well-being* (pp. 139–165). Oxford: Oxford University Press.

Di Tella, R., MacCulloch, R. J., & Oswald, A. J. (2001). Preferences over inflation and unemployment: Evidence from surveys of happiness. *American Economic Review, 91*(1), 335–341.

Di Tella, R., MacCulloch, R. J., & Oswald, A. J. (2003). The macroeconomics of happiness. *Review of Economics and Statistics, 85*(4), 809–827.

Diener, E. (1984). Subjective well-being. *Psychological Bulletin, 95*, 542–575.

Diener, E., & Biswas-Diener, R. (2002). Will money increase subjective well-being? *Social Indicators Research, 57*(2), 119–169.

Diener, E., Helliwell, J. F., & Kahneman, D. (2010). *International differences in well-being*. Oxford: Oxford University Press.

Diener, Ed., Carol Nickerson, Richard E. Lucas, and Ed Sandvik. 2002. "Dispositional Affect and Job Outcomes." *Social Indicators Research* 59(3): 229–259.

Diener, E., Suh, E. M., Lucas, R. E., & Smith, H. L. (1999). Subjective well-being: Three decades of progress. *Psychological Bulletin, 125*, 276–302.

Dolan, P., Layard, R., & Metcalfe, R. (2011). *Measuring subjective well-being for public policy*. Retrieved from http://eprints.lse.ac.uk/35420/1/measuring-subjective-wellbeing-for-public-policy.pdf

Easterlin, R. A. (1974). Does economic growth improve the human lot? In P. A. David & M. W. Reder (Eds.), *Nations and households in economic growth: Essays in honor of Moses Abramovitz*. New York: Academic Press.

Easterlin, R. A., McVey, L. A., Switek, M., Sawangfa, O., & Zweig, J. S. (2010). The happiness–income paradox revisited. *Proceedings of the National Academy of Sciences, 107*(52), 22463–22468.

Easterlin, R. A., Morgan, R., Switek, M., & Wang, F. (2012). China's life satisfaction, 1990–2010. *Proceedings of the National Academy of Sciences, 109*(25), 9775–9780.

Easterlin, R. A., & Sawangfa, O. (2010). Happiness and economic growth: Does the cross section predict time trends? Evidence from developing countries. In E. Diener, J. F. Helliwell, & D. Kahneman (Eds.), *International differences in well-being* (pp. 166–216). Oxford: Oxford University Press.

Estes, R. J. (1995). *Praxis: Resources for social and economic development: A database of world-wide resources pertaining to national and international social development* "published" on Lynx and the World Wide Web. Retrieved from http://caster.ssw.upenn.edu/~restes/praxis.html

Ferrer-i-Carbonell, A., & Gërxhani, K. (2011). Financial satisfaction and (in) formal sector in a transition country. *Social Indicators Research, 102*(2), 315–331.

Fogel, R. W. (1986). Nutrition and the decline in mortality since 1700: Some preliminary findings. In S. L. Engerman & R. E. Gallman (Eds.), *Long-term trends in American economic growth* (pp. 439–555). Chicago: University of Chicago Press.

Fogel, R. W. (1993). New sources and new techniques for the study of secular trends in nutritional status, health, mortality, and the process of aging. *Historical Methods, 26*(Winter), 1–44.

Fowler, J. H., & Christakis, N. A. (2008). Dynamic spread of happiness in a large social network: Longitudinal analysis over 20 years in the Framingham Heart Study. *British Medical Journal, 337*(768), a2338.

Frey, B. S. (2011). Happy people live longer. *Science, 331*(6017), 542–543.

Frey, B. S., & Stutzer, A. (2002). What can economists learn from happiness research? *Journal of Economic Literature, 40*(2), 402–435.

Grable, J. E., Cupples, S., Fernatt, F., & Anderson, N. (2013). Evaluating the link between perceived income adequacy and financial satisfaction: A resource deficit hypothesis approach. *Social Indicators Research, 114*, 1109.

Graham, C., Chattopadhyay, S., & Picon, M. (2010). The Easterlin and other paradoxes: Why both sides of the debate may be correct. In E. Diener, J. F. Helliwell, & D. Kahneman (Eds.), *International differences in well-being* (pp. 247–288). Oxford: Oxford University Press.

Graham, C., Eggers, A., & Sukhtankar, S. (2004). Does happiness pay?: An exploration based on panel data from Russia. *Journal of Economic Behavior & Organization, 55*(3), 319–342.

Guven, C. (2012). Reversing the question: Does happiness affect consumption and savings behavior? *Journal of Economic Psychology, 33*(4), 701–717.

Hansen, T., Slagsvold, B., & Moum, T. (2008). Financial satisfaction in old age: A satisfaction paradox or a result of accumulated wealth? *Social Indicators Research, 89*(2), 323–347.

Heady, B., Muffels, R., & Wooden, M. (2008). Money does not buy happiness: Or does it? A reassessment based on the combined effects of wealth, income and consumption. *Social Indicators Research, 87*, 65–82.

Hsieh, C. M. (2004). Income and financial satisfaction among older adults in the United States. *Social Indicators Research, 66*, 249–266.

Jackson, T., Marks, N., Ralls, J., & Stymne, S. (1998). *Sustainable economic welfare in the UK, 1950–1996*. London: New Economics Foundation.

Jones, W. O., & Merat, C. (1962). Consumption of exotic consumer goods as an indicator of economic achievement in ten countries of tropical Africa. *Food Research Institute Studies, 3*(1), 35–60. February.

Joo, S. (2008). Personal financial wellness. In J. J. Xiao (Ed.), *Handbook of consumer finance research* (pp. 21–34). New York: Springer.

Joo, S., & Grable, J. E. (2004). An exploratory framework of the determinants of financial satisfaction. *Journal of Family and Economic Issues, 25*(1), 25–50.

Kahneman, D., & Deaton, A. (2010). High income improves evaluation of life but not emotional well-being. *Proceedings of the National Academy of Sciences, 107*(38), 16489–16493.

Kahneman, D., & Krueger, A. B. (2006). Developments in the measurement of subjective well-being. *Journal of Economic Perspectives, 20*(1), 3–24.

Komlos, J. (1995). *The biological standard of living on three continents: Further exploration in anthropometric history*. Boulder, CO: Westview.

Krueger, A. B. (Ed.). (2009). *Measuring the subjective well-being of nations: National accounts of time use and well-being*. Chicago: University of Chicago Press.

Kuznets, S. (1933). National income. In E. R. A. Seligman & A. Johnson (Eds.), *Encyclopedia of the social sciences* (Vol. 11, pp. 205–224). New York: Macmillan.

Kuznets, S. (1946). *National income: A summary of findings*. New York: National Bureau of Economic Research.

Layard, R., Mayraz, G., & Nickell, S. (2010). Does relative income matter? Are the critics right? In E. Diener, J. F. Helliwell, & D. Kahneman (Eds.), *International differences in well-being* (pp. 139–165). Oxford: Oxford University Press.

Lee, D., Sirgy, M. J., Larsen, V., & Wright, N. D. (2002). Developing a subjective measure of consumer well-being. *Journal of Macromarketing, 22*(2), 158–169.

Lucas, R. E., Diener, E., & Suh, E. (1996). Discriminant validity of well-being measures. *Journal of Personality and Social Psychology, 71*, 616–628.

Lyubomirsky, S., King, L., & Diener, E. (2005). The benefits of frequent positive affect: Does happiness lead to success? *Psychological Bulletin, 131*(6), 803.

Lyubomirsky, S., Tkach, C., & DiMatteo, M. R. (2006). What are the differences between happiness and self-esteem? *Social Indicators Research, 78*(3), 363–404.

Malhotra, N. K. (2006). Consumer well-being and quality of life: An assessment and directions for future research. *Journal of Macromarketing, 26*(1), 77–80.

McGranahan, D. V., Richard-Proust, C., Sovani, N. V., & Subramanian, M. (1970). *Contents and measurement of socio-economic development: An empirical inquiry. Report No. 70.10*. Geneva: United Nations Research Institute for Social Development.

Michalos, A. C. (2008). Education, happiness and wellbeing. *Social Indicators Research, 87*(3), 347–366.

Morris, M. D. (1979). *Measuring the condition of the world's poor: The physical quality of life index*. New York: Pergamon.

Nordhaus, W. D., & Tobin, J. (1973). Is growth obsolete? In M. Moss (Ed.), *The measurement of economic and social performance* (pp. 509–532). New York: Columbia University Press.

Oishi, S. (2012). *The psychological wealth of nations: Do happy people make a happy society*. Malden, MA: Wiley-Blackwell.

Oishi, S., Diener, E., & Lucas, R. E. (2007). The optimum level of well-being: Can people be too happy? *Perspectives on Psychological Science, 2*(4), 346–360.

Oishi, S., Kesebir, S., & Diener, E. (2011). Income inequality and happiness. *Psychological Science, 22*(9), 1095–1100.

Osberg, L. (2001, November 17). *Isn't it well being that we want to improve? The metric of evaluation*. Paper presented at From Theory to Practice: International Conference on Evaluation Methodology, Ottawa, ON.

Osberg, L., & Sharpe, A. (1998, October 30–31). *An index of economic well-being for Canada*. Paper presented at the CSLS Conference on the State of Living Standards and Quality of Life in Canada, Ottawa, ON.

Oswald, A. (1997). Happiness and economic performance. *Economic Journal, 107*(November), 1815–1831.

Oswald, A. J., Proto, E., & Sgroi, D. (2009). *Happiness and productivity. IZA Discussion Paper No 4645*. Bonn: Institute for the Study of Labor.

Pancer, E. (2009). What is consumer well-being? An historical analysis. In R. Hawkins (Ed.), *Proceedings of the 14th Biennial Conference on Historical Analysis and Research in Marketing*. Wolverhampton, UK: CHARM.

Pavot, W., & Diener, E. (1993). Review of the satisfaction with life scale. *Psychological Assessment, 5*, 164–172.

Pigou, A. C. (1929). *The economics of welfare* (3rd ed.). London: Macmillan. first published 1920.

Schyns, P. (2001). Income and satisfaction in Russia. *Journal of Happiness Studies, 2*, 173–204.

Seghieri, C., Desantis, G., & Tanturri, M. L. (2006). The richer, the happier? An empirical investigation in selected European countries. *Social Indicators Research, 79*, 455–476.

Sirgy, M. J. (2008). Ethics and public policy implications of research on consumer well-being. *Journal of Public Policy & Marketing, 27*(2), 207–212.

Sirgy, M. J., & Lee, D. (2006). Macro measures of Consumer Well-Being (CWB): A critical analysis and a research agenda. *Journal of Macromarketing, 26*(1), 27–44.

Sirgy, M., Lee, D., Grzeskowiak, S., Chebat, J., Johar, J., Hermann, A., et al. (2008). An extension and further validation of a community-based consumer well-being measure. *Journal of Macromarketing, 28*(3), 243–257.

Sirgy, M. J., Lee, D., & Kressmann, F. (2006a). A need-based measure of Consumer Well Being (CWB) in relation to personal transportation: Nomological validation. *Social Indicators Research, 79*(2), 337–367.

Sirgy, M. J., Lee, D., & Rahtz, D. (2007). Research on Consumer Well-Being (CWB): Overview of the field and introduction to the special issue. *Journal of Macromarketing, 27*(4), 341–349.

Sirgy, M. J., Michalos, A. C., Ferriss, A. L., Easterlin, R. E., Patrick, D., & Pavot, W. (2006b). The quality-of-life (QOL) research movement: Past, present, and future. *Social Indicators Research, 76*, 343–466.

Steckel, R. H., & Floud, R. (1997). *Health and welfare during industrialization*. Chicago: University of Chicago Press.

Stevenson, B., & Wolfers, J. (2008). *Economic growth and subjective well-being: Reassessing the Easterlin paradox (No. w14282)*. Cambridge, MA: National Bureau of Economic Research.

Stone, R. (1986). Nobel memorial lecture 1984. The accounts of society. *Journal of Applied Econometrics, 1*(1), 5–28.

Sun, F., Xiao, J. J. (2012). Perceived social policy fairness and subjective well-being. *Social Indicators Research, 107*(1), 171–186.

UNDP. (2002). *Human development report 2002: Deepening democracy in a fragmented world.* New York: Oxford University Press.

UNDP. (2013). *The rise of the south: Human progress in a diverse world. Human Development Report 2013.* New York: United Nations Development Program.

United Nations Department of Economic and Social Affairs. (1961). *Report on the world social situation.* New York: United Nations.

United Nations Department of Social Affairs. (1952). *Preliminary report on the world social situation.* New York: United Nations.

Van Praag, B. M. S., & Frijters, P. (1999). The measurement of welfare and well-being: The Leyden approach. In D. Kahneman, E. Diener, & N. Schwarz (Eds.), *Well-being: The foundations of hedonic psychology* (pp. 413–433). New York: Russell Sage.

Veenhoven, R. (2002). Why social policy needs subjective indicators. *Social Indicators Research, 58*(1-3), 33–46.

Vera-Toscano, E., Ateca-Amestoy, V., & Serrano-del-Rosal, R. (2006). Building financial satisfaction. *Social Indicators Research, 77*, 211–243.

Wong, C. K., Wong, K. Y., & Mok, B. H. (2006). Subjective well-being, societal condition and social policy–The case study of a rich Chinese society. *Social Indicators Research, 78*(3), 405–428.

Xiao, J. J. (2012). Chapter 24: Family economic well-being. In G. W. Peterson & K. R. Bush (Eds.), *Handbook of marriage and the family* (3rd ed.). New York: Springer.

Xiao, J. J. (2013). Chapter 8: Money and happiness: Implications for investor behavior. In H. Kent Baker & V. Ricciardi (Eds.), *Investor behavior: The psychology of financial planning and investing* (pp. 153–169). Hoboken, NJ: John Wiley & Sons.

Xiao, J. J., Chen, C., & Chen, F. (2014). Consumer financial capability and financial satisfaction. *Social Indicators Research, 118*(1), 415–432.

Zimmerman, S. L. (1995). *Understanding family policy: Theories and applications* (2nd ed.). Thousand Oaks, CA: Sage.

Chapter 2
Consumer Interests and Economic Wellbeing

Abstract This chapter discusses consumer economic wellbeing from a political perspective: how consumers pursue their rights in the marketplace through a public decision-making process to preserve and improve their economic wellbeing. In this chapter, we discuss consumer interests, consumer issues, consumer rights, and consumer representation. Because consumer right to privacy is a relatively new right, we summarize research on this right in a separate section. In addition, we also discuss the concept of consumer sovereignty and strategies for individual consumers to protect themselves in the marketplace.

2.1 Consumer Interests

A straightforward definition of consumer interest is difficult to find in the literature. In an earlier paper, a scholar divides consumer interests into two categories, economic interests and marketing interests. He considers economic interest superordinate and marketing interest subordinate. He encourages consumer advocates to pay more attention to economic interests, which means supporting economic policies that encourage continuity of economic activities, open markets, and price stability (Schooler 1982).

An influential scholar of consumer economics, Scott Maynes (1988), discusses consumer interest in an overview of a book entitled *Frontiers on Consumer Interest Research*, which is organized by American Council on Consumer Interests (ACCI), the major academic organization in consumer economics that publishes *Journal of Consumer Affairs*. Maynes states that consumer interest can be considered from several alternative interpretations: (1) anything that furthers the attainment of consumer rights; (2) any policies, practices, institutions, and ideas that are based on the approval of informed consumers, an idea originated in Maynes (1976); (3) cost-benefit assessments of proposals or institutions as a means of assessing efficiency and considerations of fairness proposed by Morgan (1985); and (4) removing consumer concerns and problems. The first definition is supported by the ACCI research committee and used to organize the *Frontiers* book.

Mayer and Brobeck (1997) describe difficulties in defining consumer interests because of three reasons: it could be objective or subjective; different groups of

J.J. Xiao, *Consumer Economic Wellbeing*, International Series on Consumer Science, DOI 10.1007/978-1-4939-2821-7_2

consumers may have different, sometimes conflicting interests; and individual consumers may have multiple, conflicting interests. However, they believe using consumer interest is helpful in four situations: when consumers obtain necessities; when consumers get best values from their money through purchases; when market process is improved by competition, representation, information, and redress; and when consumer interests are contrasted with other interests, such as corporate interests, labor interests, and environmental interests.

A marketing professor discusses characteristics of consumer interests that are diffusions of interest (a consumer's interests may be diffused by diverse roles one plays and diverse products one purchases), intensity (individuals' awareness as consumers may be lower than awareness of other roles played in society), organizational difficulties (not as effectively organized as other specialized groups such as business or labor groups), conflicting interests (may emerge among two individuals or groups when seeking to possess the same objects), and specificity of special interests (compared to consumers, business owners have more direct and specific interests in their producer role). He defines consumer interest as "the balancing by government of the interests of individuals in their roles as consumers and the interests of individuals and organizations in their roles as providers of labor and capital in the economic system" (p. 25). He argues that consumer interest is difficult to define and if needed, it should be defined in the context of governing (Forbes 1987).

Difficulties of defining consumer interest can be explained by the multiple meanings of consumer and interest. As discussed in Chap. 1, "consumer" has both narrow and broad definitions. The narrow definition of consumer refers to people who use market goods only, whereas the broad definition of consumer refers to people who consume. According to Merriam-Webster's Desk Dictionary (1995 ed.), interest has at least the following meanings: right, welfare, concern, and financial charge, among several others. When consumer interest is used in the literature of consumer research, it means consumer right, consumer welfare, or consumer concern. From a political science perspective, consumer interest means consumer right. If we use a narrow definition of consumer and consider multiple meanings of interest, consumer interest can be defined as wellbeing of consumers when purchasing and using market goods. Politically and legally, consumer interest can be expressed by consumer rights, while consumer rights originate from consumer issues in most cases.

2.2 Consumer Issues

Consumer problems refer to consumer dissatisfaction when using market goods and services. Consumer issues refer to consumer problems that become public issues. In the literature, the two terms are used interchangeably. As an influential scholar of consumer protection, Maynes et al. (1977) discusses consumer problems in market economy, which are asymmetric power between businesses and consumers, issues faced by disadvantaged consumers, informationally imperfect consumer markets, problems caused by monopoly, consumer grievances, and underrepresented consumer interests. Consumer sovereignty is suggested by Adam Smith in his claim that consumption has been the virtual goal of economic activities. However, because of these consumer problems, there is a long way to achieve the goal of consumer sovereignty.

Consumer issues differ substantially across nations. Thorelli (1988) compares consumer issues in developed and less developed countries. He first creates a framework for cross-cultural comparison, the ecology of markets. Then he compares the market systems in developed and less developed countries in the following dimensions: consumer characteristics and values, products, consumer search strategies, seller strategies, market institutions, and market system performance. Consumer problems in less developed countries identified by him are product safety, fraudulent and imitation goods, false or misleading information, corruption, high marketing costs, little organized consumer action, hyperinflation, and multinational corporations. In developed countries, consumer problems are product safety, consumer information, consumer education, quality, nonmetropolitan markets, one size fits all vs. individualization, decline of trust, participation, quality of competition, and prospects of consumer movement. Common consumer problems in both developed and less developed countries are misleading advertising and protectionism. Although his paper was published more than 20 years ago, many problems and differences between developed and less developed countries remain true.

2.3 Consumer Rights

Consumer rights can be categorized as moral rights and legal rights. Consumer moral rights are entitlements consumers should possess in the marketplaces when they do businesses with commercial companies. Consumer legal rights are those legalized moral rights that are specified by government laws and regulations. President Kennedy is an important name in the literature of consumer rights because he was the first person worldwide to propose the concept of consumer rights and also propose the first four specific consumer rights. He did so when delivering a presidential address of the union to congress on March 15, 1962, the date used as International Consumer Day and now celebrated by many countries. The four rights that consumers should have are the right to safety, information, choice, and voice. As recalled by the president's ghostwriter, these rights were a list of important issues faced by the nation and compiled by advisors of the president at the time (Lampman 1988). In the following years, President Nixon proposed "buyer rights" to Congress on October 30, 1969. This right is labeled a consumer right to redress by consumer researchers. President Ford proposed consumers' right to consumer education, which is based on a secondary source in 1975 but recognized by consumer researchers and others including President Clinton in 1994. President Clinton proposed consumers' right to service when he proclaimed the National Consumer

Week on October 23–29, 1994. In addition, International Organization of Consumer Union (now renamed Consumers International) proposed consumers' right to a clean environment in 1984.

Proposing the concept of a consumer bill of rights and the aforementioned consumer rights have long-term impacts on consumer protection in the USA and the world for three reasons. First, this proposal represents one of the few times any president directly addressed consumer rights, which were novel and revolutionary at the time. Secondly, the four rights serve as a working agenda for the social reform of the 1960s and 1970s, and many relevant consumer protection laws relevant to these rights have been proposed and passed in congress and became consumer protection laws. Finally, the issues associated with these rights continue to be relevant in current times (Swagler 1997).

However, consumer rights proposed by presidents have limitations. The rights are from a perspective of consumer protection by government but do not empower consumers from the bottom up. Another limitation is that the rights can be contradictory, such as right to safety and the right to choose (Swagler 1997). In addition, the list of rights is not comprehensive and overlooks some important rights, such as consumer right to privacy.

Consumer rights proposed by presidents are considered the first of three major steps in public policy making. The other two steps are legislations on special consumer topics and more specific administrative rules. In addition, to achieve efficiency and effectiveness, consumer rights also need to consider the balance between social costs and benefits (Lampman 1988).

International consumer advocacy communities endorsed the concept of consumer rights. For instance, the International Organization of Consumer Unions, which changed its name to Consumers International (CI) in 1995, worked with the United Nations (UN) for 10 years and finally the UN adopted the "United Nations Guidelines for Consumer Protection" in 1985. The 1999 expanded version of the guideline reflects the influence of consumer rights discussed above. The guideline asserts that consumers should be protected in the following aspects: physical safety; promotion and protection of consumer economic interests; standards for the safety and quality of consumer goods and services; distribution facilities for essential consumer goods and services; measures enabling consumers to obtain redress; education and information programs; and promotion of sustainable consumption (United Nation 2003). Interestingly, consumer right to voice is not included in the guideline.

Consumer rights posted on the website of Consumers International (2010) reflect important dimensions of consumer rights endorsed by international consumer advocates:

1. The right to satisfaction of basic needs—To have access to basic, essential goods and services: adequate food, clothing, shelter, health care, education, public utilities, water, and sanitation.
2. The right to safety—To be protected against products, production processes, and services that are hazardous to health or life.

3. The right to be informed—To be given the facts needed to make an informed choice, and to be protected against dishonest or misleading advertising and labeling.
4. The right to choose—To be able to select from a range of products and services, offered at competitive prices with an assurance of satisfactory quality.
5. The right to be heard—To have consumer interests represented in the making and execution of government policy, and in the development of products and services.
6. The right to redress—To receive a fair settlement of just claims, including compensation for misrepresentation, shoddy goods, or unsatisfactory services.
7. The right to consumer education—To acquire knowledge and skills needed to make informed, confident choices about goods and services while being aware of basic consumer rights and responsibilities and how to act on them.
8. The right to a healthy environment—To live and work in an environment which is non-threatening to the wellbeing of present and future generations.

Comparing the eight rights on the CI website and eight rights proposed by American scholars (Lampman and Douthitt 1997), they are very similar. The only difference is that the right to convenience, proposed by Clinton, is substituted by CI for the right to basic needs.

UN's consumer rights guidelines inspirited many countries to create consumer protection laws. In the *Encyclopedia of the Consumer Movement* (Brobeck 1997), consumer protection movements in many countries are described. For example, influenced by the UN's guideline and experiences of developed countries such as the USA and demanded by the economic growth and open door polices, in 1984 China created its China Consumer Association, a quasi government agency that has hundreds of branches at provincial, city, district, and county levels. In January 1994, the Chinese national consumer protection law took effect (Xiao 1997).

2.4 Consumer Right to Privacy

Consumer right to privacy is not included in the list of consumer rights endorsed by CI because this is a comparatively new right that shows significances in the last two decades. For this reason, this section is devoted to this important topic. The concept of the right to privacy could be traced back to more than 100 years ago in a paper published in *Harvard Law Review* (Warren and Brandeis 1890). Westin's (1967) book on privacy influenced research, legislation, and business in the last five decades. The earlier papers with consumer privacy in the title were published in the 1970s (Hersbergen 1973; Rosen 1977). Several comprehensive reviews compiled recent research on consumer privacy (Lanier and Saini 2008; Rapp et al. 2009; Xu 2009).

2.4.1 Definition of Consumer Privacy

Privacy has been generally defined as "the claim of individuals, groups, or institutions to determine for themselves when, how, and to what extent information about them is communicated to others" (Westin 1967, p. 7). Consumers have three primary areas of concern: transparency and their levels of awareness when personal data are collected and disseminated; security and the protocols in place to ensure that information is protected from outside intruders; and liability and available remedies if data are improperly used or errors occur in records (Milne and Gordon 1993).

2.4.2 Privacy as a Consumer Right

The first academic journal paper on privacy as a consumer right is written by Goodwin (1991). According to the author, consumers' right to privacy was proposed by government officials, business practitioners, and academic writers in the later 1980s. Consumer privacy is defined in terms of control over information disclosure and the environment in which a consumer transaction occurs. These two dimensions generate a 2×2 matrix, identifying four states of privacy based on control over environment, information disclosure, both, or neither. *Total control* refers to the state in which the consumer can control both who is present and who will know about the transaction or behavior. Transactions that fall into this category require the least amount of regulation for privacy protection. Most cash transactions without requesting consumer identification information fall into this cell. *Environmental control* represents a state of privacy where the consumer retains control over the presence of others in his/her environment but loses control over disclosure of information. Examples of this privacy state include videotext or catalog shopping transactions, where the consumer remains at home, undisturbed, while information may be recorded invisibly. *Disclosure control* refers to the state in which the consumer's environment is disturbed, but person-specific information remains undistributed. Marketing examples include mall or door-to-door surveys, with anonymity granted to respondents. This state of privacy may be the easiest to conceptualize and regulate. *No control* represents the lowest degree of privacy within this framework: The consumer controls neither who is present nor the distribution of the information gathered by the intruder. Marketing examples include unsolicited telephone and personal contacts by telemarketers, salespersons, or market researchers (Goodwin 1991).

The two mechanisms used to ensure that consumers are in control of their information are "opt-in" and "opt-out" (Fletcher 2003). Opting-in gives consumers more control over what data firms are allowed to acquire and which advertisers can use consumers' personal information, along with the types of marketing communications consumers ultimately receive. Opting-out is also control oriented but requires awareness of the lists and databases with which consumers are associated and overt efforts to seek removal (Rapp et al. 2009).

2.4.3 Consumer Concerns About Privacy

Based on national surveys, the Privacy Segmentation Index was developed in the early 1990s to segment the US population along a continuum from high to low privacy concerns, resulting in three groups. The first segment is classified as high/fundamentalists who call for new legislation to stop erosion of their rights. The second is termed medium/pragmatists who register moderate interest in privacy issues but are willing to give access to and use of their personal data for certain purposes. The final segment is the low/unconcerned who suffer little anxiety about information (Dolnicar and Jordaan 2007).

Researchers propose a concept of *marketing avoidance*—consumer efforts to conceal themselves and to deflect marketing. The theoretical analyses find that in markets where the marginal cost of solicitation is sufficiently low, efforts by low-benefit consumers to conceal themselves will increase the cost-effectiveness of solicitations and lead sellers to market more. However, concealment by high-benefit consumers leads sellers to market less. Furthermore, concealment by low-benefit consumers increases direct privacy harm and consumer welfare is higher with deflection than concealment (Hann et al. 2008).

2.4.4 Marketing and Consumer Privacy

Three marketing channels have potential to invade consumer privacy, direct mail, Internet, and neuromarketing.

Privacy and direct mail: Researchers identify four critical attributes to determine consumer participation in direct mail campaigns: targeting, volume, permission, and compensation. They find that the level of compensation is deemed most essential, followed by volume of mail with a preference for less, and then better targeting with a desire for mailings that are directed to specific needs. The permission factor is least important to consumers (Milne and Gordon 1993). A later study shows that consumers may be less concerned about privacy than consumer advocates and policymakers expected. Only 25 % of informants want to remove identifying information from all mailing lists and this percentage has dropped when marketers' purposes and tactics are clarified (Milne and Rohm 2000).

Privacy and Internet: Most consumers are unaware of how their private information will be handled and used. Consumers avoid websites that require personal data for registration, leading some to falsify or provide incomplete details (Sheehan and Hoy 1999). Consumers may employ a decision calculus that weighs potential exposure problems associated with passing along private information against the perceived value of the content available on the website (Rapp et al. 2009). A popular method for gathering consumer data involves Internet banners and pop-up advertisements (Palmer 2005). When online shoppers click on promotional materials, they leave a cookie trail, which digitally marks search movement records on consumers' computer systems (Charters 2002). These cookies remain in machines and allow webmasters to recognize users on return visits in order to tailor advertisements specifically to their interests. Privacy issues arise since marketers access and combine these data to amass consumer profiles across potentially thousands of websites. Such issues are magnified because cookies typically are downloaded without permission, and Internet users may be unaware of blocking options that could relieve their discomfort or believe that they have no choice if they wish to navigate particular sites (Palmer 2005). A researcher examines how the interactive effects of the disclosure and practice of cookie use as a method of nonconsensual identification might influence online users' affect or behavior. He finds that both cookie use and disclosure have increased but the covert use of cookies is still a concern. Consumers' negative reactions to cookie use are significantly reduced by a priori cookie disclosure by the visited website (Miyazaki 2008).

Privacy and neuromarketing: The new potential invasion of privacy involves use of neuroimaging to scan the brains of individuals under various testing conditions (Wilson et al. 2008). As brain scanning and interpretation advance, privacy issues may intensify. Previous practices suggest that widespread sharing may occur if the information is linked to consumer preferences or if it enhances data gathered already by direct advertising or Internet usage. An added concern is that the rate of incidental pathology findings in subjects from neuroscientific studies is 1–2 %, and provision of these data to firms such as insurance agencies could place consumers under a new form of risk that may bar them from needed services, rather than facilitate access (Rapp et al. 2009).

2.4.5 Conceptualizations of Consumer Privacy

Privacy has been considered a dynamic and dialectic concept that subsumes a wide variety of conceptualizations (Margulis 2003a, b). The conceptualizations of information privacy can be done through three different ways. The first way, referred to as the *information exchange* lens, conceptualizes privacy as a "privacy calculus" which contributes to the understanding of the trade-offs that consumers are willing to make when they exchange their personal information for certain benefits (Klopfer and Rubenstein 1977; Stone and Stone 1990). The second way, referred to as the *social contract* lens, frames the discussion of the bond of trust between organizations and individuals over information privacy based on the *Integrative Social Contract Theory* (Donaldson and Dunfee 1994, 1995, 1999). The third way, referred to as the *information control* lens, emphasizes the role of control perception in explaining the privacy phenomenon (e.g., Westin 1967; Margulis 2003b).

Integrating these theories, a researcher proposes a conceptual model of the organization-consumer information interaction in the context of business-to-consumer electronic commerce (B2C e-commence). According to this model, consumers' information disclosure decision is determined by four general factors:

(1) privacy attitudes such as privacy concerns; (2) privacy related beliefs such as perceived risks, trust, and perceived information control; (3) the type of personal information requested; and (4) social norms. On the other hand, in response to consumers' increasing privacy concerns, e-commerce websites implement privacy measures to comply with privacy laws, develop privacy policy and join privacy and security seal programs, and deploy privacy-enhancing technologies to protect consumers' personal information (Xu 2009).

Researchers propose a framework for analyzing consumer privacy from justice perspectives. They argue that consumers are willing to disclose personal information if three justices are met. The three justices are distributive, procedural, and interactional justices. *Distributive justice* is concerned with the perceived fairness of outcomes that one receives. Consumers may be willing to provide personal information after cost-benefit analyses (if benefits of providing personal information are greater than the costs) or social comparisons (comparing outcomes from different corporations for providing similar personal information). *Procedural justice* refers to the perceived fairness of the procedures and how these procedures are enacted. One example is consumers' ability to remove their names from marketing lists before they are used or shared. *Interactional justice* refers to the fairness of interpersonal treatment that an individual receives from another. In the context of consumer transaction, this method can be used by corporations in gathering information from consumers and how consumers are treated interpersonally (Culnan and Bies 2003).

2.4.6 Government Protection of Consumer Privacy

The privacy literature describes three major privacy protection approaches: privacy-enhancing technology, industry self-regulation, and government legislation (Xu 2009). The privacy laws of the European Union (EU) and the USA represent the two major privacy regulatory models—the comprehensive legislative approach and the self-regulatory approach. These two different privacy regulatory models highlight two different views of privacy: a fundamental rights view of privacy (i.e., "privacy as a human right") and an instrumentalist view of privacy (i.e., "privacy as a commodity"). The first camp views privacy as a fundamental human right, like the right to liberty or life (Sopinka 1997; Walczuch and Lizette 2001). The fundamentalist position holds that privacy is tied to a cluster of rights, such as autonomy and dignity (Beaney 1966). The second camp holds privacy to be of instrumental value rather than a fundamental right; that is, the value of privacy comes because it sustains, promotes, and protects other things that we value.

The FTC implemented several rules under the Financial Services Modernization Act (1999) regarding financial privacy, along with similar protections for consumers under the Fair Credit Reporting Act (1970) and the Children's Online Privacy Protection Act (1998). The FTC (1998) has advanced five interrelated guidelines for data collection and usage. These core principles consist of notice (notification by marketers and advertisers of intentions with regard to collected information), choice (consumer right to decide if and how private information can be used), access (consumers' ability to view and obtain collected data), security (marketer or advertiser obligation to ensure that personal data are protected), and redress (enforcement mechanisms in place to assure compliance). Legislators have considered several bills to enhance consumer privacy protection (Franzak et al. 2001).

The Organization for Economic Cooperation and Development (OECD) offer alternative guidelines referred to as Fair Information Practices (FIPs), giving consumers control over disclosure and subsequent use of personal information according to their needs and desires (Culnan 2000).

2.4.7 *Business Self-Regulation on Consumer Privacy*

Self-regulation involves the setting of standards by an industry group or certifying agency and the voluntary adherence to the set standards by members or associates. Under this self-regulatory approach, industries develop rules and enforcement procedures that substitute for government regulation (Swire 1997) and often issue certifications in the form of seals of approval which assure that the businesses indeed conform to the fair information practices they purport to (Culnan and Bies 2003). An example of an industry self-regulation is the Direct Marketing Association (DMA) that makes compliance with its privacy principles a condition of its membership (DMA 2003). Other examples include privacy seals on e-commerce and e-service websites such as those given by Online Privacy Alliance or TRUSTe (Xu 2009).

2.5 Consumer Representation

2.5.1 *Consumer Advocates at National Level*

Consumer rights are actively proposed, lobbied, and promoted by consumer advocates. In the USA, consumer advocacy organizations represent consumer interests and protect consumer interests in public policy making. Major consumer organizations include the Consumer Federation of America, Consumer Union, National Consumers' League, Public Interest Research Groups, among others. More than two dozen consumer advocacy organizations active in the USA are described in *Encyclopedia of Consumer Movement* (Brobeck 1997). Several individuals have made significant contributions to the consumer movement that have changed the landscape of consumer protection in the USA, among them are Ralph Nader, Esther Peterson, and Colston Warne (Brobeck 1997).

Stephen Brobeck, a long-term executive director of Consumer Federation of America, describes strategies his organization uses in consumer advocacy. When consumer advocates pursue consumer policies, they need to make distinctions among facts, preferences, and universal values. Facts relate not only to physical characteristics of products but also to their consumer impacts, which can be accomplished by product testing. Preferences are subjective qualities that manifest themselves in consumer choices of products, which vary among individual consumers. Universal values refer to accessibility, affordability, quality, safety, convenience, and customer service, which are universal throughout almost all parts of the world today and should be reflected in consumer policies. He identifies several dilemmas in advocating pro-consumer policies. First, it is not always easy to establish important facts such as discrimination in auto loan lending. Second, consumer preferences are not always consistent with universal values such as taking out an auto loan but actually being unable to afford it. Third, there are trade-offs among the universal values such as high safety being related to less accessibility. Forth, universal values vary depending on the needs of individual and groups of consumers. Affordability is more important for a low-income consumer but safety is more important for a middle-income consumer. Finally, university values related to products may conflict with other societal values (raising speed limits to increase transportation efficiency tends to diminish auto safety). He suggests a three-step process in advocating consumer policies. The first is to learn about consumer preferences. The second step is to evaluate these policies in terms of universal consumer values by assessing both efficiency and equity considerations. The third step is to consider broader societal impacts. He uses a case of automobile fuel efficiency standards to demonstrate how these steps are used in advocating consumer policies (Brobeck 2006).

Drawing on social movement theory, supporters of consumer movement are divided into those seeking benefits for themselves, for others, or for the public at large. In addition, organizational leaders can be divided into volunteers and professionals. Using these distinctions, four types of consumer organizations are categorized (Herrmann 1991). The first type is called volunteer-led organizations with beneficiary constituencies (examples: food price protests and rent strikes). The second type is volunteer-led organizations with conscience constituencies (examples: state and local consumer groups). The third type is professionally led organizations with a beneficiary constituency (example: Consumer Union). The fourth type is professionally led organizations with conscience constituencies (example: Nader organizations). These four types appeared historically in this order in the USA and also occurred in other countries as they moved through the various stages of economic development. Descriptions and characteristics of several types of consumer organizations are described in Herrmann et al. (1988).

2.5.2 *Consumer Advocates at State and Local Level*

Consumer advocacy groups at the state level exist in all states, although they typically have no paid staff and few resources (Xiao and Richardson 2003). Thus, these groups often operate out of private homes and use post office boxes. According to a 1992 survey, the number of these groups exceeded 400. Quite a few strong state and local advocacy groups exist, usually in large cities and heavily populated states (Brobeck 1997).

Some consumer advocacy groups specialize in problems of the poor (e.g., high-interest credit terms, high fees to cash checks) or some other specific issue (e.g., provision of utilities). Many specialized consumer advocacy groups have high credibility with legislators, members of the executive branch, and the press. Most state and local consumer interest groups perform at least one of the three general functions: complaint resolution, consumer education and information dissemination, and lobbying and regulatory intervention to influence government decisions affecting consumers.

Grassroots consumer groups share several important characteristics (Xiao and Richardson 2003). First, all are completely or largely autonomous. Second, nearly all grassroots leaders believe that government plays a critically important role in consumer protection. Third, most groups concentrate on pocketbook concerns, such as deceptive and abusive sales practices, price gouging, and defective products. Lastly, despite limited resources, most grassroots groups are highly visible because they receive much press coverage (Brobeck 1997).

State consumer protection advocacy organizations are the oldest major type of grassroots consumer groups. These organizations are usually run and supported by middle-class professionals. The principal focus of these groups is persuading states to establish effective consumer protections. One of the most effective of these organizations has been the Virginia Citizens Consumer Council (VCCC). Major accomplishments of this group include enactment of the Virginia Consumer Protection Act and the establishment of local consumer protection offices, passage of a strong new-car "lemon law," and mandated public representation on health regulatory boards.

Local consumer action groups are the second major type of grassroots consumer groups. The complaint-organizing model developed by Consumer Education and Protective Association (CEPA) in Philadelphia in the late 1960s influenced many of these organizations. CEPA organized consumers by requiring those with complaints to participate in the resolution of the grievances of others as a condition of receiving help with their own problem. This method of resolution included a complaint letter stating the consumer's grievance and requested settlement, followed by a delegation of CEPA members to discuss the grievance with the merchant, ending with the organization of weekly "educational pickets" until the merchant agreed to resolve the problem. Besides using the complaint-organizing model, these groups also undertake a broad range of advocacy and educational activities. Several famous organizations of such type include Consumer Action in San Francisco, Chicago Consumer Coalition, Consumer Protection Association in Cleveland, and Seattle Consumer Action Network.

The third type of grassroots consumer group is the Public Interest Research Groups (PIRGs). In the 1970s and early 1980s, PIRGs were organized on college and university campuses in more than 20 states. In the early years, virtually all funding came from student activity fees. Later, to supplement these resources, PIRGs undertook nationwide door-to-door canvassing, raising millions of dollars annually. Several national PIRG groups also provide support to state and local groups. This program emphasizes statewide advocacy on consumer, environmental, good government, and student issues.

The fourth type of grassroots consumer groups is Citizen Utility Boards (CUBs), inspired by Nader and organized largely by PIRGs. These statewide consumer utility advocacy groups were funded through a requirement that private utilities allow CUBs to use bill mailings to solicit voluntary dues-paying members. The role of CUBs has been limited because other utility advocacy groups that received state funding—consumer utility counsels—were already established in most states. In addition, the CUB concept was weakened by a US Supreme Court decision that forbids states to require utilities to give advocacy groups access to their mailings. The CUBs that still exist either have access to certain state mailings or raise funds using conventional methods employed by other nonprofit organizations.

Other grassroots consumer groups consist of state consumer federations that include the cooperative and labor communities, state or local offices of national groups that have consumer issues as part of their agendas such as AARP, consumer groups affiliated with university law schools such as the Center for Public Representation at University of Wisconsin Law School, and organizations resulting from consumer boycotts, such as the Chicago Consumer Coalition.

The activities of these local consumer groups are consistent with two historic American traditions: citizen activism and citizen participation in volunteer organizations. They have created and contributed to a "consumer consciousness," an awareness by consumers that their interests are distinct from those of sellers and that as consumers they have rights in their dealings with sellers and the ability to enforce these rights (Brobeck 1997).

2.5.3 Consumerism, a Term with Changing Meanings

The earliest use of consumerism, found in 1944, referred to the interest of eliminating wastes and needless tolls and was associated with the cooperative movement at the time (Swagler 1994). Since the 1960s, *consumerism* has been used with two basic meanings. The first refers to a social movement or ideology that seeks the consumer interest. The period of 1960–1970 was the heyday of the third wave of the US consumer movements, during which this meaning was most popular in press and professional literature. The second basic meaning of consumerism, which was used by some authors at the same time period including a 1960 best seller *The Waste Maker* by Vance Packard, refers to excessive materialism. Since the 1980s this meaning is more common in the popular and professional literature, including Pope John Paul II's 1991 encyclical *Centesimus Annus* (Swagler 1994). In recent years, consumerism became a positive marketing term, focusing on what consumers want to buy and a managerial determination to make it available (Rotfeld 2010). Consumer professionals need to identify different meanings when they read the literature about consumerism.

2.5.4 Consumer Movement

The consumer movement consists of organized efforts of individuals and private, not-for-profit organizations to enhance the rights and collective welfare of consumers. The primary goal of the movement is to advance efficiency and equity in the marketplace (Herrmann and Mayer 1997).

Throughout the US history, there were three waves of consumer protection movements within the twentieth century (Cohen 2003, 2010; Herrmann and Mayer 1997). All three waves coincided with broader periods of reform—whether the Progressive Era of the early twentieth century, the New Deal of the 1930s and 1940s, or the Great Society of the 1960s. In all three of these twentieth-century activist moments, women made up many of the masterminds and often the shock troops of the consumer movement. Moreover, another social group frequently excluded from traditional politics, African Americans, became activists in the realm of consumption. Among the three waves, the third wave is considered the most influential and significant. This third wave of the consumer movement succeeded on two levels. On the first level, it passed landmark legislation to better protect consumers in the marketplace. On the second level, it invigorated federal regulatory authority in consumer interest, dramatically increasing the amount of economic and particularly social regulation on behalf of ordinary Americans with new agencies such as the Environmental Protection Agency (EPA), the Occupational Safety and Health Administration (OSHA), and the CPSC. Some analysts estimate that between 1970 and 1975, social regulation rose by more than 200 % (Cohen 2003, 2010).

Is it the time for the fourth wave of the consumer movement? It may be under way because of the current financial crisis and legislation progress in the interest of consumers. In recent years, several pro-consumer laws on credit card, health care, and financial product protection have been passed and implemented. The major reason is that the current financial crisis has adversely and severally affected consumer life. Consumers are most easily politicized in tough economic times, when they are feeling economically insecure and worried about their vulnerabilities as producers and consumers (Cohen 2010).

One important feature of all three waves of consumer movements in the USA is diminished public confidence in business and heightened confidence in government that results in new regulatory controls. Other characteristics of consumer movements in the USA include institutionalization (consumer affair departments are created in federal and state government and in large corporations), specialization (some consumer organizations have been established themselves as experts in particular areas such as food safety and nutrition, health care, automobile safety, credit cards), professionalization (consumer leaders have become full-time professionals who can build a career in consumer affairs or public interest advocacy), changing strategies (consumer advocates make less efforts to influence consumer product choices and more of an attempt to alter seller behavior directly through legislative and regulatory means), and internationalization (US consumer protection practices have influenced and also have been influenced by other countries; consumer issues related to international trade and environmental protection are international in nature) (Herrmann and Mayer 1997; Mayer 1989).

2.6 Consumer Sovereignty

Consumer sovereignty refers to the situation in which consumers exert ultimate control over the economy. Under consumer sovereignty, consumer preferences determine the composition of goods that are produced in the economy. Through spending decisions, individual consumers control both the allocation of resources and the distribution of goods across the economy (Hildebrand 1951). Three assumptions fall under this situation: first, consumers are rational to make optimal choices; second, consumers are fully informed to make optimal choices; and third, consumers are able to purchase goods in a competitive marketplace. This concept has been questioned by social scientists in many aspects. The first question is whether consumer sovereignty produces an economic outcome different from what government could solely provide. The answer is no, evidenced by failures of many socialist countries. Moreover, this idea faces several practical rejections. First, consumers are simply irrational. Second, they are too ignorant to make informed choices. Third, marketers may alter consumer preferences to buy unnecessary goods. Fourth, consumers may not seek behavior that results in optimal public interest such as environmental issues. Current economic forces such as globalization will enhance, rather than detract from, consumer sovereignty as consumers are presented with more options and more opportunities than ever before (Saving 2006).

From a historic perspective, consumer sovereignty is a term traced to a book by William Harold Hutt (1936). Hutt defines consumer sovereignty as follows (1936, p. 257): "The consumer is sovereign when, in his role of citizen, he has not delegated to political institutions for authoritarian use the power which he can exercise socially through his power to demand (or refrain from demanding)." He later rephrases his definition (1940, p. 66): "it [consumers' sovereignty] simply refers to the controlling power exercised by free individuals, in choosing between ends, over the custodians of the community's resources, when the resources by which those ends can be served are scarce." Hutt argues the parallelism between consumer sovereignty and the sovereignty of the ballot box. Consumers vote with their dollars. Hutt holds it as quite possible that individuals have little idea of their best interests or of their highest welfare. He also considers the idea that society lacks the ability to agree on what patterns of consumption would be a better central precept. This recognition forms the basis for the social value of tolerance. The key value to be realized by consumer sovereignty is not welfare maximization of any sort, but rather the simple tolerance of the desires of others. While emphasizing the pragmatism of tolerance in the short run, Hutt hopes that in the long run consumer sovereignty might make a contribution to social improvement (Persky 1993).

A researcher has conducted a study to see whether there is direct evidence supporting economists' faith in consumer sovereignty in a simple context that compares values of gifts and similar goods purchases by consumers themselves. Data collected from college students show that consumers' own purchases generate between 10 and 18 % more value than items received as gifts, which implies that consumers make better choices in this context and the consumer rationality assumption under consumer sovereignty is supported. However, the consumer rationality assumption is violated in many intertemporal and probabilistic contexts cited in this study (Waldfogel 2005).

From a legal perspective, antitrust and consumer protection laws support one another as components of an overarching unity. This overarching unity is consumer sovereignty, described as "the state of affairs in which consumers have an unimpaired ability to make decisions in their individual interests and markets operate efficiently in responding to the collective effect of those decisions" (Averitt and Lande 1997, pp. 722–723). Antitrust and consumer protection laws share a common purpose to facilitate the exercise of consumer sovereignty or effective consumer choice. Antitrust law is intended to ensure that a meaningful range of options is available to consumers through market competition. Consumer protection laws seek to protect the ability of consumers to freely choose among such options. Using telecommunication policies as a case, in the USA, issues of consumer sovereignty are being addressed through an uncoordinated stream of piecemeal litigation, primarily through interpretation of numerous savings clauses. By contrast, other nations are demonstrating a greater ability or willingness to conduct a holistic review and coordination of consumer protection remedies (Cherry 2010).

A researcher provides a conceptual analysis on limited consumer sovereignty in human services by using geriatric nursing home patients as a case. These care recipients cannot enforce their legal right to quality service; their quality-effective demand is low. Formal economic analyses often characterize the weak position of the care recipient as an information asymmetry problem. An additional obstacle, however, is the recipient's inability to safeguard his or her personal interest due to physical, mental, or social incapacities; that is, "limited consumer sovereignty." Incapacitated individuals cannot enforce quality even when quality information is available. This creates a fundamental incentive problem in the monitoring of quality. This population also depends on services that are complex and non-verifiable, making external monitoring difficult. To improve consumer sovereignty in areas with low-quality effective demand, the author proposes several measures such as enhancing service recipients' voices and choices and facilitating the outside monitoring by able individuals and groups (Eika 2009).

Consumer sovereignty may be enhanced through international trade and economic opening in developing countries. Researchers demonstrate Brazil's move toward greater openness in its foreign trade and capital account since the 1980s, reflects a weakening of the exercise of national sovereignty for economic objectives, while consumer sovereignty has been correspondingly increased. There are costs and benefits to Brazil from both kinds of sovereignty. Increasing constraints on macroeconomic policy making have been accompanied by an increase in the choices open to many individuals. The latter increase, however, has been limited by a highly skewed distribution of income, which has persisted despite the profound changes in economic policy (Baer and Coes 2002).

From a perspective of business ethics, researchers argue that consumer sovereignty in an increasingly high-tech world is more of a fiction than a fact. The world of high tech is increasingly responsible for changes in the opportunity, ability, and motivation of business firms to compete and consumers to make rational decisions. Consumer sovereignty cannot be used to maintain a thriving economy; instead performance standards designed to meet the demands of various stakeholders of the organization are needed (Sirgy and Su 2000).

2.7 Strategies for Individual Consumers

2.7.1 Consumer Rights Perceived by Consumers

How do ordinary consumers think about consumer rights and responsibilities? Based on a qualitative study among ordinary consumers who were not active politically or consumer advocates in Sydney, Australia, in the setting of credit card debt, a researcher proposes a framework on sociohistorically shaped political myths, in which four quatrains are labeled: individual autonomy, social equality, consumer sovereignty, and corporate dominance. Several types of consumers based on this framework with cases of consumers are interviewed. The researcher concludes that a broader political ideology—one that intertwines consumption practices with a causal narrative of business, society, and state—infuses consumer opinions. Consumers negotiate tensions between each of these four myths—for example, individual autonomy versus social equality, and consumer sovereignty versus corporate dominance. This ideology triggers moral judgments among consumers about themselves and others that inform their perceptions of deservedness and apportions degree of responsibility and blame across consumer, business, and government participants (Henry 2010).

2.7.2 Consumer Acumen

To prepare competent consumers for future generations, McGregor (2011a) proposes a concept of *consumer acumen*. The concept is modeled after the emerging literature on business acumen. Consumer acumen adds to consumer literacy with keen, penetrating consumer intelligence that informs quick perception and discernment of changing economic contexts and improves consumer decision making. Consumer acumen can be defined as the art of linking two things: (1) the insightful assessment of the external consumer landscape with (2) the actual execution of consumer management strategies to attain desired consumer goals. Six dimensions of consumer acumen are proposed: the ability to scan and interpret the complex economy, see patterns and make connections, think big picture, engage in intense mental activity, holistically manage ambiguity and expectations, and assume consumer leadership.

McGregor (2011b) discusses consumer education philosophies for training future competent consumers. She argues that the basic premise is that the nature of people's socialization into their role as a consumer will depend upon the consumer educator's philosophy of education—what is the purpose of education. She distinguishes between two overarching intents of consumer education: (a) empowerment for self-interest relative to the power of businesses and/or (b) empowerment gained from supporting citizens to become more socially, ethically, and morally responsible consumers. She also explores the relationship between eleven dominant educational philosophies and four types of consumer education. She believes that consumer educators could benefit from becoming philosophically savvy and philosophically inclusive if they wish to address the pressing moral and ethical multi-dilemmas emerging in our consumer society.

2.7.3 Unscrewed: Strategies for Individual Consumers to Redress

Burley (2006) in his book *Unscrewed*, based on his own life and business experience, presents strategies to balance powers between consumers and businesses and to actively assure the consumer right to redress. He uses true stories to demonstrate his ideas. He calls these strategies "unscrewed solutions" with five P's: principle, purpose, promise, power tools, and plan. The principle states that a company will do only what is in its financial self-interest. The purpose is to reclaim money, assets, or equity while minimizing time and effort. The promise is to show the determination to the offending business that the consumer will spend an unlimited amount of time and energy to get what he or she deserves refunded or replaced. The power tools are five conventional technologies (telephone, fax, computer and printer, Internet, and e-mail) and one nontechnical method (personal visit) to leverage a consumer's position with the offending business. The plan includes an acceptable goal, adversary research, a specific strategy, a realistic timeline, and an honest assessment of the situation. In addition, he develops techniques for dealing with small businesses, big businesses, and government and megacorporations. Techniques to deal with small businesses are town crier intent, complaint ad intent, customer discouragement, inform competitors, and tenacity for complaining. Strategies to negotiate with big business are using 800 calls, continuing faxes, complaining on offending business's website, using consumer review sites, and calling investor relation departments as a stakeholder. Methods to talk with government and megacorporations include informing the supervisor (to low-level staff), news releases intent (to high-level officials), and political withdrawal (to affected officials).

2.8 Summary

This chapter is about consumer politics. Consumer politics refers to the public policy decision-making process in which how consumers represent their interests to gain reasonable legal rights in the marketplace. Consumer interest is a term with multiple meanings. In the context of the consumer political environment, it refers to consumer rights.

To achieve consumer economic wellbeing, consumers need government regulations to ensure basic consumer rights. In the USA consumer rights are realized by relevant government laws and regulations. Many consumer rights originate from consumer issues that adversely affect consumers' economic interests. President Kennedy proposed consumer right as a concept along with four consumer rights in the 1960s. Later, several US presidents and consumer organizations proposed several consumer rights and the UN adopted the concept and developed a guideline of consumer rights for other countries to follow when they make consumer protection laws.

Consumer right to privacy has received attention by public policy makers, business practitioners, and consumer leaders in recent decades. More consumers start to realize that their personal information is valuable and should be protected by law.

Consumers are represented by consumer advocates in national organizations such as the Consumer Federation of America and its member organizations in the USA. These organizations mainly work with issues important to low- and middle-income consumers and advocate for consumers in legislation at national, state, and local levels in the public policy-making process. Additionally, these organizations provide helpful information for consumers through their publications, such as the *Consumer Report* published by Consumer Union.

Consumer sovereignty is a concept served as a basic assumption in the work of some economists. The concept assumes that comparing businesses and consumers in the market, consumers dominate the game, which is conceptually possible but in reality is not.

In a typical market economy, especially the buyer market, consumers should be considered the high priority. Individual consumers should know that they can protect their basic rights by first knowing what these rights are and how to pursue them if needed. Individual consumers also need to know where to seek help when they need to voice their concerns and obtain new rights when new issues come out because of new technologies, new products, or new services.

References

Averitt, N. W., & Lande, R. H. (1997). Consumer sovereignty: A unified theory of antitrust and consumer protection law. *Antitrust Law Journal, 65*, 713–756.

Baer, W., & Coes, D. V. (2002). National sovereignty and consumer sovereignty: Some consequences of Brazil's economic opening. *Quarterly Review of Economics and Finance, 42*(5), 853–863.

Beaney, W. M. (1966). Right to privacy and American law. *Law and Contemporary Problems, 31*, 253–271.

Brobeck, S. (Ed.). (1997). *Encyclopedia of the consumer movement*. Santa Barbara, CA: ABC CLIO.

Brobeck, S. (2006). Defining the consumer interest: Challenges for advocates. *The Journal of Consumer Affairs, 40*(1), 177–185.

Burley, R. (2006). *Unscrewed: The consumer's guide to getting what you paid for*. Berkeley, CA: Ten Speed Press.

Charters, D. (2002). Electronic monitoring and privacy issues in business-marketing: The ethics of the double click experience. *Journal of Business Ethics, 35*(February), 243–254.

Cherry, B. (2010). Consumer sovereignty: New boundaries for telecommunications and broadband access. *Telecommunications Policy, 34*(1/2), 11–22.

Cohen, L. (2003). *A consumers' republic: The politics of mass consumption in postwar America*. New York: Knopf.

Cohen, L. (2010). Colston E. Warne Lecture: Is it time for another round of consumer protection? The lessons of twentieth-century U.S. history. *Journal of Consumer Affairs, 44*(1), 234–246.

Consumers International. (2010). *Consumer rights*. Retrieved from http://www.consumersinternational.org/ who-we-are/consumer-rights

Culnan, M. J. (2000). Protecting privacy online: Is self-regulation working? *Journal of Public Policy and Marketing, 19*(Spring), 20–26.

Culnan, M. J., & Bies, R. J. (2003). Consumer privacy: Balancing economic and justice considerations. *Journal of Social Issues, 59*(2), 323–342.

DMA. (2003, April). *Privacy promise member compliance guide*. Retrieved April 1, 2005, from http://www.the-dma.org/privacy/privacypromise.shtml

Dolnicar, S., & Jordaan, Y. (2007). A market-oriented approach to responsibly managing information privacy concerns in direct marketing. *Journal of Advertising, 36*(Summer), 123–149.

Donaldson, T., & Dunfee, W. T. (1994). Towards a unified conception of business ethics: Integrative social contracts theory. *Academy of Management Review, 19*, 252–284.

Donaldson, T., & Dunfee, W. T. (1995). Integrative social contracts theory: A communication conception of economic ethics. *Economics and Philosophy, 11*, 85–112.

Donaldson, T., & Dunfee, W. T. (1999). *Ties that bind: A social contracts approach to business ethics*. Cambridge, MA: Harvard Business School Press.

Eika, K. (2009). The challenge of obtaining quality care: Limited consumer sovereignty in human services. *Feminist Economics, 15*(1), 113–137.

Fletcher, K. (2003). Consumer power and privacy: The changing nature of CRM. *International Journal of Advertising, 22*, 249–272.

Forbes, J. D. (1987). *The consumer interest: Dimensions and policy implications*. New York: Croom Helm.

Franzak, F., Pitta, D., & Fritsche, S. (2001). Online relationship and the consumer's right to privacy. *Journal of Consumer Marketing, 18*(7), 631–641.

FTC. (1998). *Privacy online: A report to congress*. Washington, DC: Author.

Goodwin, C. (1991). Privacy: Recognition of a consumer right. *Journal of Public Policy and Marketing, 10*(1), 149–166.

Hann, I. H., Hui, K. L., Lee, S. Y. T., & Png, I. P. (2008). Consumer privacy and marketing avoidance: A static model. Management Science, 54(6), 1094–1103.

Henry, P. C. (2010). How mainstream consumers think about consumer rights and responsibilities. *Journal of Consumer Research, 37*(December), 670–687.

Herrmann, R. O. (1991). Participation and leadership in consumer movement organizations. *Journal of Social Issues, 47*(1), 119–134.

Herrmann, R. O., & Mayer, R. N. (1997). U.S. consumer movement: History and dynamics. In S. Brobeck (Ed.), *Encyclopedia of the consumer movement* (pp. 584–601). Santa Barbara, CA: ABC-CLIO.

Herrmann, R. O., Walsh, E. J., & Warland, R. H. (1988). The organizations of the consumer movement: A comparative perspective. In E. S. Maynes (Ed.), *The frontier of research in the consumer interest* (pp. 470–494). Columbia, MO: American Council on Consumer Interests.

Hersbergen, R. L. (1973). Regulating commercial exploitation of name lists and direct mail solicitation under the fair credit reporting act-a victory for consumer privacy? *Ohio Northern Law Review, 1*(1), 1–30.

Hildebrand, G. H. (1951). Consumer sovereignty in modern times. *American Economic Review, 41*(2), 19–33.

Hutt, W. (1936). *Economists and the public: A study of competition and opinion*. London: Honathan Cape. reprinted New Brunswick: Transaction Publishers, [1990].

Hutt, W. (1940). The concept of consumers' sovereignty. *Economic Journal, 50*, 66–77.

Klopfer, P. H., & Rubenstein, D. L. (1977). The concept privacy and its biological basis. *Journal of Social Issues, 33*, 52–65.

Lampman, R. J. (1988). JFK's four consumer rights: A retrospective view. In E. S. Maynes (Ed.), *The frontier of research in the consumer interest* (pp. 19–33). Columbia, MO: American Council on Consumer Interests.

Lampman, R. J., & Douthitt, R. A. (1997). The consumer bill of rights: Thirty-five years later. *Advancing the Consumer Interest, 9*(2), 4–6.

Lanier, C. D., & Saini, A. (2008). Understanding consumer privacy: A review and future directions. *Academy of Marketing Science Review, 12*(2). Retrieved December 9, 2010, from http://www.amsreview.org/articles/lanier02-2008.pdf

Margulis, S. T. (2003a). On the status and contribution of Westin's and Altman's theories of privacy. *Journal of Social Issues, 59*(2), 411–429.

Margulis, S. T. (2003b). Privacy as a social issue and behavioral concept. *Journal of Social Issues, 59*(2), 243–261.

Mayer, R. N. (1989). *The consumer movement: Guardians of the marketplace*. Boston: Twayne.

Mayer, R. N., & Brobeck, S. (1997). Consumer interest. In S. Brobeck (Ed.), *Encyclopedia of the consumer movement* (pp. 153–155). Santa Barbara, CA: ABC-CLIO.

Maynes, E. S. (1976). *Decision-making for consumers: An introduction to consumer economics*. New York: Macmillan.

Maynes, E. S. (1988). The first word, the last word. In E. S. Maynes (Ed.), *The frontier of research in the consumer interest* (pp. 3–16). Columbia, MO: American Council on Consumer Interests.

Maynes, E. S., Morgan, J. N., Vivian, W., & Duncan, G. J. (1977). The local consumer information system: An institution-to-be? *Journal of Consumer Affairs, 11*(1), 17–33.

McGregor, S. L. T. (2011a). Consumer acumen: Augmenting consumer literacy. *Journal of Consumer Affairs, 45*(2), 344–357.

McGregor, S. L. T. (2011b). Consumer education philosophies: The relationship between education and consumption. *Journal for International Education Research and Development Education, 34*(4), 4–8.

Milne, G. R., & Gordon, E. M. (1993). Direct mail privacy-efficiency trade-offs within an implied social contract framework. *Journal of Public Policy and Marketing, 12*(2), 206–215.

Milne, G. R., & Rohm, A. (2000). Consumer privacy and name removal across direct marketing channels: Exploring opt-in and opt-out alternatives. *Journal of Public Policy and Marketing, 19*(2), 238–249.

Miyazaki, A. D. (2008). Online privacy and the disclosure of cookie use: Effects on consumer trust and anticipated patronage. *Journal of Public Policy & Marketing, 27*(1), 19–33.

Morgan, J. N. (1985). What is the consumer interest? In K. P. Schittgrund (Ed.), *Proceedings, 31st Annual Conference of the American Council on Consumer Interests* (pp. 1–7). Columbia, MO: ACCI.

Palmer, D. E. (2005). Pop-ups, cookies, and spam: Toward a deeper analysis of the ethical significance of Internet marketing practices. *Journal of Business Ethics, 58*(May), 271–280.

Persky, J. (1993). Consumer sovereignty. *The Journal of Economic Perspectives, 7*(1), 183–191.

Rapp, J., Hill, R. P., Gaines, J., & Wilson, R. M. (2009). Advertising and consumer privacy: Old practices and new challenges. *Journal of Advertising, 38*(4), 51–61.

Rosen, C. E. (1977). Institutional intimidation and consumer privacy. *Journal of Consumer Affairs, 11*(2), 94–100.

Rotfeld, H. J. (2010). A pessimist's simplistic historical perspective on the fourth wave of consumer protection. *Journal of Consumer Affairs, 44*(2), 423–429.

Saving, J. L. (2006). Consumer sovereignty in the modern global era. *Journal of Private Enterprise, 22*(1), 107–119.

Schooler, R. D. (1982). The consumer's interests – The superordinate and the subordinate. *The Journal of Consumer Affairs, 16*(1), 166.

Sheehan, K. B., & Hoy, M. G. (1999). Flaming, complaining, abstaining: How online users respond to privacy concerns. *Journal of Advertising, 28*(Fall), 37–51.

Sirgy, M. J., & Su, C. (2000). The ethics of consumer sovereignty in an age of high tech. *Journal of Business Ethics, 28*(1), 1–14.

Sopinka, J. (1997). Freedom of speech and privacy in the information age. *Information Society, 13*(2), 171–184.

Stone, E. F., & Stone, D. L. (1990). Privacy in organizations: Theoretical issues, research findings, and protection mechanisms. *Research in Personnel and Human Resources Management, 8*(3), 349–411.

Swagler, R. (1994). Evolution and applications of the term consumerism: Theme and variations. *Journal of Consumer Affairs, 28*(2), 347–360.

Swagler, R. (1997). Consumer rights. In *Encyclopedia of the consumer movement* (pp. 168–169). Santa Barbara, CA: ABC-CLIO.

Swire, P. P. (1997). Markets, self-regulation, and government enforcement in the protection of personal information. In W. M. Daley & L. Irving (Eds.), *Privacy and self-regulation in the information age* (pp. 3–19). Washington, DC: Department of Commerce.

Thorelli, H. D. (1988). Consumer problems: Developed and less developed countries. In E. S. Maynes (Ed.), *The frontier of research in the consumer interest* (pp. 523–546). Columbia, MO: American Council on Consumer Interests.

United Nation. (2003). *United Nations guidelines for consumer protection*. New York: Author.

Walczuch, R. M., & Lizette, S. (2001). Implications of the new EU Directive on data protection for multinational corporations. *Information Technology & People, 14*(2), 142.

Waldfogel, J. (2005). Does consumer irrationality trump consumer sovereignty. *Review of Economics and Statistics, 87*(4), 691–696.

Warren, S. D., & Brandeis, L. D. (1890). The right to privacy. *Harvard Law Review, 4*(5), 193–220.

Westin, A. F. (1967). *Privacy and freedom*. New York: Atheneum.

Wilson, M., Gaines, J., & Hill, R. P. (2008). Neuromarketing and consumer free will. *Journal of Consumer Affairs, 42*(Fall), 389–410.

Xiao, J. J. (1997). Consumer movement in China. In S. Brobeck, R. Mayer, & R. Herrmann (Eds.), *Encyclopedia of the consumer movement* (pp. 104–109). Santa Barbara, CA: ABC-CLIO.

Xiao, J. J., & Richardson, L. (2003). Consumer protection at the state level. In K. Meier & E. T. Garman (Eds.), *Regulation and consumer protection* (4th ed., pp. 403–422). Cincinnati, OH: Thompson Learning.

Xu, H. (2009). Consumer responses to the introduction of privacy protection measures: An exploratory research framework. *International Journal of E-Business Research, 5*(2), 21–47.

Chapter 3
Consumer Financial Capability and Economic Wellbeing

Abstract Consumer financial capability is an important factor for consumer economic wellbeing. Financial capability is an ability of applying appropriate financial knowledge and performing desirable financial behaviors to achieve financial goals and enhance financial wellbeing. Empirical research finds that financial literacy in many countries is much lower than expected. Consumers have also engaged in less than desirable financial behaviors. The chapter first discusses concepts of consumer financial capability, financial literacy, and financial behavior. And then introduces two specific behavior theories; the theory of planned behavior that is to help understand consumer behavior and the transtheoretical model of behavior change (TTM) that is to help change consumer behavior. The section also discusses how to apply these theories to help improve consumer financial knowledge, behaviors, and capabilities. Future research directions on how to improve consumer financial capability are then discussed in the following section.

3.1 Financial Capability

Financial capability can be considered an ability of applying appropriate financial knowledge and perform desirable financial behaviors to achieve financial wellbeing. In recent years, led by the UK (Atkinson et al. 2006), several countries such as Austria (Fessler et al. 2007), Canada (Arrowsmith and Pignal 2010), Ireland (O'Donnell and Keeney 2009), and the USA (Lusardi 2011) have moved their focus from promoting financial literacy to financial capability among consumers.

In an introduction to a special issue on financial capability for *Journal of Economic Psychology*, two guest editors briefly summarized the current status of financial capability research. According to them, research on financial capability and financial literacy seeks to understand and to improve how consumers make financial decisions. On the one hand, this concerns knowledge of consumers. On the other hand, it concerns the actual behavior of consumers and its prerequisites such as skills and attitudes. Financial literacy mainly focuses on the understanding of economic and financial concepts (e.g., compound interest) and knowledge about financial instruments (e.g., mutual funds vs. stocks). Research on financial literacy has often shown a bleak picture: in many countries, many respondents have little

J.J. Xiao, *Consumer Economic Wellbeing*, International Series on Consumer Science, DOI 10.1007/978-1-4939-2821-7_3

literacy. Financial illiteracy is often found to be related to being underprivileged (e.g., low education and belonging to a minority group) and to unfavorable economic outcomes (e.g., less saving, poor retirement savings arrangements). In many countries, financial education programs have been established over the last decades. However, evidence on their effectiveness is mixed: while programs with specific goals (e.g., matched-savings programs) show positive effects, programs intended to enhance general financial literacy show less clear effects (Hoelzl and Kapteyn 2011). Financial capability is also considered a broader concept that highlights action and behavior of the individual, and the relevance of outside institutions and regulations (Johnson and Sherraden 2007).

Financial capability is examined in several ways by researchers. Financial capability can be distinguished in three areas that influence behavior: (1) knowledge and understanding, (2) skills, and (3) confidence and attitudes (Kempson et al. 2005). In the UK survey of financial capability, this concept is measured in five categories of financial behaviors: (1) managing money: making ends meet, i.e., having little problems dealing with financial obligations; (2) managing money: keeping track, i.e., having an overview of expenses; (3) planning ahead, i.e., being future oriented; (4) choosing products, i.e., deciding reasonably in financial matters; and (5) staying informed, i.e., seeking information about financial products and the economy (Atkinson et al. 2006).

Some researchers argue that variations in financial capability are more related to psychological than informational differences. They list several candidate biases that would hinder the transformation of sufficient information into goal-directed behavior: mental accounting, information overload, status quo bias, procrastination, regret, and loss aversion. These cognitive biases may not be easy to overcome, and more research on debiasing in financial behavior is needed. They argue that financial capability programs should not only rely on content delivering, but also consider behavior modifications (De Meza et al. 2008).

The UK was the first country in the world to conduct a national financial capability survey. Based on the Baseline Survey of Financial Capability (BSFC), researchers describe the distribution of financial capability to look for groups of people with similar skills (Atkinson et al. 2006). They also explore ways of identifying people most at risk of becoming over indebted (Kempson and Atkinson 2006). The financial capability of people with literacy and numeracy needs is also analyzed with the BSFC data (Atkinson 2007). These British researchers have shown that there is considerable diversity in the financial capability scores of adults with literacy and numeracy needs. It would not be appropriate to assume that financial capability needs are an inevitable consequence of literacy or numeracy needs. For example, 17 % of working age adults with no educational qualifications have financial capability scores that put them in the top 20 % of people for making ends meet and 10 % of them are in the top 20 % for planning ahead. These results show quite clearly that *keeping track* of finances is not an area of concern for most of the adults that have been studied. Yet budgeting in particular is an aspect of financial capability that very often gets special attention in courses that cover personal finances.

The 2009 US National Financial Capability Study consists of three linked surveys: (1) National Survey; (2) State-by-State Survey; (3) Military Survey. Lusardi (2011) has reported the findings of the National Survey, administered to respondents between May and July 2009. The overarching research objectives of the US financial capability survey are to benchmark key indicators of financial capability and evaluate how these indicators vary with underlying demographic, behavioral, attitudinal, and financial literacy characteristics. Financial capability cannot be judged simply by looking at one indicator. Rather, it covers several aspects of behavior. Consistent with the surveys that have been done in other countries, these behavior aspects include how people manage their resources, how they make financial decisions, the skill set they use in making such decisions, and the search and information elaboration that goes into those decisions. Lusardi focused on four main areas to assess Americans' financial capability: (1) Making ends meet; (2) Planning ahead; (3) Choosing and managing financial products; and (4) Financial literacy and self-assessed skills. This survey was conducted again in 2012 that demonstrated a snapshot of financial capability of American consumers (FINRAIEF 2013).

Another UK researcher has proposed a different way to measure consumer capability by using an index of combing financial behavior and outcome. Using data from the British Household Panel Survey, the results show the lowest financial capability among young unemployed single adults living in households with other unrelated non-working adults. In contrast, older men and women in full-time work with an employed spouse have the most financial capability (Taylor 2011).

A group of researchers have used a different approach to measure financial capability. This is a comprehensive measure that includes objective financial literacy, subjective financial literacy, desirable financial behavior, risky financial behavior and perceived financial capability. Using data from the 2009 US State-by-State Survey of Financial Capability, the results indicate a positive association between perceived financial capability and financial satisfaction. The findings suggest that desirable financial behavior increases financial satisfaction, whereas risky financial behavior decreases financial satisfaction. Subjective financial literacy is also found to contribute positively to financial satisfaction. The positive association between objective financial literacy and financial satisfaction is found in bivariate analyses but not in multivariate analyses. The results imply that, to enhance consumer financial well-being, consumer financial education programs should emphasize action taking and encourage consumers to avoid risky financial behavior, engage in desirable financial behavior, and improve financial self-efficacy (Xiao et al. 2014a). Research indicates money management ability contributes to perceived financial independence of young adults (Xiao et al. 2014d).

Using a similar approach, researchers examine age differences in financial capability. In this study, financial capability is measured by five variables: objective financial literacy, subjective financial literacy, desirable financial behavior, perceived financial capability, and financial capability index (a sum of Z scores of the former four variables). Financial capability is expected to increase with age and data from the 2012 National Financial Capability Study is used for data analyses. Multiple regression results indicate that age differences in four financial capability variables show similar patterns. After controlling for demographic and economic characteristics, young adults aged 18–24 had the lowest scores for objective financial literacy, subjective financial literacy, perceived financial capability, and financial capability index. Age patterns of financial behavior are complicated that need future research to understand them (Xiao et al. 2015).

The same measure of financial capability is used to examine the association between financial education and financial capability among American consumers. Based on data from the 2012 National Financial Capability Study, results show that, after controlling for demographic and financial variables, respondents who have ever received financial education have higher scores in objective financial literacy, subjective financial literacy, desirable financial behavior, perceived financial capability, and financial capability index. In addition, high school, college, and workplace financial education variables also show positive associations with the five financial capability variables. The results imply that financial education in high school, college and workplaces may enhance consumer financial capability (Xiao and O'Neill 2014).

3.2 Financial Literacy

According to standard economic theory, consumers are fully informed and can make rational choices in long term financial planning to maximize their utilities over life-cycle stages. However, empirical research indicates that consumers, in fact, are not fully informed and cannot make rational choices even when the information is available (Campbell et al. 2011).

Research on consumer financial literacy has been conducted among consumer economists with a long history (Hira 2010; Burns 2008). Lusardi (2011), an economics professor and leading researcher on financial literacy, provides a review of economic literature on financial literacy. Over the last two decades, researchers have started to explore whether individuals are well equipped to make financial decisions. Research shows that many US consumers display low levels of financial literacy (Bernheim 1995; 1998). Most Americans fail to understand basic financial concepts, particularly those relating to bonds, stocks, and mutual funds (Hilgert et al. 2003). A study of Washington state residents finds that people frequently fail to understand terms and conditions of consumer loans and mortgages (Moore 2003). The National Council on Economic Education's report shows a widespread lack of knowledge regarding fundamental economic concepts among high school students (NCEE 2005), confirming similar findings by the Jump$tart Coalition for Personal Financial Literacy (Mandell 2008). Lack of financial sophistication is not only an American problem; researchers have documented low levels of financial literacy in several other countries as well (Smith and Stewart 2008). Similarly, respondents from a large scale survey in Europe have scored poorly on financial numeracy and literacy scales (Christelis et al. 2010). Consistent with findings in the USA, UK borrowers have a poor understanding of mortgages and interest rates (Miles 2004).

Lusardi and Mitchell (2014) have developed a life-cycle saving model that addresses the role of financial literacy. This model predicts that financial literacy is endogenously determined over the life cycle. Consumers invest in financial knowledge to the point where their marginal time and money costs of doing so are equated to their marginal benefits. These predictions suggest that consumers who receive financial education would increase their ability to manage their money and perform financially better than their counterparts who do not receive financial education. Previous research has also shown that financial education is associated with financial literacy and encourages desirable financial behaviors among consumers (Xiao et al. 2012; Xiao and O'Neill 2014). Earlier financial literacy predicts later financial behavior evidenced in a study of college students (Xiao et al. 2014c).

In the research of financial literacy, subjective and objective measures are distinguished by researchers. Research finds that the two types of measures have different effects on consumer financial behaviors. For example, a study based on a sample of first-year college students shows that subjective financial knowledge does more to prevent risky credit behaviors than objective financial knowledge (Xiao et al. 2011a, b).

3.3 Financial Behavior

Financial behavior refers to human behaviors relevant to money management (Xiao 2008). Common financial behaviors include behaviors related to earning, spending, borrowing, and saving. Financial behaviors should demonstrate consumer financial capability. Higher financial capability should be associated with desirable financial behaviors. The premise of desirable financial behavior should be a certain level of financial knowledge relevant to the interested behavior. Desirable financial behavior should enhance consumer economic wellbeing. Financial behaviors that cause negative consequences of economic wellbeing are undesirable, and are sometimes harmful behaviors. For example, paying bills later than a due date is a undesirable behavior because the consumer will pay the late payment fee and bear other negative financial consequences such as lowering the credit score.

Research on financial behavior can be categorized as special topic research and general topic research. Specific financial behaviors have been researched extensively such as spending, borrowing, and saving behaviors. Some researchers also treat financial behavior as a construct and have developed scales to measure it. Using data from a nationally representative sample of adults, researchers have developed a scale of financial management behaviors. The scale has four subscales: cash management, credit management, savings and investment, and insurance. They have also examined the psychometric properties of the scale and find that the scale is highly associated with other measures of financial management behaviors and predictive of participants' actual levels of savings and consumer debt (Dew and Xiao 2011). Reviews of financial behavior theories and research and their implications for consumer financial education can be found in Xiao et al. (2010, 2011).

Professionals who care about consumer economic wellbeing should better understand consumer financial behaviors and help consumers develop desirable financial behaviors. In the research literature, there are many theories for understanding consumer behaviors and helping consumers develop desirable behaviors. Two of them are the theory of planned behavior and transtheoretical model of behavior change that have been applied to consumer financial behaviors in recent years (Xiao 2008).

3.4 Understanding Behavior

3.4.1 Theory of Planned Behavior

The theory of planned behavior is an extension of the theory of reasoned action (Ajzen 1991). The theory of reasoned action was first introduced by Fishbein in 1967 and then defined, developed, and tested in the 1970s. It was summarized in a book by Fishbein and Ajzen (1975). The purpose of this theory is to predict and understand human behavior. According to the theory of reasoned action, a person's behavior is determined by her/his behavior intention. The intention is determined by this person's attitude toward the behavior, the subjective norm, and the relative importance between the attitude and the subjective norm. The development of the theory of reasoned action was motivated by the fact that existing attitude theories could not predict behavior (Ajzen and Fishbein 1980). Later, the theory developer added to the model an additional factor, perceived control, to determine the behavior intention and behavior, and renamed the model as the theory of planned behavior (Ajzen 1991).

The theory of planned behavior focuses on factors that determine individuals' actual behavioral choices. According to this theory, three factors influence behavioral intentions: attitudes about the target behavior, subjective norms, and perceived behavioral controls. In turn, behavioral intention influences one's behavior patterns (Ajzen 1991; Ajzen and Fishbein 1980). An attitude toward a behavior is recognized as a person's positive or negative evaluation of a relevant behavior and is composed of a person's salient beliefs regarding the perceived outcomes of performing a behavior. A subjective norm refers to a person's perception of whether significant referents approve or disapprove of a behavior.

To capture non-volitional aspects of behavior, the theory of planned behavior incorporates an additional variable—perceived behavioral control, which is not typically associated with traditional attitude-behavioral models (e.g., Fishbein and Ajzen 1975). The perceived behavioral control describes the perceived difficulty level of performing the behavior—reflecting both past experience as well as anticipated barriers. As a general rule, the more favorable the attitude toward performing a behavior, the greater the perceived social approval, and the easier the performance of the behavior is perceived to be, the stronger the behavioral intention will be. In turn, the greater the behavioral intention, the more likely the behavior will be performed. In addition, the perceived control may affect the behavior directly (Ajzen 1991).

The theory of planned behavior and its former version, the theory of reasoned action, have been applied in many subject areas such as weight loss, occupational orientation, family planning, consumer behavior, voting, alcoholism (Ajzen and Fishbein 1980), hunting (Hrubes et al. 2001), genetically modified food buying (Cook et al. 2002), technology adoption (Lynne et al. 1995), consumer complaining (East 2000), and online surveys (Bosnjak et al. 2005), among others. A comprehensive reference list of papers using the theory of reasoned action and the theory of planned behavior was compiled by Icek Ajzen and posted on his website (http://www-unix.oit.umass.edu/~aizen/index.html).

Several meta-analyses have been conducted to evaluate the efficacy of the theory of planned behavior and its former version, the theory of reasoned action. An evaluation research review examining 185 independent studies indicated that the theory in general is valid (Armitage and Conner 2001). However, this evaluation study has identified several issues relevant to the application of the theory. First, self-reports are not a reliable information source. If possible, researchers should use objective and observed variables to measure behavior. Second, perceived control is a concept different from self-efficacy, unlike the common assumption that they are the same measure with two different names. Compared to perceived control, self-efficacy is a better predictor of behavior. Third, there are alternative measures for intention, such as desire and self-prediction, in which intention and self-prediction are better predictors for behavior compared to desire. Fourth, subjective norm is a weak predictor of intention compared to two other variables, attitude and perceived control. Therefore, alternative categorizations are needed, such as moral and descriptive norms.

3.4.2 Applications to Financial Behavior

Several studies have applied the theory of planned behavior to consumer behavior in financial services such as investment decisions, mortgage use, and credit counseling. The theory is used to investigate investment decisions with data from a sample of British consumers. The results show that friends and relatives and easy access to funds strongly contributed to investment decisions (East 1993). Using data from a sample of mortgage clients, researchers examine customer service switching behavior. They find that interactions between perceived control and intention, between perceived control and attitude, and between attitude and subjective norms significantly affected behavior intention (Bansal and Taylor 2002). Using survey and account data from a sample of clients of a national consumer counseling agency, researchers examine factors that are associated with consumer behavior in completing a debt management plan. They find that attitude toward a behavior and perceived control affect the actual behavior, but subjective norm does not. In addition, satisfaction with the debt management program service, a factor not specified in the theory, also contributes to actual behavior (Xiao and Wu 2008). The similar results are also found in Guo et al. (2009).

The theory of planned behavior has also been applied to consumer behavior in the setting of e-commerce, such as online shopping and e-coupon use. Based on the theory, researchers decompose belief constructs and include the interaction term of salient belief in the revised model. Based on data collected from a sample of college students, they find these additional variables contribute to consumer online shopping intentions (Lim and Dubinsky 2005). Furthermore, researchers apply the theory to consumer online purchase intentions. Based on data collected from a national sample of computer users, they find that intention to use the Internet for information search serves as a mediating variable between antecedents (such as attitude, perceived control, and past experience) and the outcome variable, online purchase intention. Attitude and past experience also directly contribute to the purchase intention (Shim et al. 2001). A researcher proposes a theoretical framework to explain consumer coupon and e-coupon behavior based on the theory of planned behavior (Fortin 2000). Researchers compare the theory of reasoned action and the theory of planned behavior in the context of e-coupon use intentions and find the theory of planned behavior explains the intention best (Kang et al. 2006).

Additionally, a group of researchers apply the theory of planned behavior to investigate how college students form financial behaviors such as cash, credit, and saving management. Based on their findings, all three antecedents of the behavior intention specified by the theory are associated with the intention and the intention contributes to the behavior (Shim et al. 2009; Xiao et al. 2011b).

3.5 Changing Behavior

3.5.1 Transtheoretical Model of Behavior Change (TTM)

The transtheoretical model of behavior change (TTM) was developed in the 1970s by James Prochaska, a psychology professor at University of Rhode Island, and his colleagues (Prochaska 1979; Prochaska et al. 1992). They formed the model by highlighting major psychological theories in a uniform framework for the purpose of helping people change their undesirable behaviors. "Transtheoretical" in the title means to transform theories into applications, which implies that this model was developed for the applied purpose of counseling. The model was first applied to cessation of smoking and then to a variety of other health-related behaviors, including alcohol abuse, drug abuse, high fat diets and weight control, psychological distress, and sun exposure (Prochaska et al. 1994). A few studies applied the TTM to other areas, such as organizational change (Prochaska 2000) and collaborative service delivery (Levesque et al. 1999). More information about this model and its accomplishments can be found from the website of ProChange Behavior Systems: http://prochange.com/.

Major constructs of the TTM include stage of change, process of change, self-efficacy, and decisional balance. The TTM identifies five stages of behavior change: precontemplation, contemplation, preparation, action, and maintenance. If a person is not willing to change in 6 months, s/he is in precontemplation. If a person is willing to change in 6 months, s/he is in contemplation. If s/he is willing to change in 30 days, s/he is in preparation. If s/he has started to change for less than 6 months, s/he is in action. If s/he has been changing for over 6 months but less than 18 months, s/he is in maintenance. If s/he has changed the behavior for more than 18 months, we consider her/his behavior has been changed. Some people may relapse to previous stages. At times, behavior change may take several cycles. The TTM also identifies ten processes of change, in which *processes* are strategies or interventions for facilitating the behavior change. Table 3.1 presents definitions of the TTM change processes. According to the TTM, these strategies could be used more effectively if they are matched with appropriate stages of change.

Two indicators of success of behavior change are decisional balance and self-efficacy (or confidence). When people are at a later stage of change, they will perceive more benefits and fewer costs of behavior change, and they are more confident in avoiding an undesirable behavior when they face difficult situations.

Compared to other behavior change models, the TTM has the following unique features: (1) it integrates essentials of major psychological theories in a framework to offer more effective interventions; (2) it defines multiple stages of behavior

Table 3.1 Change strategies and tactics that match change stages

Change stage	Change strategy	Definition
Precontemplation	Consciousness raising	Finding and learning new facts, ideas, and tips that support the healthy behavior change
	Dramatic relief	Experiencing the negative emotions that go along with unhealthy behavior risks
	Environmental reevaluation	Realizing the negative impact of the unhealthy behavior or the positive impact of the healthy behavior on one's proximal social and physical environment
Contemplation	Self-reevaluation	Realizing that the behavior change is an important part of one's identity
Preparation	Self-liberation	Making a firm commitment to change
Action/Maintenance	Reinforcement management	Increasing the rewards for the positive behavior change and decreasing the rewards of the unhealthy behavior
	Helping relationships	Seeking and using social support for the healthy behavior change
	Counterconditioning	Substituting healthy alternative behaviors and cognitions for the unhealthy behaviors
	Stimulus control	Removing reminders or cues to engage in the unhealthy behavior and adding cues or reminders to engage in the healthy behavior
All stages	Social liberation	Realizing that social norms are changing in the direction of supporting the healthy behavior change

Source: Xiao et al. (2004b)

change, which is different from an action paradigm, and has the potential to reach those both ready and not ready to change a targeted behavior; (3) it matches intervention strategies to different stages of behavior change, which makes it more effective compared to other intervention programs; and (4) it focuses on enhancing self-control (Prochaska et al. 1996).

The TTM is one of a number of multi-stage theories. Among five multi-stage theories reviewed by two psychologists, the TTM is the one that most empirical studies support. Compared to motivational theories, multi-stage theories are more sophisticated (Armitage and Conner 2000). However, these authors raise several questions for multi-stage theories. These questions include: (1) psychologically, what actually happens at each stage, (2) do people go through each stage sequentially when they change their behaviors, and (3) are different stages really different in terms of determinants of the behavior change?

3.5.2 *Applications to Financial Behavior*

Application of the TTM to financial behavior started in the late 1990s. Kerkman (1998) is the first to discuss how to use TTM in financial counseling by presenting a case to demonstrate her approach. Bristow (1997) suggests that this model could be used to change people's financial behavior in Money 2000, a USDA Cooperative Extension program. Money 2000 is a successful financial education program, which has been adopted by 29 states and reported a total dollar impact of almost $20 million (O'Neill 2001). Based on data collected in 1998 among program participants in New Jersey and New York, evidence indicates that certain processes of change are used more frequently by participants who have reported behavioral changes (Xiao et al. 2004c). A group of researchers have applied the TTM in a credit counseling setting to develop a measure to help consumers change behaviors to eliminate undesirable credit card debts (Xiao et al. 2004a, b). The TTM is also applied in financial education programs for low-income consumers, in which specific educational strategies under the framework of TTM are developed (Shockey and Seiling 2004). In addition, the TTM is used to provide advice for women on being better investors (Loibl and Hira 2007).

3.6 Future Research on Consumer Financial Capability

More research can be conducted to clearly define financial capability and how to effectively measure this important concept. In addition, associations between financial capability, financial literacy, and financial behavior need attention in future research. Theoretically, we assume that the three concepts should be positively associated with each other, which should be validated with empirical data. Also, how these three concepts are associated with consumer economic wellbeing can be examined in future research.

In many studies, financial capability is measured by financial behavior such as the financial capability studies reviewed in the "financial capability" section. More in-depth research on financial behaviors can also be conducted. Researchers need to develop an inventory of financial behaviors that covers all aspects of behaviors relevant to consumer finance. In many existing studies, financial behaviors are defined for specific research purposes and many of them are not comprehensive. An inventory of financial behaviors with acceptable reliability and validity would be helpful for financial educators and researchers when they evaluate financial education programs and measure social impacts of the programs on people's behavior change and quality of life.

The two theories of consumer behavior change reviewed in this chapter have been applied to certain financial behaviors and certain populations, but they could be applied to more behaviors and more diverse populations. For example, many states have tax return sites to help low income consumers receive tax refunds. Another example is the *Go Direct* campaign launched by the U.S. Department of Treasury, which encourages electronic deposits of benefit checks issued by the U.S. Social Security Administration. Consumer economists could partner with government agencies and financial institutions to apply these theories to design effective education and outreach programs so these social initiatives would have a greater impact.

The TTM is considered a multi-stage theory with advantages to help consumers change undesirable behaviors and form positive financial behaviors stage by stage. Strategies based on this theory could be developed to work with mass populations, emphasizing certain strategies for certain behavior change stages for greater social impact, and a cost-effective approach. Mass approaches also need to be personalized. An example would be online self-assessment tools that could reach millions of people but provide each user with a personalized response, based on their individual responses (O'Neill and Xiao 2006).

The behavior theories reviewed in this chapter have been tested in numerous scientific studies and are well established. Consumer finance researchers could utilize the strategies, techniques, and tactics based on this line of research to generate practical information for financial educators and consumers.

Self-help websites based on these theories can be developed to help determined consumers change their undesirable financial behaviors themselves. Self-help manuals could also be developed for the same purpose. Use of these self-help websites and manuals could be monitored and studied to identify factors that are more effective than others in motivating and facilitating the behavior change.

One of the purposes of research on consumer financial behavior is to better understand factors that affect the formation and change of financial behaviors. Specifically, financial educators are interested in knowing the role of financial education in behavior formation and change. In addition, financial educators need to know the important characteristics of financial education programs that will not only provide financial knowledge but also encourage consumers to form positive financial behaviors and change undesirable financial behaviors. Future research should generate information that has direct implications for financial educators to develop such education programs.

Future research also needs to examine how financial education, financial behavior, and quality of life are associated. The mission of many financial educators, especially those at land grant universities, is to improve people's quality of life by providing effective financial education. They hope the education will have a direct impact on these people's financial behaviors and eventually help improve the financial well-being of these people. Data on financial education, financial behavior, and quality of life could be collected to provide insights in to this topic.

Desirable financial behavior may enhance health. Researchers examine which employees are more likely to improve their health, controlling for differences in initial health, demographics, job type, and income. They find that existing retirement-contribution patterns and future health improvements are highly correlated. Employees who have saved for the future by contributing to a 401(k) show improvements in their abnormal blood-test results and health behaviors approximately 27 % more often than noncontributors do (Gubler and Pierce 2014). Desirable behaviors in different life domains may enhance each other. A study shows that improved health is associated with desirable financial behaviors among a sample of financially stressed consumers (O'Neill et al. 2005). This line of research could be expanded in the future.

There are two issues that are not addressed by the behavior theories reviewed in this chapter: the structure of financial behaviors and interactions between financial behaviors. The first issue asks if there is a pattern when consumers adopt various financial behaviors. Some previous studies suggest the adoption of financial behaviors may have a hierarchical pattern and consumers adopt some financial behaviors before others. According to a study by Federal Reserve staff (Hilgert et al. 2003), it seems consumers adopt cash management behavior first, and then credit behavior, followed by saving and investing behavior. Studies on saving motives (Xiao and Noring 1994) and financial asset shares (Xiao and Anderson 1997) also show such a pattern. Is this pattern valid in general? If so, what is the theoretical foundation? The second issue is to ask if positive financial behaviors enhance each other. Do positive financial behaviors beget positive financial behaviors? If so, we may focus on promoting one particular financial behavior and hope the formation of that behavior will influence the formation of other positive financial behaviors. Some evidence shows that self-perceived financial behavior performance is associated with self-reported positive financial behavior (Xiao et al. 2006). More theoretical and empirical studies are needed to address these issues.

3.7 Summary

Governments in many countries are now concerned about consumer capability since economic and social changes make individual consumers bear more responsibility for their own financial security in the long term, such as economic security at retirement. Financial capability assumes that consumers can apply appropriate financial knowledge and perform desirable financial behaviors to achieve and sustain their economic wellbeing. Financial literacy can be gained by lifelong learning and taking advantage of public educational services provided by government and non-government organizations. Financial behaviors can be understood and modified to desirable directions by using research findings based on behavior theories such as the theory of planned behavior and the transtheoretical model of behavior change.

References

Ajzen, I. (1991). The theory of planned behavior. *Organizational Behavior and Human Decision Processes, 50*, 179–211.

Ajzen, I., & Fishbein, M. (1980). *Understanding attitudes and predicting social behavior*. Englewood Cliffs, NJ: Prentice-Hall.

Armitage, C. J., & Conner, M. (2000). Social cognition models and health behavior: A structured review. *Psychology and Health, 15*, 173–189.

Armitage, C. J., & Conner, M. (2001). Efficacy of the theory of planned behavior: A meta-analytic review. *British Journal of Social Psychology, 40*, 471–499.

Arrowsmith, S., & Pignal, J. (2010). Initial findings from the 2009 Canadian financial capability survey. Task Force on Financial Literacy.

Atkinson, A. (2007). *Financial capability amongst adults with literacy and numeracy needs. Working paper*. Bristol: University of Bristol.

Atkinson, A., McKay, S., Kempson, E., & Collard, S. (2006). *Levels of financial capability in the UK: Results of a baseline survey. Consumer Research Report 47*. London: Financial Services Authority.

Bansal, H. S., & Taylor, S. F. (2002). Investigating interactive effects in the theory of planned behavior in a service-provider switching context. *Psychology & Marketing, 19*, 407–425.

Bernheim, D. (1995). Do households appreciate their financial vulnerabilities? An analysis of actions, perceptions, and public policy. *Tax Policy and Economic Growth, 3*, 11–30.

Bernheim, D. D. (1998). *Financial illiteracy, education, and retirement saving (No 96–7)*. Pennsylvania, PA: Wharton School Pension Research Council, University of Pennsylvania.

Bosnjak, M., Tuten, T. L., & Wittmann, W. W. (2005). Unit (non)response in web-based access panel surveys: An extended planned-behavior approach. *Psychology & Marketing, 22*(6), 489–505.

Bristow, B. J. (1997). *Promoting financial well-being: Running a successful MONEY 2000 campaign*. Ithaca, NY: Cornell Cooperative Extension.

Burns, S. A. (2008). Promoting applied research in personal finance. In J. J. Xiao (Ed.), *Handbook of consumer finance research* (pp. 411–418). New York, NY: Springer.

Campbell, J. Y., Jackson, H. E., Madrian, B. C., & Tufano, P. (2011). Consumer financial protection. *Journal of Economic Perspectives, 21*(1), 91–113.

Christelis, D., Jappelli, T., & Padula, M. (2010). Cognitive abilities and portfolio choice. *European Economic Review, 54*(1), 18–38.

Cook, A. J., Kerr, G. N., & Moore, K. (2002). Attitudes and intentions towards purchasing GM food. *Journal of Economic Psychology, 23*(5), 557–572.

De Meza, D., Irlenbusch, B., & Reyniers, D. (2008). *Financial capability: A behavioural economics perspective. Consumer Research Report 69*. London: Financial Services Authority.

Dew, J., & Xiao, J. J. (2011). The financial management behavior scale: Development and validation. *Journal of Financial Counseling and Planning, 22*(1), 43–59.

East, R. (1993). Investment decisions and the theory of planned behavior. *Journal of Economic Psychology, 14*(2), 337–375.

East, R. (2000). Complaining as planned behavior. *Psychology & Marketing, 17*, 1077–1095.

Fessler, P., Schürz, M., Wagner, K., & Weber, B. (2007). Financial capability of Austrian households. *Monetary Policy & the Economy Q, 3*, 50–67.

FINRAIEF. (2013). *Financial capability in the United States: Report of findings from the 2012 National Financial Capability Study*. Washington, DC: FINRA Investor Education Foundation.

Fishbein, M., & Ajzen, I. (1975). *Belief, attitude, intention, and behavior: An introduction to theory and research*. Reading, MA: Addison-Wesley.

Fortin, D. R. (2000). Clipping coupons in cyberspace: A proposed model of behavior for deal-prone consumers. *Psychology & Marketing, 17*, 515–534.

Gubler, T., & Pierce, L. (2014). Healthy, wealthy, and wise: Retirement planning predicts employee health improvements. *Psychological Science, 25*(9), 1822–1830.

Guo, L., Xiao, J. J., & Tang, C. (2009). Understanding the psychological process underlying customer satisfaction and retention in a relational service. *Journal of Business Research, 62*, 1152–1159.

Hilgert, M. A., Hogarth, J. M., & Beverly, S. G. (2003). Household financial management: The connection between knowledge and behavior. *Federal Reserve Bulletin, 89*, 309–322.

Hira, T. (2010). The NEFE quarter century project: Implications for researchers, educators, and policy makers from a quarter century of financial education. Retrieved from http://www.nefe.org/LinkClick.aspx?fileticket=A2P8jPulqkw%3d&tabid=934.

Hoelzl, E., & Kapteyn, A. (2011). Financial capability. *Journal of Economic Psychology, 32*(4), 543–545.

Hrubes, D., Ajzen, I., & Daigle, J. (2001). Predicting hunting intentions and behavior: An application of the theory of planned behavior. *Leisure Sciences, 23*, 165–178.

Johnson, E., & Sherraden, M. S. (2007). From financial literacy to financial capability among youth. *Journal of Sociology & Social Welfare, 34*(3), 119–146.

Kang, H., Hahn, M., Fortin, D. R., Hyun, Y. J., & Eom, Y. (2006). Effects of perceived behavioral control on the consumer usage intention of e-coupons. *Psychology & Marketing, 23*(10), 841–864.

Kempson, E., & Atkinson, A. (2006). *Overstretched: People at risk of financial difficulty*. London: Genworth Financial Inc.

Kempson, E., Collard, S., & Moore, N. (2005). *Measuring financial capability: An exploratory study. Consumer Research Report 37*. London: Financial Services Authority.

Kerkman, B. C. (1998). Motivation and stages of change in financial counseling: An application of a transtheoretical model from counseling psychology. *Financial Counseling and Planning, 9*(1), 13–20.

Levesque, D. A., Prochaska, J. M., & Prochaska, J. O. (1999). Stages of change and integrated service delivery. *Consulting Psychology Journal, 51*, 226–241.

Lim, H., & Dubinsky, A. J. (2005). The theory of planned behavior in e-commerce: Making a case for interdependencies between salient beliefs. *Psychology & Marketing, 22*, 833–855.

Loibl, C., & Hira, T. K. (2007). New insights into advising female clients on investment decisions. *Journal of Financial Planning, 20*(3).

Lusardi, A. (2011). Americans' financial capability (No. w17103). National Bureau of Economic Research.

Lusardi, A., & Mitchell, O. S. (2014). The economic importance of financial literacy: Theory and evidence. *Journal of Economic Literature, 52*(1), 5–44.

Lynne, G. D., Casey, C. F., Hodges, A., & Rahmani, M. (1995). Conservation technology adoption decisions and the theory of planned behavior. *Journal of Economic Psychology, 16*(4), 581 598.

Mandell, L. (2008). Financial literacy of high school students. In J. J. Xiao (Ed.), *Handbook of consumer finance research* (pp. 163–184). New York, NY: Springer.

Miles, D. (2004). *The UK Mortgage Market: Taking a longer-term view*. London: Final Report and Recommendations.

Moore, D.L. (2003). Survey of financial literacy in Washington State: Knowledge, behavior, attitudes, and experiences. Washington State Department of Financial Institutions.

NCEE. (2005). *What American teens and adults know about economics*. Washington, DC: National Council on Economic Education.

O'Donnell, N., & Keeney, M. J. (2009). *Financial capability: new evidence for Ireland (No. 1/ RT/09)*. Dublin: Central Bank of Ireland.

O'Neill, B. (2001). Updated MONEY 2000™: Impact data. Message to MONEY 2000™ electronic mail group, MONEY2000-NATIONAL-L@cce.cornell.edu.

O'Neill, B., & Xiao, J. J. (2006). Financial fitness quiz findings: Strengths, weaknesses, and disconnects. *Journal of Extension, 44*(1).

O'Neill, B., Xiao, J. J., Sorhaindo, B., & Garman, E. T. (2005). Financial distressed consumers: Their financial practices, financial well-being, and health. *Financial Counseling and Planning, 16*(1), 73–87.

Prochaska, J. O. (1979). *Systems of psychotherapy: A transtheoretical analysis*. Homewood, IL: Dorsey.

Prochaska, J. M. (2000). A transtheoretical model for assessing organizational change: A study of family service agencies' movement to time limited therapy. *Families in Society, 80*(1), 76–84.

Prochaska, J. O., DiClemente, C. C., & Norcross, J. C. (1992). In search of how people change: Applications to addictive behaviors. *American Psychologist, 47*(9), 1102–1114.

Prochaska, J. O., Redding, C. A., Harlow, L. L., Rossi, J. S., & Velicer, W. F. (1994). The transtheoretical model of change and HIV prevention: a review. *Health Education Quarterly, 21*, 4.

Prochaska, J. O., Redding, C. A., & Evers, K. E. (1996). The transtheoretical model and stages of change. In K. Glanz, F. M. Lewis, & B. K. Rimer (Eds.), *Health behavior and health education: Theory, research, and practice* (2nd ed., pp. 60–84). San Francisco, CA: Jossey-Bass.

Shim, S., Easlick, M. A., Lotz, S. L., & Warrington, P. (2001). An online prepurchase model: The role of intention to search. *Journal of Retailing, 77*, 397–416.

Shim, S., Xiao, J. J., Barber, B., & Lyons, A. (2009). Pathway to life success: A conceptual model of financial well-being for young adults. *Journal of Applied Developmental Psychology, 30*, 708–723.

Shockey, S. S., & Seiling, S. B. (2004). Moving into action: Application of the transtheoretical model of behavior change to financial education. *Financial Counseling and Planning, 15*(1), 41–52.

Smith, B., & Stewart, F. (2008). Learning from the experience of OECD countries: Lessons for policy, programs and evaluations. In A. Lusardi (Ed.), *Overcoming the saving slump: How to increase the effectiveness of financial education and saving programs* (pp. 345–367). Chicago: University of Chicago Press.

Taylor, M. (2011). Measuring financial capability and its determinants using survey data. *Social Indicators Research, 102*(2), 297–314.

Xiao, J. J. (2008). Applying behavior theories to financial behavior. In J. J. Xiao (Ed.), *Handbook of consumer finance research* (pp. 69–81). New York, NY: Springer.

Xiao, J. J., Ahn, S., Serido, J., & Shim, S. (2014c). Earlier financial literacy and later financial behavior of college students. *International Journal of Consumer Studies*. Online First.

Xiao, J. J., & Anderson, J. G. (1997). Hierarchical financial needs reflected by household financial asset shares. *Journal of Family and Economic Issues, 18*(4), 333–356.

Xiao, J. J., Chatterjee, S., & Kim, J. (2014b). Factors associated with financial independence of young adults. *International Journal of Consumer Studies, 38*, 394–403.

Xiao, J. J., Chen, C., & Chen, F. (2014c). Consumer financial capability and financial satisfaction. *Social Indicators Research, 118*(1), 415–432.

Xiao, J. J., Chen, C., & Sun, L. (2014d). Age differences in consumer financial capability. International Journal of Consumer Studies. Forthcoming.

Xiao, J. J., Collins, M., Ford, M., Keller, P., Kim, J., & Robles, B. (2010). A review of financial behavior research: Implications for financial education. Commissioned report submitted to National Endowment on Financial Education.

Xiao, J. J., Ford, M. E., & Kim, J. (2011a). Consumer financial behavior: An interdisciplinary review of selected theories and research. *Family and Consumer Science Research Journal, 39*(4), 399–414.

Xiao, J. J., Newman, B. M., Prochaska, J. M., Leon, B., Bassett, R., & Johnson, J. L. (2004a). Applying the transtheoretical model of change to debt reducing behavior. *Financial Counseling and Planning, 15*(2), 89–100.

Xiao, J. J., Newman, B. M., Prochaska, J. M., Leon, B., & Bassett, R. (2004b). Voice of consumers in credit card debts: A qualitative approach. *Journal of Personal Finance, 3*(2), 56–74.

Xiao, J. J., & Noring, F. E. (1994). Perceived saving motives and hierarchical financial needs. *Financial Counseling and Planning, 5*, 25–44.

Xiao, J. J., & O'Neill, B. (2014). Financial education and financial capability. In V. J. Mason (ed.), *Proceedings of the Association for Financial Counseling and Planning Education* (pp. 58–68).

Xiao, J. J., O'Neill, B., Prochaska, J. M., Kerbal, C. M., Brennan, P., & Bristow, B. J. (2004c). A consumer education program based on the transtheoretical model of change. *International Journal of Consumer Studies, 28*(1), 55–65.

Xiao, J. J., Serido, J., & Shim, S. (2012). Financial education, financial knowledge, and risky credit behaviour of college students. In D. Lamdin (Ed.), *Financial decisions across the lifespan: Problems, programs, and prospects* (pp. 113–128). New York, NY: Springer.

Xiao, J. J., Sorhaindo, B., & Garman, E. T. (2006). Financial behavior of consumers in credit counseling. *International Journal of Consumer Studies, 30*(2), 108–121.

Xiao, J. J., Tang, C., Serido, J., & Shim, S. (2011b). Antecedents and consequences of risky credit behavior among college students: Application and extension of the theory of planned behavior. *Journal of Public Policy & Marketing, 30*(2), 239–245.

Xiao, J. J., & Wu, J. (2008). Completing debt management program in credit counseling: An application of the theory of planned behavior. *Financial Counseling and Planning, 19*(2), 29–45.

Part II
Consumer Economic Environments

Chapter 4
Government and Consumer Economic Wellbeing

Abstract Government can enhance consumer economic wellbeing through various approaches. One major approach is to regulate the market to rebalance powers between consumers and businesses. The focus of this chapter is government regulation related to consumer protection. In this chapter, regulation is first defined and categorized. Relevant regulation theories are then discussed. A theory of public policy setting is introduced and the role of American presidents in making consumer protection laws is discussed. After briefly introducing consumer laws, government regulations in the fields of consumer safety and finance are introduced. State level consumer protection laws in the USA are also introduced. Finally, government consumer protection measures are compared at the international level.

4.1 Government Regulation for Consumer Protection

A book entitled *Regulation and Consumer Protection*, edited by Meier et al. (2003), offers a comprehensive review of government regulation and consumer protection in the USA. Regulation is defined as any attempt by government to control the behavior of citizens, corporations, or other governments. Regulation takes numerous forms such as pricing regulation, franchising or licensing, standard setting, direct allocation of resources, incentive providing, fair competition promoting, and information providing (Meier 2003).

Regulation is described as a policymaking process of a subsystem. Dynamic interactions between concerned subcommittees, agencies, and interests groups serve as a subsystem and chief executives, legislatures, and courts serve as external, environmental factors influencing this subsystem. Besides this regulation policymaking subsystem, there are other factors such as economic, technological, historical, cultural, and public opinions to influence the policy decision-making process (Licari 2003).

Increasing regulatory responses to consumers is considered one direction for regulation reforms. Two formal mechanisms proposed to increase the responsiveness of regulatory agencies to consumers are the Agency for Consumer Advocacy and the use of public funds to support consumer participation in agency procedures. The idea of creating the Agency for Consumer Advocacy was discussed in the 1970s but never materialized because of various political reasons (Smith 2003).

J.J. Xiao, *Consumer Economic Wellbeing*, International Series on Consumer Science, DOI 10.1007/978-1-4939-2821-7_4

4.2 Categorizing Consumer Protection Measures

Consumer protection measures fall into four categories: choice restriction, choice enlargement, individual empowerment, and collective empowerment (Friedman 1991). Choice restriction focuses primarily on health and safety areas related to specific products and populations such as children. The choice enlargement measure is mainly to provide mandated, consumer needed information on products and services. Individual empowerment refers to improving consumer competency through consumer education. Collective empowerment is to provide resources for consumer advocacy organizations and bring consumer voices into the public policy making process. These measures offer consumer oriented government protection. To better protect consumers, the government also regulates business behaviors to improve consumer wellbeing, such as promoting competition in the market, fighting marketing frauds, and restricting unfair business practices against consumers.

4.3 Regulation Theories

4.3.1 Captured Theory

Stigler (1971) believes that as a rule, regulation is acquired by the industry and is designed and operated primarily for its benefit, which can be labeled "acquired" regulation. He also acknowledges two main alternative views of the regulation of industry. The first view is that regulation is instituted primarily for the protection and benefit of the public at large or some large subclass of the public. The second view is that industry regulation is the outcome of a political process that defies rational economic explanation. Government regulation can be in the form of direct subsidies, entry control, price control, etc. The regulations are achieved by profit maximizing dependent upon three political limitations: smaller firms usually receive larger shares of benefits, the procedural safeguards required of public processes are costly, and the political process automatically admits powerful outsiders to the industry's councils. These limitations need to be considered in calculating the profitability of regulating an industry. Costs of obtaining legislation are different from the market process for three reasons. First, the decisions must be made simultaneously by a large number of persons. Second, the democratic decision process must involve all parties of the community, not simply those who are directly concerned with a decision. The industry seeking political power must go to the appropriate seller, the political party, and prepare to pay two things a party needs: votes and resources. Occupational licensing is used as a case to demonstrate the costs of legislation seeking in his paper.

4.3.2 *Libertarian Paternalism*

In the literature of regulation, paternalism refers to strict government regulation that restricts business and consumer behaviors. Libertarian paternalism is a relatively weak, soft, and nonintrusive type of paternalism because choices are not blocked, fenced off, or significantly burdened (Thaler and Sunstein 2003, 2009). In government regulation, a nudge is any aspect of the choice architecture that alters people's behavior in a predictable way without forbidding any options or significantly changing economic incentives. To count as a mere nudge, the intervention must be easy and cheap to avoid. Nudges are not mandates. Six principles of good choice architecture, NUDGES, are presented below (Thaler and Sunstein 2009):

- iNcentives (Need to ask who uses, chooses, pays, and profits. Salience of costs and benefits can be manipulated to draw people's attention. Example: health-care costs).
- Understanding mappings (to improve user's ability to map to improve their welfare. Effective mapping is needed for complicated decisions. For the mapping purpose, propose government intervention: RECAP: record, evaluate, and compare alternative prices. Example: information disclosure).
- Defaults (use the default option for the welfare of users. Example: 401k plan participation).
- Give feedback (to notify users if they are doing well or making mistakes. Example: immediate picture made by digital camera).
- Expect error (use design to correct possible user errors or correct possible errors. Example: different sized nozzles for different fuels in gas stations).
- Structure complex choices (when choices become more numerous and vary on more dimensions, people are more likely to adopt simplifying strategies. Policy makers need to develop good choice architecture since it provides structure and structure affects outcomes. Example: paint wheel in paint stores).

4.4 Policy Agenda Setting

Mayer (1991) has examined the public policy agenda-setting process regarding consumer issues. Consumer problems can be defined as consumer dissatisfactions at the individual level. Consumer issues are those individual problems that become public issues and draw attention by the public, mass media, and policy makers. How are consumer problems developed into consumer issues and consumer laws? There are two competing views. First, these problems are publicized by the mass media, which arouses public opinion, and only then do public policymakers address them. A second, less unidirectional view holds that the process is sometimes reversed, with issues originating from policymakers.

To research the agenda-setting process, three agendas are specified: the media, public, and policy agenda. The media agenda refers to what is given high priority by the mass media and can be measured by news coverage, documentaries, and editorials. The public agenda refers to the set of issues that are foremost in the minds of the citizenry and can be measured by public opinion polls and complaints directed at businesses and government. The policy agenda consists of the issues that government decision makers believe are necessary to deliberate and can be measured by presidential speeches, bills filed by legislators, and rule-making proceedings initiated by regulatory agencies. Mayer (1991) finds that during the 1960–1987 period, consumer issues were first raised on the policy agenda; later federal attention to consumer problems had become legitimized by early executive and legislative action. Throughout this period, some consumer issues were placed on the media, public, and policy agendas by accidents and scandals, but these isolated events did not explain the overall pattern of consumer issues. These evidences support that the public policy agenda-setting process follows a multidirectional model instead of unidirectional model.

4.5 Presidents and Consumer Protection

Several US presidents have played an important role in consumer protection regulation (Waterman and Garman 1997). Democratic presidents are usually more supportive of the consumer movement's agenda than Republican ones. Two underlying factors influence the positions of all presidents on consumer issues. One is the extent to which the public demands new consumer protections. When this demand is evident, presidents almost always either take the lead in promoting new protections or accede to them. The second factor is general economic conditions. If economic growth slows, businesses restructure, and foreign economic competition increases, presidents will be concerned about the economic impacts of any new protections. In addition, businesses can be influential through their campaign contributions and lobbies on consumer protection law creations and implementations.

Throughout US history, the following presidents are considered pro-consumers, who actively assisted the passage and enactment of important consumer protection laws. Theodore Roosevelt played a vital role to help pass the two early consumer protection laws, the Meat Inspection Act and the Pure Food and Drug Act, both in 1906. Franklin Delano Roosevelt was not only instrumental to the passage of the enhanced Federal Food, Drug, and Cosmetic Act, but also established a Consumer Advisory Board within the National Recovery Administration. John F. Kennedy delivered the first consumer message to congress in which he proposed the concept of consumer rights and also specified four consumer rights. Lyndon Johnson was considered the greatest champion of consumer protection issues; he created a new White House position—special assistant for consumer affairs—established the President's Committee on Consumer Interests, issued several consumer reform proposals, and signed several important consumer protection acts into law. Richard Milhouse Nixon delivered a special message to congress on consumer protection, proposed the "Buyer's Bill of Rights," and added the right to redress to the list of consumer rights. Gerald Ford proposed the "right to consumer education". Carter supported the proposal for a federal consumer protection agency that failed to pass Congress. Bill Clinton proposed the "right to service" and focused on one single consumer issue, the health-care reform. Barack Obama signed into law the Credit CARD Act of 2009 and the Dodd-Frank Act of 2010, which created the Consumer Financial Protection Bureau and enacted mortgage protections. On the contrary, Ronald Reagan was anti-regulation, made major budget cuts in consumer agencies, and appointed leaders with antiregulatory views to consumer regulatory agencies. However, the younger George Bush's Office of the Comptroller of the Currency declared state anti-predatory lending statutes preempted as to national banks.

4.6 Consumer Protection Laws

Consumer law includes two components: public consumer law and private consumer law (Rustad 2007). Public consumer law is a subset of administrative law that governs the relationships between business and government. Federal and state agencies enforce public law consumer regulations through civil penalties as well as criminal fines that go to the state or federal treasury. The purpose of public consumer law at both the federal and state level is to detect and punish conduct inimical to a large number of consumers, not the individual. Another purpose is to deter misconduct. In addition, public agencies sometimes obtain settlements in the form of consent decrees that include some compensation to injured consumers.

Private consumer law encompasses remedies initiated by aggrieved consumers to redress personal injuries, financial losses, or property damages caused by defective goods, products, or services. Public consumer law seeks to regulate the consumer market and protect consumers from predatory or unfair practices, whereas private lawsuits are the only practical means to get consumer's money back. Consumers may use small claims courts that are special courts intended to enable consumers to represent themselves in an informal proceeding but have a cap or limit on the amount consumers can claim. Consumers may need to retain an attorney to pursue bigger and more complex cases (Bevans 2011; Rustad 2007). Class actions also enable the aggregation of many small claims so that they can be litigated in a single case more efficiently.

4.7 Consumer Safety Protection

4.7.1 Food Safety

Congress has assigned food safety mandates to nine federal agencies lodged in four different Cabinet Departments and two independent agencies. Among them, two agencies have primary responsibilities for food safety for American consumers, the Food Safety and Inspection Service in the Department of Agriculture is responsible for enforcing regulations on meat and poultry and the Food and Drug Administration in the US Department of Health and Human Services is responsible for all other food products (Carsky 2003).

4.7.2 Drug Safety

The Food and Drug Administration (FDA) that is housed in the US Department of Health and Human Services regulates drug safety. The mission of the FDA is to ensure that (1) foods are safe, wholesome, and sanitary; human and veterinary drugs, biological products, and medical devices are safe and effective; cosmetics are safe; and electronic products that emit radiation are safe; (2) regulated products are honestly, accurately, and informatively represented; and (3) these products are in compliance with the law and FDA regulations; noncompliance is identified and corrected, and any unsafe or unlawful products are removed from the market (Grant and Olmstead 2003).

4.7.3 Consumer Product Safety

The Consumer Product Safety Commission, an independent regulatory agency charged with protecting consumers from hazards associated with an estimated 15,000 different consumer products, regulates consumer product safety. According to the Consumer Product Safety Act (1972), the agency's purpose is to protect the public against unreasonable risks of injury associated with consumer products. It has authorities to set mandatory standards, ban products, order recalls of unsafe products, or institute labeling requirements. The agency enforces six statues, the Consumer Product Safety Act, Federal Hazardous Substances Act, Poison Prevention Packaging Act, Flammable Fabrics Act, Refrigerator Safety Act, and Fire Safe Cigarette Act (Fise 2003).

4.7.4 Transportation Safety

The National Highway Traffic Safety Administration that is housed in the US Department of Transportation regulates transportation safety. Its major regulatory areas include safety, damageability, and fuel economy. The agency has authority to set minimum safety standards that must be met by manufacturers of cars and related products such as tires, child safety seats, and motorcycle helmets in the USA. The agency also administers a grant program for the states to conduct various traffic safety programs such as anti-drunk driving, safety belt use, speed control, motorcycle safety, and emergency medical services programs (Stone 2003).

4.7.5 Environment Safety

The National Environmental Policy Act (1969) established the prevention and reduction of environmental damage as a goal of all federal agencies when carrying out the routine business of government. The act requires all federal agencies prepare an environmental impact statement any time their activities might damage the environment. Environmental safety is regulated by the Environmental Protection Agency (EPA), an independent agency that reports directly to the president. EPA is the largest regulatory agency, administering regulations under more than two-dozen statues. Policy tools used by EPA include prohibitions, command and control regulations, licensing and use restrictions, market-like incentives, fiscal inducements, and information provision. Regulatory areas include air quality, water quality, hazardous wastes, and pesticides (Ringquist 2003).

4.8 Consumer Financial Protection

4.8.1 Antitrust Regulation

The purpose of antitrust regulation is to encourage competitions in marketplace. Antitrust regulation is enforced by two agencies, the Antitrust Division housed in the US Department of Justice and the Federal Trade Commission (FTC), an independent agency. The Antitrust Division enforces the Sherman Act while the FTC carries out the Federal Trade Commission Act. They share jurisdiction over the Clayton Act. The FTC can attack most of the business practices banned by the Sherman Act as unfair methods of competition. The regulatory areas include monopolization, collusion, mergers, and price discrimination, and exclusionary practices (Anderson 2003).

4.8.2 Fair Trade Regulation

Federal Trade Commission (FTC), an independent federal agency in the USA, has jurisdiction over virtually all industries for this purpose, regulates unfair and deceptive practices in the marketplace. FTC was very active in protecting consumers in the 1970s as responses to requests by consumer advocates. FTC enforces laws to protect consumers for fair dealing such as warranty under Magnuson-Moss Warranty Act, and preventing deception and unfairness and protecting privacy under the FTC Act. Because the FTC is an independent federal agency, it is not subject to the direction of the president. The president's role is limited to appointing commissioners, naming the chair from among the commissioners, and influencing the congressional appropriations for the FTC. In the 1980s, under the influence of

President Reagan, the FTC made a series of decisions to indicate it was retreating from its aggressive consumer protection policies. When President Clinton was in office, the agency focused on consumer protection issues about information highway (Silbergeld 2003).

4.8.3 Depository Institution Regulation

Depository institutions refer to commercial banks, savings associations, savings banks, and credit unions. There is a set of federal agencies that regulate depository institutions such as the Office of the Comptroller of the Currency, Federal Reserve System, Federal Deposit Insurance Corporation, Office of Thrift Supervision (which was eliminated by the Dodd-Frank Act and folded into the OCC), and National Credit Union Administration. All states have their own banking departments. The federal government's major goal in regulating banks is to protect banks, their depositors, and the communities in which they operate from failures. Another regulatory goal is to promote competition in banking. A final goal of federal regulation is to protect consumers of bank credit and services from discrimination, deception, and abuse of their rights (Xiao 2003).

4.8.4 Credit Regulation

Credit markets are regulated by a set of federal agencies similar to those that regulate depository institutions (see the previous section). Consumer credit protection laws cover areas in consumer information, consumer protection, and fair and efficient credit allocation. These regulations require lenders to inform consumers about interest rates and finance charges on credit. The regulations also protect consumers from potential abuse by imposing a loan rate ceiling, restrict debt collection procedures, and establish procedures for billing errors. The regulations also ensure an effective and fair credit allocation by prohibiting lenders from discriminating against consumers based on borrowers' socio-demographic characteristics (Hong and Heck 2003).

Many state usury laws have been effectively preempted as to many consumer loans (e.g., credit cards) by federal laws that provide that when a lender in one state issues a consumer loan to a consumer in another state, the lender's state usury laws apply to the loan. In response, many lenders have established their offices in states like Delaware and South Dakota to take advantage of favorable usury laws and "export" them to their transactions with consumers in other states. As a result, usury laws have become much less significant than they once were, except for in-state transactions, like payday loans (Jeff Sovern, September 18, 2014, personal communication). Consumer credit laws may need to be revised too to better protect consumers. A law researcher argues that the Truth in Lending Act (TILA) that is intended to enable consumers to borrow wisely not only fails the subprime borrowers in that goal, but is interpreted to require lenders to provide misleading disclosures that might have persuaded borrowers that their loans are more affordable than they would turn out to be and proposes strategies to improve consumer disclosure environments (Sovern 2014).

4.8.5 Housing Regulation

The housing delivery system involves a complex set of interrelationships between the private market activity of producers, sellers and buyers, and government policy-makers and regulators. Although housing markets are local, there is multi-level regulation of housing. The areas of housing regulation include construction, accessibility, safety, and environmental issues. Regulation on housing construction at the federal level is mainly enforced by the Department of Housing and Urban Development. Regulations related to accessibility primarily focus on discrimination, such as the Fair Housing Act that prohibits discrimination in housing based on several socioeconomic characteristics. Safety issues in housing include fire protection, lead-based paint cleanup, stair safety, and response to natural hazards. Environmental issues in housing include energy conservation, indoor air quality, and wetlands (Meeks 2003).

4.8.6 Security Regulation

Security markets are regulated mainly by the Securities and Exchange Commission (SEC), which is an independent agency in the USA. Regulatory tools used by SEC are disclosure, enforcement, and self-regulation. The Securities Act (1933) and the Securities Exchange Act (1934) require disclosure when an issue of securities is registered with the SEC prior to a public sale. SEC has authority to insure disclosure by companies and to bring actions against market professionals through administrative action, filing for an injunction, and referring a case to the Department of Justice for criminal prosecution when violations of the security laws occur. The Securities Enforcement Remedies and Penny Stock Reform Act (1990) gives SEC the authority to impose disgorgement sanctions in administrative hearings or the surrendering of profits earned through illegal market activities. While SEC has strong rule-making powers to structure and regulate trading activities, it works with the markets to maintain a system of self-regulation that is overseen by the SEC (Khademian 2003).

4.8.7 Financial Service Regulation

The idea of a federal agency to focus on consumer protection in financial products was proposed by Warren (2007) in *Democracy*, a policy discussion journal started in 2006. A later version with a reference list was published in *Journal of Consumer*

Affairs (Warren 2008). She argues that if the Consumer Product Safety Commission can ensure there are no unsafe consumer products in the marketplace, a similar agency should exist for financial products. The reason is because regulation on financial products is lacking and consumers are hurt financially by many unfair business practices and marketing frauds (for example, teaser rates, negative amortization, increased use of fees, cross-default clauses, penalty interest rates, and two-cycle billing) in many financial services such as mortgage and credit card areas, which are evidenced by mass consumer bankruptcies, foreclosures, and debt delinquencies. Consumer protection laws can be used for consumer confusion instead of consumer protection. For example, information disclosure becomes a way to confuse rather than inform consumers. One-page credit card contracts in the 1980s have grown to over 30-pages of incomprehensible text. Another major reason for the new agency is that existing regulatory agencies are inadequate. Many subprime products are not regulated by relevant federal agencies and regulatory agencies are unmotivated to protect consumers since these agencies' major missions are to ensure the soundness and safety of financial institutions. Many scholars and policy analysts proposed ideas to reform America for a better place for Americans in *Democracy* but this is the only one that brought the idea of the new consumer protection agency to reality.

After reviewing heavy evidence on issues of consumer inabilities and businesses taking advantage of consumer inabilities in product designs in credit markets, Bar-Gill and Warren (2008) propose that the new agency should include at least three features: reliance on ex ante regulation rather than ex post litigation, rulemaking located within a regulatory agency rather than a legislature, and regulation based on the product sold rather than the identity of the seller.

In 2010, the Dodd-Frank Wall Street Reform and Consumer Protection Act law was passed in Congress and signed into law by President Obama, authorizing the creation of the Consumer Financial Protection Bureau to regulate consumer financial products. The legislative process of creating this new agency has been documented in a book with great details (Kirsch and Mayer 2013; Kirsch et al. 2014). Unlike Warren hoped as an independent agency, the new agency is housed in the Federal Reserve but will have independent authorities to set rules and take enforcement actions. The missions of the bureau are to conduct rule-making, supervision, and enforcement for Federal consumer financial protection laws; to restrict unfair, deceptive, or abusive acts or practices; to take consumer complaints; to promote financial education; to research consumer behavior; to monitor financial markets for new risks to consumers; and to enforce laws that outlaw discrimination and other unfair treatment in consumer finance, which are described at the agency's website (http://www.consumerfinance.gov/the-bureau/).

Rationales for consumer financial protection through government regulation are presented by a group of scholars at Harvard University (Campbell et al. 2011). From a perspective of standard economics, government regulation can remedy issues caused by market failures such as externalities, information asymmetries, market powers, and coordination failures. In addition, mounting evidence from behavioral economics show that consumers have limitations in financial literacy and cognitive abilities in financial decision making that would result in suboptimal financial decisions and hurt their financial wellbeing. In addition, because of the diversity of consumer economics and cognitive abilities, lower income and lower educated consumers end up paying higher prices for many financial products. To address these issues, government regulations can be helpful. They recommend that the new agency should be focused on providing information to consumers in a way consumers can understand and make correct actions. The improved disclosure should not only improve consumer understanding of the information but also prevent paying high prices. They also provide other suggestions for the new agency such as encouraging two-pricing schemes, allowing flexibilities in regulation, allowing financial innovations that enhance consumer wellbeing, and avoiding unintended negative consequences for consumers caused by the political process. For example, they believe that politicians' desire to extend credit access to lower-income households is a contributing factor in the development of the subprime mortgage market, the recent housing and credit bubbles, and ultimately the financial crisis in 2007–09.

4.9 State and Local Consumer Protection

4.9.1 State and Local Consumer Protection Agencies

Xiao and Richardson (2003) describe consumer protection at the state and local level in the USA. A number of agencies exist in state and local consumer protection. These include consumer protection agencies, Offices of Attorneys General, agencies that protect utility consumers, various state agencies, and local agencies.

The most common consumer protect agency at the state level is a division or unit under the state Attorney General's office. Some have a consumer protection division or section at the second layer of the office and other states have a consumer protection unit under the civil division or section in the office. Some states have an active consumer protection division or unit under other state departments and only a few states (California, Connecticut, Massachusetts, New York, South Carolina) have a separate *office of consumer affairs* (Xiao and Richardson 2003).

Consumer protection agencies at the state and local level vary considerably in size and resources. A survey conducted by an association of state consumer agency officials shows that among their member agencies, the smallest office consists of a part-time staff member with a budget of $5,000 while one of the largest agency's budgets is $22 million. Populations served range from 40,000 to 35 million. These agencies provide services for consumers such as conducting educational outreach/public information campaigns, maintaining web sites that accept online complaints, having toll-free numbers for consumer information and referral services, providing complaint mediation assistance, and enforcing regulations for consumer protection. Of the 60 agencies responding to the survey, total complaints filed with those agencies in 2003–2004 was 445,676. The total amount recouped for consumers through complaint mediation, enforcement cases, and regulatory action in 2003/4 was over

$88.5 million. Each closed case netted consumers an average return of $513 per complaint (NACAA/CFA 2005).

Consumer agency staffers who handle complaints first attempt to persuade the parties to reach a mediated settlement. Should this prove impossible, agencies pursue a variety of alternatives. Many agencies can issue subpoenas to uncooperative merchants as well as secure civil citations when violations of law are clear and no further investigation is needed. Administrative adjudicative hearings and arbitration proceedings are sometimes available to bring cases to closure. Besides handling consumer complaints, these agencies also conduct consumer and merchant education programs, enforce consumer protection laws, play the role of consumer advocacy before legislatures, assume licensing and other responsibilities, and cooperate with other agencies to resolve consumer issues (Gregg 1997).

The attorney general at the state level is an elected position. Attorneys general have to answer primarily to voters, not governors, and are responsible for most consumer protection activities, including enforcement and handling consumer complaints. The unique role of attorney general combines regulatory authority with the executive authority of an elective office, and this makes the gubernatorial executive presence less essential in this area. Many states have a consumer protection section or unit within the Office of the Attorney General, rather than in the executive branch of government. At the heart of the attorney general's role is the duty to enforce the state's specific consumer protection laws. In most states, those responsibilities now extend to an array of related functions that continue to grow in importance as the offices evolve. Among these functions are the resolution of consumer disputes, public outreach and consumer education, and policy and legislative advocacy. In addition, states cooperate in pursuit of a common objective in consumer protection. Based on the multi-state investigations, the attorney general has developed voluntary guidelines, proposals for federal reforms, and model state legislation to address industry-wide problems (Blanke 1997).

Regulated utilities are monopoly franchises and generally fall under the governing authority of an elected or an appointed Public Service Commission (PSC) or Public Utilities Commission (PUC). PSCs may regulate taxicabs along with various other duties. To ensure that the consumer interest is represented in the utility regulation process, many states have utility consumer advocates. A majority of states have an agency affiliated with the PSC, typically called the People's Counsel or Consumer Counsel, whose mandate is to represent consumers before the PSC. State utility consumer advocates are empowered by state laws to protect public utility ratepayers from monopoly abuses and profiteering. Acting independently of each state's Public Utility Commission, these advocates represent ratepayers in more than 40 states and the District of Columbia. In 19 states, the state attorney general provides utility consumer advocate representation. Since the 1970s, these advocacy agencies have saved utility consumers billions of dollars through interventions in ratemaking proceedings and through court actions. The advocates have also established legal precedents for consumer rights relating to the quality and terms of public utility service. Instead of having a utility consumer advocate agency fully independent of the PUC, California and some other states maintain "intervenor compensation" programs to award after-the-fact fees to grassroots consumer advocacy groups for their participation in regulatory proceedings (Spratley 1997).

Consumer protection duties in the states are complicated by the existence of a number of specialized state agencies with authority over certain industries. Executive branch appointees usually regulate most insurance and financial institutions, typically through an insurance commission, a banking commission, a securities commission, or some combination thereof. Some states also have specialized financial regulation of consumer credit companies and consumer finance companies, often in the attorney general's office or through an independent executive agency. On a selective basis, states venture into regulation of many other industries, and the apparatus for regulation may be placed in a variety of offices in the executive branch. Examples include a department of weights and measures, licensing and occupational regulation, and agricultural regulation (Xiao and Richardson 2003).

Consumer protection at the local government level is often a "hit or miss" situation. Some cities and counties have consumer protection agencies that administer various laws and have the traditional functions of licensing, health inspection, or weights and measures. As a rule, however, most cities and counties, except the largest ones, do not have a central consumer agency to handle consumer complaints, much less administer and enforce consumer protection laws. Where they exist, these local agencies are often important locally for their roles in public policymaking and consumer information. Most enforcement of consumer protection laws and regulations at the local level is provided through the offices of district attorneys or state attorneys. District and state attorneys are typically appointed or elected and are administratively separate from the mayor or county executive. The agenda of local law enforcement officials is generally concerned with criminal law, leaving everyday consumer protection as a low priority almost uniformly across the USA (Xiao and Richardson 2003).

4.9.2 State Consumer Protection Laws

Several model consumer protection laws were proposed by various organizations during the late 1960s and early 1970s. Since these were only model statutes, state legislatures were free to adopt them either in their entirety, in some amended form, or not at all, depending on what, if any, provisions were deemed beneficial for consumers in a particular state (Xiao and Richardson 2003).

The *Uniform Deceptive Trade Practices Act* (*UDTPA*) was drafted in 1964 and revised in 1966. The UDTPA preceded the Federal Trade Commission's proposal that states draft their own consumer protection laws. It represented an attempt at circumventing inconsistency among the consumer protection laws that had begun developing in those states acting on their own initiative. The UDTPA provided a list of 11 prohibited trade practices and contained a "catch-all provision" prohibiting "...conduct which similarly creates a likelihood of confusion or misunderstanding." The UDTPA, in its model form, allows injured consumers to seek injunctive relief from future violations of the act, however, it did not provide for monetary damages or restitution. While UDTPA provided limited relief for consumers in the states that passed it, UDTPA was only a beginning effort to protect consumers.

In 1967 the FTC, in conjunction with the Committee on Suggested State Legislation of the Council of State Governments, drafted the *Unfair Trade Practices and Consumer Protection Act* (*UTPCPA*). The UTPCPA grants authority to state attorneys general to adopt regulations, issue subpoenas, and conduct hearings. It also permits the attorney general to seek injunctive relief and civil penalties in some circumstances, and to seek forfeiture of a corporate franchise for violations of the act. The FTC drafted an amended version in 1971 that greatly enhanced protection for consumers as it provided, for the first time, private causes of action by individual consumers against violators of the act and it permitted the attorney general to seek restitution on behalf of injured consumers.

The *Uniform Consumer Sales Practices Act* (*UCSPA*) was approved by the National Conference of Commissioners on Uniform State Laws in 1971. This statute was intended to provide merchants with predictable standards for their conduct, and to bring about uniformity among state laws on consumer sales practices by making them consistent with the Federal Trade Commission policy. This model statute prohibits both unconscionable and deceptive sales practices, and provides a non-exclusive list of 11 deceptive sales practices (which are quite similar to the 11 prohibited trade practices delineated in the UDTPA), as well as factors a court would consider in evaluating a claim of *unconscionability*, which offers strong consumer protection.

By 1981, all states and the District of Columbia had adopted one of the three above proposed statutes in either its model form or a hybrid version. These state laws, modeled after the Federal Trade Commission Act, were dubbed "Little FTC Acts," and provided enforcement at the state level, generally through the state attorney general's office. These acts embodied the substance of the FTC act, in that they adopted the FTC's mandates and interpretations, and provided restitution and other remedies appropriate to consumer needs. Although the Little FTC Acts vary somewhat from state to state, practices that are illegal in one state will likely be illegal in all others as well.

Virtually all state consumer protection acts now provide the aggrieved consumer with a private cause of action, a provision absent in the federal FTC Act that gives both individual consumers and government entities the ability to file lawsuits. The states' acts permit either the aggrieved consumer or the attorney to seek restitution damages. Approximately 35 states' acts provide remedies that exceed actual damages, including double damages, treble damages, punitive damages, or minimum statutory damages. Also, approximately 40 states' acts permit a prevailing plaintiff to recover attorney fees (Xiao and Richardson 2003).

4.10 International Comparisons of Consumer Protection

Mayer (2003) provides a comprehensive overview on international consumer protection. He analyzes consumer protection from an international perspective by using four factors: the level of gross domestic product (GDP), the level of government involvement in the economy, the degree of political openness to the participation of consumers, and the cultural emphasis on collective welfare versus individual freedom and opportunity. Based on these factors, he divides countries into seven categories: Anglo-Capitalists, Northern European Corporatists, Trade Integrationists, Former Central Planners, Earnest Strivers, Hopeful Starters, and an unnamed seventh category which is desperately poor and/or racked by civil strife.

Anglo capitalists have high GDP, low government involvement with the economy, high involvement with strong private associations, and value individual freedom and opportunity and private property. Examples of these countries include the USA, the UK, Canada, and Australia. Consumer protection policies are justified in these countries to the extent that they contribute to the efficient functioning of free markets. Policies to promote safety, representation, and redress are encouraged since they are to correct market failures. These countries have active consumer protection organizations but many of them are self-supported. These countries respect freedom of individual choice. In the USA there are fewest legal limitations for driving, drinking and smoking, compared to other western countries.

Northern European Corporatists have high GDP, moderate government involvement in economy, high involvement with strong labor unions and parties, and value group welfare and protection of the vulnerable. Examples include Sweden, Norway, the Netherlands, and Germany. These countries are called "welfare states" and have centralized protection agencies and specialized consumer representatives, such as the consumer ombuds in the Nordic countries, which are funded by the government. Consumer cooperatives are active in these countries to make private sellers more responsive to consumer needs. These countries take efforts to provide basic consumer necessities to less fortunate consumers and to protect vulnerable consumers. They enforce "paternalistic" policies governing safety.

Trade Integrationists have upper-middle GDP, are moderate with their emphasis on promoting exports, and are moderate with single party dominance. Their values are too diverse to generalize. Examples include Italy, Japan, Malaysia, and Mexico. Consumer protection in these countries can be considered part of their participation in the international trading system rather than as a response to domestic consumer demand. Trade Intergrationists are creating consumer protection standards to match the international conventions. There are fewer private, independent consumer advocacy groups within these countries.

Former Central Planners have upper and lower-middle GDP, are high but decreasing with privatization, have low but increasing strength for democratic institutions, and value that government provides basic necessities and public goods. Examples include Poland, Hungary, Russia, and Latvia. These countries are transitioning to market economies. Supplies of consumer goods are in shortage, which results in black markets. These countries have motivations to implement consumer protection policies under citizens' beliefs that leaders of these countries should be held more accountable. Additionally, they want to match their western counterparts when applying for international trade organizations such as the European Union.

Earnest Strivers have upper and lower-middle GDP, government involvement in the economy is moderate, which encourages foreign investment, democratic level is low with a strong influence of military, and they value social hierarchy and the importance of group and family. Examples include Indonesia, Philippines, El Salvador, and Turkey. These countries are struggling to help their citizens to meet their basic needs and started to demand laws and protection institutions to ensure other consumer rights such as safety, information, choice, representation, education, and redress.

Hopeful starters have lower-middle and low GDP, government involvement is moderate but decreasing with structural adjustment, democratic institution strength is low with strong ethnic divisions, and they value ethnic identity, traditionalism, and fatalism. Examples include India, Kenya, Guyana, and Bangladesh. Large portions of the population of these countries lack basic necessities such as clean water, food, and fuel. To these countries, western-style consumer protections seem like superfluous luxuries. Consumer organizations in these countries have focused on extremely basic consumer problems such as infant milk formula and an essential drugs list. In addition, their well-being may be hurt by their preference for foreign-made products by which products banned, severely restricted, or past peak usability are dumped into their markets.

4.11 Summary

To ensure the efficient and fair operation of the market economy and to rebalance powers between consumers and businesses, governments issue and enforce consumer protection laws and regulations. Regulations can be categorized as choice restrictions, choice enlargement, individual empowerment, and collective empowerment.

There are several theories on regulation discussed throughout this chapter. The capture theory believes that regulations are favored by the regulated industries to better protect these industries' interests. However, this theory may reflect only partial truth of the reality. The libertarian paternalism theory emphasizes nudge, a minor regulation with few restrictions but a great amount of flexibility for the purpose of enhancing consumer economic wellbeing. The theory of public agenda setting describes the public policy making process in the USA. The chapter also discusses the role of presidents in the role of consumer protection legislation. President Kennedy is considered the consumer champion who proposed the concept of consumer rights and also proposed four consumer moral rights that are still influential in the law making process in the USA and throughout the world. Consumer protection laws assume that consumers are on a weak side in the marketplace compared to their business counterparts and deserve legal protections in many situations.

The US consumer protection measures can be categorized into two broad areas, safety and finance. The US government has many laws and corresponding agencies to provide these protections. Areas of consumer safety protection cover food, drug, transportation, consumer product, and the environment. Areas of consumer financial protection include antitrust, fair trade, depository institution, credit, housing, security, and financial service. Consumer protection laws also cover warranties and privacy. Consumer protection laws vary from state to state in the USA. From an international perspective, the consumer protection measures are diverse in terms of philosophies, focuses, and approaches, which are closely relevant to the economic development levels, political and social systems, and cultural values and histories of individual countries.

References

Anderson, J. (2003). Chapter 4: Antitrust regulation. In K. J. Meier, E. T. Garman, & L. R. Keiser (Eds.), *Regulation and consumer protection: Politics, bureaucracy, and economics* (4th ed., pp. 75–108). Mason, OH: Thomson.

Bar-Gill, O., & Warren, E. (2008). Making credit safer. *University of Pennsylvania Law Review, 157*, 1–101.

Bevans, N. R. (2011). *Consumer law & protection: A practical approach for paralegals and the public*. Durham, NC: Carolina Academic Press.

Blanke, D. (1997). State attorneys general. In S. Brobeck (Ed.), *Encyclopedia of the consumer movement*. Santa Barbara, CA: ABC-CLIO.

Campbell, J. Y., Jackson, H. E., Madrian, B. C., & Tufano, P. (2011). Consumer financial protection. *Journal of Economic Perspectives, 21*(1), 91–113.

Carsky, M. L. (2003). Chapter 10: Food safety regulation. In K. J. Meier, E. T. Garman, & L. R. Keiser (Eds.), *Regulation and consumer protection: Politics, bureaucracy, and economics* (4th ed., pp. 235–258). Mason, OH: Thomson.

Fise, M. E. R. (2003). Chapter 11: Consumer product safety regulation. In K. J. Meier, E. T. Garman, & L. R. Keiser (Eds.), *Regulation and consumer protection: Politics, bureaucracy, and economics* (4th ed., pp. 259–280). Mason, OH: Thomson.

Friedman, M. (1991). Research on consumer protection issues: The perspective of the "human sciences". *Journal of Social Issues, 47*(1), 1–19.

Grant, A., & Olmstead, S. (2003). Chapter 9: Regulating drugs. In K. J. Meier, E. T. Garman, & L. R. Keiser (Eds.), *Regulation and consumer protection: Politics, bureaucracy, and economics* (4th ed., pp. 212–233). Mason, OH: Thomson.

Gregg, B. B. (1997). State and local consumer affairs offices. In S. Brobeck (Ed.), *Encyclopedia of the Consumer Movement*. ABC-CLIO: Santa Barbara, CA.

Hong, G.-S., & Heck, K. Z. (2003). Chapter 14: Credit regulation. In K. J. Meier, E. T. Garman, & L. R. Keiser (Eds.), *Regulation and consumer protection: Politics, bureaucracy, and economics* (4th ed., pp. 331–352). Mason, OH: Thomson.

Khademian, A. M. (2003). Chapter 16: Securities market regulation and investor protection. In K. J. Meier, E. T. Garman, & L. R. Keiser (Eds.), *Regulation and consumer protection: Politics, bureaucracy, and economics* (4th ed., pp. 367–386). Mason, OH: Thomson.

Kirsch, L., & Mayer, R. N. (2013). *Financial justice: The people's campaign to stop lender abuse*. Santa Barbara, CA: ABC-CLIO.

Kirsch, L., Mayer, R. N., & Silber, N. I. (2014). The CFPB and payday lending: New agency/old problem. *Journal of Consumer Affairs, 48*(1), 1–16.

Licari, M. J. (2003). Chapter 2: The policy process. In K. J. Meier, E. T. Garman, & L. R. Keiser (Eds.), *Regulation and consumer protection: Politics, bureaucracy, and economics* (4th ed., pp. 11–40). Mason, OH: Thomson.

Mayer, R. N. (1991). Gone yesterday, here today: Consumer issues in the agenda-setting process. *Journal of Social Issues, 47*(1), 21–39.

Mayer, R. N. (2003). Chapter 19: Consumer protection—a global perspective. In K. J. Meier, E. T. Garman, & L. R. Keiser (Eds.), *Regulation and consumer protection: Politics, bureaucracy, and economics* (4th ed., pp. 423–440). Mason, OH: Thomson.

Meeks, C. B. (2003). Chapter 15: Housing regulation. In K. J. Meier, E. T. Garman, & L. R. Keiser (Eds.), *Regulation and consumer protection: Politics, bureaucracy, and economics* (4th ed., pp. 353–366). Mason, OH: Thomson.

Meier, K. J. (2003). Chapter 1: Myths of regulation and consumer protection. In K. J. Meier, E. T. Garman, & L. R. Keiser (Eds.), *Regulation and consumer protection: Politics, bureaucracy, and economics* (4th ed., pp. 1–10). Mason, OH: Thomson.

Meier, K. J., Garman, E. T., & Keiser (Eds.). (2003). *Regulation and consumer protection: Politics, bureaucracy, and economics* (4th ed.). Mason, OH: Thomson.

NACAA/CFA. (2005). Thirteenth Annual NACAA/CFA Consumer Complaint Survey Report. http://www.nacaa.net/pdf/survey.pdf.

Ringquist, E. J. (2003). Chapter 7: Environmental protection regulation. In K. J. Meier, E. T. Garman, & L. R. Keiser (Eds.), *Regulation and consumer protection: Politics, bureaucracy, and economics* (4th ed., pp. 143–180). Mason, OH: Thomson.

Rustad, M. L. (2007). *Everyday law for consumers*. Boulder, CO: Paradigm.

Silbergeld, M. (2003). Chapter 5: The revitalization of the federal trade commission. In K. J. Meier, E. T. Garman, & L. R. Keiser (Eds.), *Regulation and consumer protection: Politics, bureaucracy, and economics* (4th ed., pp. 109–120). Mason, OH: Thomson.

Smith, K. B. (2003). Chapter 20: Reforming regulation. In K. J. Meier, E. T. Garman, & L. R. Keiser (Eds.), *Regulation and consumer protection: Politics, bureaucracy, and economics* (4th ed., pp. 441–474). Mason, OH: Thomson.

Sovern, J. (2014). Fixing consumer protection laws so borrowers understand their payment obligations. *Journal of Consumer Affairs, 48*(1), 17–33.

Spratley, W. A. (1997). State utility consumer advocates. In S. Brobeck (Ed.), *Encyclopedia of the consumer movement*. Santa Barbara, CA: ABC-CLIO.

Stigler, G. J. (1971). The theory of economic regulation. *Bell Journal of Economics and Management Science, 2*, 3–21.

Stone, J. L. (2003). Chapter 12: Automobile safety regulation. In K. J. Meier, E. T. Garman, & L. R. Keiser (Eds.), *Regulation and consumer protection: Politics, bureaucracy, and economics* (4th ed., pp. 281–302). Mason, OH: Thomson.

Thaler, R. H., & Sunstein, C. R. (2003). Libertarian paternalism. *American Economic Review, 93*(2), 175–179.

Thaler, R. H., & Sunstein, C. R. (2009). *Nudge: Improving decisions about health, wealth, and happiness*. New York, NY: Penguin.

Warren, E. (2007). Unsafe at any rate. *Democracy, Summer, 5*, 8–19.

Warren, E. (2008). Product safety regulation as a model for financial services regulation. *Journal of Consumer Affairs, 42*(3), 452–460.

Waterman, R. W., & Garman, E. T. (1997). Presidents and the consumer movement. In S. Brobeck (Ed.), *Encyclopedia of the consumer movement* (pp. 433–438). Santa Barbara, CA: ABC-CLIO.

Xiao, J. J. (2003). Chapter 13: Depository institutions regulation. In K. J. Meier, E. T. Garman, & L. R. Keiser (Eds.), *Regulation and consumer protection: Politics, bureaucracy, and economics* (4th ed., pp. 303–330). Mason, OH: Thomson.

Xiao, J. J., & Richardson, S. L. (2003). Chapter 18: State and local consumer protection. In K. J. Meier, E. T. Garman, & L. R. Keiser (Eds.), *Regulation and consumer protection: Politics, bureaucracy, and economics* (4th ed., pp. 403–422). Mason, OH: Thomson.

Chapter 5
Business and Consumer Economic Wellbeing

Abstract In the marketplace, consumers and businesses are two major players. Consumers play dual roles to contribute to the economy, most of whom working for businesses to earn incomes and purchasing products from businesses. A perfect market works when participating players follow a set of rules that ensure efficient and fair operation of the economy. In reality, the market is imperfect and both good and bad business behaviors occur. Good business behavior is defined as business practices that are not only consider their own interests but also consumer interests or interests of other parties directly or indirectly involved in the transactions. Bad business behaviors are defined as business practices that hurt consumer wellbeing and public interests such as marketing frauds and rip offs. This chapter reviews several concepts that lead to good business behaviors such as corporate social responsibility and quality of life marketing, etc. It also examines the research literature relevant to marketing frauds, rip offs, and consumer victims.

5.1 Concepts Toward Good Business Behavior

5.1.1 Corporate Social Responsibility

Corporate social responsibility (CSR) is an important concept to signify good business behaviors. Although there are different definitions of corporate social responsibility, CSR implies particular attention to the ethical, social, and environmental implications of business. Business practices of corporate social responsibility include social, environmental, and economic dimensions. As demonstrated in a CSR study, specific practices include donating money and time to communities, local sourcing and hiring, paying taxes, using recyclable materials, having anti-waste programs, having fair labor policies, having fair supplier policies, and having fair consumer policies (Kolk et al. 2010).

Carroll and Shabana (2010) provide a comprehensive review on the concept and business practices of corporate social responsibility. The notion of corporate social responsibilities was mentioned in the 1940s. The theoretical discussion and debates became active in the 1970s (Frederick 1978). In 1990s and 2000s, the literature discussed more about globalization and CSR and related CSR with sustainability issues.

J.J. Xiao, *Consumer Economic Wellbeing*, International Series on Consumer Science, DOI 10.1007/978-1-4939-2821-7_5

Among several alternative definitions of CSR, the following is used often: "The social responsibility of business encompasses the economic, legal, ethical, and discretionary [later referred to as philanthropic] expectations that society has of organizations at a given point in time" (Carroll 1979, p. 500, 1991, p. 283). Among four aspects of responsibilities, the economic and legal responsibilities are required, the ethical responsibilities are expected, and the discretionary/philanthropic responsibilities are desired. The essence of CSR and what it really refers to are the ethical and philanthropic obligations of the corporation toward society. Kotler and Lee (2005) agree and define CSR as a commitment to improve community wellbeing through discretionary business practices and contributions of corporate resources. More discussions on academically derived definitional constructs can be found in Carroll (1999).

Enhancing CSR is beneficial for businesses because of its functions of (1) reducing cost and risk; (2) strengthening legitimacy and reputation; (3) building competitive advantage; and (4) creating win–win situations through synergistic value creation (Kurucz et al. 2008).

The business case for CSR refers to the arguments that provide rational justification for CSR initiatives from a primarily corporate economic/financial perspective. Business-case arguments contend that firms that engage in CSR activities will be rewarded by the market in economic and financial terms. A narrow view of the business case justifies CSR initiatives when they produce direct and clear links to firm financial performance. Mostly, the narrow view of the business case focuses on immediate cost savings. By contrast, the broad view of the business case justifies CSR initiatives when they produce direct and indirect links to firm performance. The advantage of the broad view over the narrow view is that it allows the firm to benefit from CSR opportunities. The broad view of the business case for CSR enables the firm to enhance its competitive advantage and create win–win relationships with its stakeholders, in addition to realizing gains from cost and risk reduction and legitimacy and reputation benefits, which are realized through the narrow view (Carroll and Shabana 2010). Research shows that there is an ideal level of CSR, which managers can determine via cost-benefit analysis and that there is a neutral relationship between CSR and financial performance (McWilliams and Siegel 2001).

Evidences of the impact of CSR on financial performance of a firm are mixed. For example, investment in research and development (R&D) may be an important determinant of firm performance. When this factor is considered in the analysis, CSR has a neutral impact on financial performance (McWilliams and Siegel 2000). On the whole, research seems to indicate the existence of a positive relationship between CSR and financial performance; however, some inconsistencies linger. In light of the broad view of the business case for CSR these inconsistencies may be attributed not only to methodological differences and interpretation biases, but also to the existence of mediating variables and situational contingencies (Carroll and Shabana 2010).

CSR in the international context shows interesting country differences. A study aims to explore CSP topics in eight largest retailers in China, in which four are

Chinese and four are non-Chinese companies. The analysis of CSR/sustainability dimensions communicated in both Chinese and English languages shows substantial differences between the Chinese and international contexts. Interestingly, the largest divergence can be found for international retailers between their Chinese and corporate attention for CSR (home versus host settings), most notably in the case of Carrefour, and to a lesser extent, Wal-Mart. In the Chinese context, there are differences between the Chinese and international retailers as well (domestic versus foreign firms), with the former reporting more on economic dimensions, including philanthropy, and the latter more on product responsibility—contentious labor issues and the environment receive relatively limited attention in both groups in China (Kolk et al. 2010).

From an economic perspective, researchers in a critical literature review conclude that CSR can only achieve a second-best level of public goods provision. They identify three types of CSR, moral hazard CSR, not-for-profit CSR, and strategic CSR and argue that the match of preferences between shareholders and stakeholders including consumers motivates different models with different implications. Based on their review of empirical studies, CSR does not reduce costs, ceteris paribus. For hypotheses related to strategic CSR, they find mixed evidence in favor of labor markets as drivers of CSR, while consistent evidence shows that consumers bear at least some of the costs. Their review also suggests that consumer demands for CSR are diverse and political factors affect CSR provision (Kitzmueller and Shimshack 2012).

5.1.2 Quality of Life Marketing

Quality of life (QOL) marketing is defined as marketing practice designed to enhance the wellbeing of customers while preserving the wellbeing of the firm's other stakeholders (Sirgy 1996). The dimension pertaining to the enhancement of customer wellbeing is labeled the beneficence component of QOL marketing, while the preservation of the wellbeing of the firm's other stakeholders is referred to as the nonmaleficence component. The consequences of marketing beneficence and nonmaleficence are high levels of customer wellbeing, customer trust and commitment, and positive corporate image and company goodwill. The beneficent and nonmaleficent components of QOL marketing are influenced by a set of environmental, organizational, and individual factors (Lee and Sirgy 2004).

5.1.3 Sustainable Marketing

Scholars relate marketing to sustainability. In an earlier paper discussing impacts of marketing on environment, a chart with two dimensions shows ecological impacts of marketing inputs. One dimension is mode of environment interaction that includes four modes: exploitation, substitution, engineering, and design. Another dimension is area of ecological impact that includes three areas, conserve or deplete resources, reduce or increase pollution, and enhance or distract environment. For each cell, benefits and costs of marketing inputs are presented (Fisk 1973).

Sustainable marketing could be achieved through the contribution of three existing marketing sub-disciplines; green marketing, social marketing and critical marketing. Green marketing facilitates the development and marketing of more sustainable products and services while introducing sustainability efforts into the core of the marketing process and business practice. Social marketing involves using the power of marketing to encourage sustainable behavior among individuals, businesses and decision makers while also assessing the impact of current commercial marketing on sustainability. This links into the critical marketing paradigm which entails analyses of marketing theory, principles and techniques using a critical theory based approach. This analysis can help guide regulation and control, develop marketing theory and practice, and challenge the dominant institutions associated with marketing and the capitalist system, encouraging a marketing system in which sustainability is a key goal (Gordon et al. 2011).

Sustainable marketing is different from responsible marketing. A researcher identifies misleading assumptions about progress through economic growth and preference satisfaction and highlights the issues to be confronted by marketers to fully address the social and ecological crisis of destructive overconsumption. He proposes an agenda for a sustainable society purpose and form for marketing (Varey 2010).

5.1.4 Ethic Marketing

Researchers propose an integrated framework that includes the nature of the product, consumer characteristics and market selection to analyze the ethical complexities of the marketing exchange. Interactions among these factors lead to various contingencies with different ethical implications for marketing managers and public policy makers. Marketers are encouraged to assess consumer interests and the ethics of marketing programs in their marketing activities (Cui and Choudhury 2003).

5.1.5 Pro-consumer Corporate Governance

A law scholar provides a comprehensive assessment of the consumer interest in the law literature. He believes that the contemporary corporate law scholarship fails to give sustained attention to consumers in favor of exploring the interests of other corporate stakeholders, especially shareholders, creditors, and workers. He proposes fundamental reforms in corporate governance in order to vindicate the consumer interest in corporate enterprise (Yosifon 2009).

5.1.6 *Pro-consumer Business Organizations*

Better Business Bureaus (BBB) are private, nonprofit organizations that provide services to assist consumers and businesses in local areas. Funded primarily by dues from business members, the mission of the BBB is to promote and foster the highest ethical relationship between business and the public through voluntary self-regulation, consumer and business education, and service excellence. There are many BBBs in the USA, Canada, and Puerto Rico that directly help millions of consumers and thousands of businesses each year (http://www.bbb.org/boston/get-to-know-us/about-us/). One unique feature of CBBB is that it operates BBBOnline. The mission of BBBOnline is to be the leader in advancing marketplace trust (http://www.bbb.org/boston/get-to-know-us/vision-mission-and-values/).

5.2 Marketing Frauds and Rip Offs

5.2.1 *Marketing Frauds*

Marketing frauds are illegal business practices that infringe upon consumer rights and hurt consumer wellbeing. Research on marketing frauds is under conducted. Some research focuses on specific types of frauds and others on characteristics of victims of marketing frauds.

A literature review study funded by FINRA Investor Education Foundation and conducted by researchers at Stanford University has identified prevalence, victims, and fraudsters of financial frauds in the marketplace (Deevy et al. 2012). Based on this study, financial fraud is a pressing concern because tens of billions of dollars lost each year to tens of millions of victims. The US Attorney General named financial fraud one of three top priorities, after terrorism and violent crime. Yet current estimates of fraud's impact likely understate the costs greatly, as under-reporting and under-admitting hamper the efforts to measure fraud. Regarding victims of frauds, everyone is susceptible to fraud, though the degree of either exposure or susceptibility may vary by fraud type. Although research has yet to identify unique markers of personal vulnerability, the demographic, behavioral, and psychological profiles of victims are relatively well studied. Profiling is important because it has the potential to allow government agencies with limited human and dollar resources to target information and protection to those who need it most. Profiling studies that analyze victims by type of scam have yielded a clearer picture of scam-specific profiles. Fraudsters are difficult to identity. Interviews, surveys, anecdotal evidence, and emerging experimental studies are beginning to identify the correlations and causes of fraudulent behavior. What information is available aligns with popular stereotypes that con men are likely to be white, young or middle-aged men from middle-class backgrounds, often characterized as "middle class failures."

Researchers at UK have conducted a literature review to identify techniques to commit frauds (Button et al. 2009). These techniques include victim selection techniques, perpetration strategies, detection avoiding strategies, and securing the gains. Victim selection techniques include the use of both open and illicit sources of information to target individuals. Typical sources are publicly available marketing lists, directories as well as so called 'suckers' lists of those who have already fallen for a scam. Perpetration strategies vary according to the specific type of fraud but some of the most common include the use of sound business skills, the latest technology, promoting professional appearances, utilizing "good" sales techniques, seeking small sums of money, and operating in a legal hinterland. There are another wide range of techniques specific to identity fraud, ranging from stealing waste to secure personal information to the use of sophisticated software to hack into victims' computers to steal personal data. Fraudsters also use a wide range of techniques to avoid detection. They often operate in jurisdictions where they are unlikely to be bothered by law enforcement. They move locations regularly to avoid detection as well as operating in a legal hinterland and seeking small sums of money.

5.2.2 Types of Marketing Frauds

Pyramid schemes. Researchers have described characteristics of pyramid schemes. Early schemes do not involve the sale of products or services. Similar to chain letters, the "opportunity" offered by early pyramid schemes passes in chainlike fashion from one participant to another. Firms operating more complex pyramid schemes offer products and services for sale to recruits and to general consumers. Many techniques are used for these schemes. Some require large up-front purchases; others pay commissions based on recruitment, with little regard for the actual purchase of a product or service; still others sell products with dubious market value; also, all claimed income levels well above what could realistically be achieved. Along with earning misrepresentations, there is a closely related set of deceptive marketing communications. The core deception is that pyramid schemes are not designed to build viable retail organizations (Vander Nat and Keep 2002).

Mail and Wire Frauds. As marketers increase their communication through both print and electronic channels, the opportunity for fraud is growing rapidly. Consequently, criminal prosecution of marketers for mail and wire fraud in federal courts has increased during recent years, resulting in greater emphasis on the elimination of fraudulent activities. An analysis of federal court cases on marketing mail and wire frauds reveals a breadth of activity related to marketing that constitutes violation of the statutes. In fact, the mail and wire fraud statutes have been applied successfully to misbehavior related to each of the marketing mix variables (i.e., product, price, distribution, and promotion). For example, direct mail brochures that contain false statements are classified as mail fraud. However, mailing a contract that related to fraudulently awarding an advertising account is also a criminal act that has been prosecuted under the mail fraud statute, although the content of the advertising campaign itself is not false or deceptive (Neese et al. 2005).

Researchers have analyzed fraud cases to help provide a basic understanding of the types of marketing activities that trigger prosecutions and convictions in federal courts. The use of the mail and wire fraud statutes has become the legal tool of choice to convict individuals and organizations that use false and misleading information to damage others. The review of marketing-related mail and wire fraud cases indicates that mass marketing is often used as part of a scheme to defraud, but fraud can also materialize through decisions made concerning other areas of the marketing mix as well. While both government and self-regulatory groups attempt to educate and prevent victims of fraud, the opportunity for fraud is unlimited. For example, the Internet provides a growing opportunity for many types of wire fraud (Neese et al. 2005).

Internet Fraud. Research indicates that the deceptive tactics available on the Internet and some of the factors that make them more or less likely to be adopted. Researchers have applied an established theory of deception to the Internet context to identify the deception tactics available online. The theory is then expanded with new hypotheses that link the selection of a specific tactic to the identity of the target and the purported identity of the deceiver. Content analysis of a broad range of documentary evidence published between 1995 and 2000 is used to build a database of 201 cases of Internet deception. The results suggest that deceivers select tactics as a function of their targets as well as their own purported identities (Grazioli and Jarvenpaa 2003).

Online Auction Fraud. Researchers examine whether online reputation systems are a useful mechanism for potential buyers to avoid fraudulent auctions. Content analysis of complaints posted in an online auction reputation system is used to improve understanding of online auction fraud and the role of reputation systems in documenting, predicting, and reducing fraud. The results show that the number of fraud allegations found in an online reputation system significantly exceeds the number of fraud allegations made through official channels. Recent negative feedback posted in an online reputation system is useful in predicting future online auction fraud. Finally, experienced online auction buyers are in a better position to use reputation system data to avoid potentially fraudulent auctions (Gregg and Scott 2006).

Effective Internet auction fraud detection has become an emergent issue in real-world scenarios in conjunction with the rapid development and prevalence of Internet auctions. Accurate detection of fraudsters can assist law enforcement agencies in preventing potential fraud cases that could result in large monetary losses. Researchers propose a hybrid approach utilizing network metrics and data-mining techniques to discover fraudsters based on Internet auction transaction records. Using experimental data gathered from the Yahoo! Auctions website, extensive experiments demonstrate that the proposed approach is capable of detecting Internet auction fraudsters both effectively and almost instantaneously with an acceptable classification accuracy rate (Chiu et al. 2011).

Identity Theft. Identity theft is an economic crime that is committed by criminals. Identity theft happens when someone steals a victim's personal information and uses it without her or his permission. It is a serious crime that can wreak havoc with victims' finances, credit history, and reputation and take time, money, and patience to resolve (Federal Trade Commission 2013).

Criminals use multiple ways to steal consumer identity information. They "dumpster dive" or rummage through the victim's garbage, the trash of businesses, or public dumps. They may work or pretend to work for legitimate companies, medical offices, clinics, pharmacies, or government agencies, and take advantage of that role to convince you to reveal personal information. Some thieves pretend to represent a trusted institution, and try to trick people by email (phishing) or phone (pretexting) into revealing personal information (Federal Trade Commission 2013).

Once identity thieves have a victim's personal information, they can drain her or his bank account, run up charges on her or his credit cards, open new utility accounts, or get medical treatment on the victim's health insurance. An identity thief might even file a tax return in the victim's name and get refund. In some extreme cases, a thief might even give the victim's name to the police during an arrest (Federal Trade Commission 2013).

A journalist wrote a book *Your Evil Twin*: *Behind the Identity Theft Epidemic* that covers this exploding crime from every possible angle. The book is filled with real-world identity theft horror stories (from both the criminal's and victim's perspective) as well as practical advice that can help consumers protect themselves. The book examines the institutions, industries, and individuals that have allowed identity theft to spread, and probes solutions now being cobbled together by the industry and government to curb this crime (Sullivan 2004).

Federal Trade Commission provides consumer step by step guides to help fight this crime. If a consumer's wallet, Social Security card, or other personal, financial, or account information is lost or stolen, she or he should contact the credit reporting companies and place a fraud alert on your credit file. The consumer should check her or his bank and other account statements for unusual activity. Consumers can exercise their legal right to a free copy of their credit report. If the identity information is lost in a data breach, the organization that lost consumer information will notify the consumer. Generally, the consumer may choose to place a fraud alert on one's credit file, monitor your accounts for unusual activity, and exercise one's right to a free copy of one's credit report. In the FTC guide, specific steps on what to do after the identify information is stolen in specific areas and how to prevent identify theft are provided (Federal Trade Commission 2013).

Consumers need to beware of the serious consequences of this crime and take measures to reduce the risk of identity theft. Survey research shows that many consumers do not follow the widely recommended practice of obtaining a credit report annually to check for errors and evidence of identity theft, even though reports are free of charge. Many of them are not securing incoming mail and still carrying identification containing one's Social Security number (O'Neill and Xiao 2005, 2008).

5.2.3 Marketing Rip Offs

Marketing rip offs are legal business practices but hurt consumer economic wellbeing in many seemingly small but collectively large ways. There are not many academic studies on this topic. Garman (2006) lists many examples of marketing rip offs in his consumer economic textbook such as rip offs in rental cars, credit and debit card registration services, identity theft insurance, health products, credit-life insurance, etc. In the book *Gotcha Capitalism*, journalist Bob Sullivan (2007) exposes the ways of various marketing rip offs and provides consumers strategies to avoid rip offs and get their deserved money back. Rip offs include high fees for ATM transactions, iron-clad cell phone contracts hard to get out, big bucks for insurance on a rental car not needed or paying a high fee for supposedly "free" wireless internet. Theoretical and empirical research on marketing rip offs targeting consumers need to be conducted by researchers who are interested in improving consumer economic wellbeing.

5.3 Characteristics of Consumer Victims

5.3.1 Victims of Investment Frauds

Researchers examine characteristics of victims of investment frauds by conducting a three-part inquiry of consumer fraud. In part 1, undercover tapes of fraud pitches are analyzed to determine how con men pitch their victims. Tape analysis reveals con criminals customize their pitch to match the psychological profile of the victim and use a complex combination of influence tactics within each pitch to persuade. In part 2, a survey is administered to victims of lottery fraud, investment fraud and non-victims of fraud. Investment fraud victims demonstrate a better understanding of basic financial literacy than non-victims. Both investment and lottery victims are more likely to have experienced a negative life event unrelated to their fraud experience. Both victim types are more likely to listen to sales pitches from unknown sales persons. Investment and lottery fraud victims both dramatically underreport fraud. In part 3, a second survey is administered to a different population of investment fraud victims and non-victims to determine if findings from survey 1 could be replicated. In fact, major findings relating to financial literacy are replicated. In addition, new findings relating to persuasion literacy are found: victims of investment fraud are less able to identify pitch lines used by con men in fraud schemes than a non-victim population. This suggests that a key strategy for deterring fraud victimization in the future might be to teach both financial literacy and persuasion literacy to investors (Shadel and Pak 2007).

5.3.2 Vulnerability of Older Consumers

Researchers discuss the older consumers' vulnerability in informed consensus in a conceptual paper (Griffiths and Harmon 2011). Building on current knowledge of factors that diminish decision-making capacity with age, they examine conditions under which aging consumers acquiesce to informed consent, when not fully informed. The conceptual framework and research propositions regarding the key factors influencing consumer vulnerability during the informed consent process are cognitive changes, sensory factors, financial changes, and the sender and receiver interaction.

In a literature review, researchers discuss the research frontier on older consumer vulnerabilities (Moschis et al. 2011). Results of studies from various fields suggest gaps in knowledge and needed research to help understand the factors that explain degrees of vulnerability among the aged to marketing communications. They present a blueprint that encompasses emergent theories and methods of studying behavior in social science to guide future research on older consumers' vulnerability.

A study on the loneliness and telemarketing fraud among older consumers find that older adults are disproportionately affected by telemarketing fraud, especially those who are socially isolated. Twenty-eight older adult telemarketing fraud victims in the study have completed a questionnaire assessing loneliness and other variables related to telemarketing fraud vulnerability. Victims tend to be male, divorced/separated, and college-educated, between ages of 60 and 70. Age and marital status are significantly associated with loneliness (Alves and Wilson 2008).

A national mail survey is conducted focusing on confidence swindles and their effects on older consumers (age 65 and over) among bunco investigators representing 331 local police departments in 39 states. The researcher concludes that elder victims of confidence swindles are more likely to be female, young-old, white, not married, and not employed outside the home. Elders with certain characteristics, such as friendliness to strangers and visible signs of financial assets on one's person, are likely to attract confidence swindlers looking for victims. Swindler teams committing crimes against elders are likely to contain more than one member, with two being most common. The tactical approach taken by confidence swindlers who target elders can be expected to vary by type of swindle with a "soft approach" likely for Pigeon Drop (in which a mark or "pigeon" is persuaded to give up a sum of money in order to secure the rights to a larger sum of money, or more valuable object) and Bank Examiner swindles (in which con artists pose as FBI agents, bank examiners, police officers, detectives or bank officials and ask consumers to withdraw your money and hand it over) and a combined approach likely for Home Improvement/Repair swindles. Home Improvement/Repair swindles of older consumers are likely to occur in middle class neighborhoods and a driveway or roofing problem is a likely focus of these swindles. Confidence swindles of elder consumers often result in substantial financial losses for the victims with $1,000 to $5,000 being likely for Pigeon Drop, Bank Examiner, and Home Improvement/Repair swindles (Friedman 1992).

Researchers use data from the 1993 Survey of Older Consumer Behavior commissioned by the American Association of Retired Persons to investigate consumer vulnerability to market fraud. Consumer vulnerability is determined based on consumers' market knowledge and awareness of unfair business practices. Results indicate that consumers are more susceptible to fraud if they are older, poor, less educated, and/or living without spouse. The cognitive deficiency paradigm proposes that consumers with limited ability to process information are more vulnerable to market fraud, while the social interaction paradigm explains consumer vulnerability based on asymmetry of social relationships and social isolation. The findings provide supporting evidence for the cognitive deficiency paradigm and activity theory but reject the hypotheses developed from the asymmetry of social relationships (Lee and Soberon-Ferrer 1997).

The receptiveness of consumers 50 years of age or older to telemarketing fraud is investigated with data from the 1996 and 1997 EXCEL Omnibus Survey commissioned by AARP. The receptiveness to telemarketing fraud is reflected by a consumer's psychological orientation (willingness to listen to sales pitch and attitude toward callers) and actual engagement in risky behavior (responding to unknown callers). The findings show that age is significantly influences these consumers' willingness to listen. Racial and ethnic minorities are more receptive to telemarketing fraud than non-Hispanic whites evidenced by positive attitudes toward callers and the number of times sending money to the callers (Lee and Geistfeld 1999).

5.3.3 Vulnerability of Young Consumers

Young consumer's vulnerability in the internet age is examined in a qualitative research. The author believes that teenagers are fully competent consumers because almost adolescents revealed competency in some aspects of consumption such as: using Internet and blogs to improve their consumption skills, comparison-shopping, and innovation by consumption and usage. However, teenagers could be considered as victims because of their vulnerability and the lack of their experiences and knowledge in terms of consumption and purchasing. In addition, today's young consumers are facing a new risk related to technologies usages. Young consumers experience vulnerability in situation where they lack control and experience an imbalance in the exchange process. This situation is compounded by multiple factors including personal characteristics (self-concept); subculture norms (teenagers are afraid to be excluded from the peer groups); experiential conditions (consumption experience and knowledge) and contextual factors (Internet, online community). Young consumer vulnerability is closely tied to identity and transformation. Indeed, when teenagers can't control their situations, they may believe that they are incompetent, weak, and vulnerable. Therefore, consumer policy should focus on empowering young consumers and facilitate the movement away from vulnerability (Batat 2010).

5.3.4 Vulnerability of Latino Immigrant Consumers

Researchers have conducted a qualitative research to identify areas of consumer fraud experienced by Latino immigrants. Types of unscrupulous practices identified include sales of automobiles, prepaid telephone cards, and counterfeit documents (Marlowe and Atiles 2005).

5.3.5 Paradigm Shift: From Fraud Victims to Victors

Friedman (1998) calls for a paradigm shift from studying victims of marketing frauds to consumers who successfully avoided marketing frauds. He has conducted two studies, one is to encourage AARP members to send him successful stories on how to avoid marketing frauds and the second is to collect marketing fraud prevention materials developed by law enforcements nationwide. He finds danger signals reported by both sources include characteristics of suspects, initial approach to respondent, the offer, suspect's pre-and post-offer action, suspect's manner of communication, and multiple aspects of the situation. He also compiles escape mechanisms offered by the two sources that are to decline to communicate, refuse the offer for the moment, refuse the offer categorically, take steps to avoid losing money after suspicious offer and contact, and report to authorities.

5.4 Summary

In an efficient and fair economy, businesses and consumers play buying and selling games following existing social norms, regulations, and laws. Good business practices provide positive confirmation for consumer wellbeing since these businesses are aware of the changing social trends and consider consequences of their practices on the wellbeing of buyers of their products as well as the world population. Concepts such as corporate social responsibility, quality of life marketing, sustainable marketing, ethic marketing can be used by businesses to foster more desirable business behaviors. Bad business practices can be either legal or illegal. Marketing frauds are illegal business practices that use unfair selling techniques to make excess profits from consumers. Rip offs are legal business practices that play a ball in the grey areas to achieve the goal of making undeserved profits. Marketing frauds and rip offs are especially harmful for vulnerable consumer populations such as old, young, low income, minority, and new immigrant consumers. For pro-consumer policy makers and socially responsible business practitioners, good business practices should be encouraged and bad business practices should be curbed.

References

Alves, L. M., & Wilson, S. R. (2008). The effects of loneliness on telemarketing fraud vulnerability among older adults. *Journal of Elder Abuse & Neglect, 20*(1), 63–85.

Batat, W. (2010). Understanding the dimensions of young consumer vulnerability in the web 2.0 society. *Child and Teen Consumption CTC*, Jun 2010, Norrköping, Sweden. pp. 250

Button, M., Lewis, C., & Tapley, J. (2009). *Fraud typologies and the victims of fraud literature review*. National Fraud Authority, Office of Fair Trading, UK. Retrieved from http://eprints.port.ac.uk/3989/1/

Carroll, A. B. (1979). A three-dimensional conceptual model of corporate social performance. *Academy of Management Review, 4*, 497–505.

Carroll, A. B. (1991, July–August). The pyramid of corporate social responsibility: Toward the moral management of organizational stakeholders. *Business Horizons, 34*, 39–48.

Carroll, A. B. (1999). Corporate social responsibility: Evolution of a definitional construct. *Business and Society, 38*, 268–295.

Carroll, A. B., & Shabana, K. M. (2010). The business case for corporate social responsibility: A review of concepts, research and practice. *International Journal of Management Reviews, 12*, 85. doi:10.1111/j.1468-2370.2009.00275.x.

Chiu, C., Ku, Y., Lie, T., & Chen, Y. (2011). Internet auction fraud detection using social network analysis and classification tree approaches. *International Journal of Electronic Commerce, 15*(3), 123.

Cui, G., & Choudhury, P. (2003). Consumer interests and the ethical implications of marketing: A contingency framework. *The Journal of Consumer Affairs, 37*(2), 364–387.

Deevy, M., Lucich, S., & Beals, M. (2012). *Scams, schemes, & swindles: A review of consumer financial fraud research.* Stanford University Financial Fraud Research Center, Stanford, CA. Retrieved from http://fraudresearchcenter.org/wp-content/uploads/2012/11/Scams-Schemes-Swindles-FINAL.pdf

Federal Trade Commission. (2013). *Taking charge: What do to if you identity is stolen*. Washington, DC: Author.

Fisk, G. (1973). Criteria for a theory of responsible consumption. *Journal of Marketing, 37*(2), 24–31.

Frederick, W. C. (1978). *From CSR1 to CSR2: The maturing of business and society thought. Working paper 279*. Pittsburgh, PA: Graduate School of Business, University of Pittsburgh.

Friedman, M. (1992). Confidence swindles of older consumers. *The Journal of Consumer Affairs, 26*(1), 20–46.

Friedman, M. (1998). Coping with consumer fraud: The need for a paradigm shift. *The Journal of Consumer Affairs, 32*(1), 1–12.

Garman, E. T. (2006). *Consumer economic issues in America* (9th ed.). Mason, OH: Thomson.

Gordon, R., Carrigan, M., & Hastings, G. (2011). A framework for sustainable marketing. *Marketing Theory, 11*(2), 143–163.

Grazioli, S., & Jarvenpaa, S. L. (2003). Consumer and business deception on the Internet: Content analysis of documentary evidence. *International Journal of Electronic Commerce, 7*, 93–118.

Gregg, D. G., & Scott, J. E. (2006). The role of reputation systems in reducing on-line auction fraud. *International Journal of Electronic Commerce, 10*(3), 95–120.

Griffiths, M. A., & Harmon, T. R. (2011). Aging consumer vulnerabilities influencing factors of acquiescence to informed consent. *The Journal of Consumer Affairs, 45*(3), 445.

Kitzmueller, M., & Shimshack, J. (2012). Economic perspectives on corporate social responsibility. *Journal of Economic Literature, 50*(1), 51–84.

Kolk, A., Hong, P., & van Dolen, W. (2010). Corporate social responsibility in China: An analysis of domestic and foreign retailers' sustainability dimensions. *Business Strategy and the Environment, 19*(5), 289–303.

Kotler, P., & Lee, N. (2005). *Corporate social responsibility: Doing the most good for your company and your cause*. Hoboken, NJ: Wiley.

Kurucz, E., Colbert, B., & Wheeler, D. (2008). The business case for corporate social responsibility. In A. Crane, A. McWilliams, D. Matten, J. Moon, & D. Siegel (Eds.), *The Oxford handbook of corporate social responsibility* (pp. 83–112). Oxford: Oxford University Press.

Lee, J., & Geistfeld, L. V. (1999). Elderly consumers receptiveness to telemarketing fraud. *Journal of Public Policy & Marketing, 18*(2), 208–217.

Lee, D., & Sirgy, M. J. (2004). Quality-of-life (QOL) marketing: Proposed antecedents and consequences. *Journal of Macromarketing, 24*(1), 44–58.

Lee, J., & Soberon-Ferrer, H. (1997). Consumer vulnerability to fraud: Influencing factors. *The Journal of Consumer Affairs, 31*(1), 70–89.

Marlowe, J., & Atiles, J. H. (2005). Consumer fraud and Latino immigrant consumers in the United States. *International Journal of Consumer Studies, 29*(5), 391–400.

McWilliams, A., & Siegel, D. (2000). Corporate social responsibility and financial performance: Correlation or misspecification? *Strategic Management Journal, 21*(5), 603–609.

McWilliams, A., & Siegel, D. (2001). Corporate social responsibility: A theory of the firm perspective. *Academy of Management Review, 26*(1), 117–127.

Moschis, G. P., Mosteller, J., & Fatt, C. K. (2011). Research frontiers on older consumers vulnerability. *The Journal of Consumer Affairs, 45*(3), 467.

Neese, W. T., Ferrell, L., & Ferrell, O. C. (2005). An analysis of federal mail and wire fraud cases related to marketing. *Journal of Business Research, 58*(7), 910–918.

O'Neill, B., & Xiao, J. J. (2008). Identity theft risk reduction factors: A post FACTA analysis. *Proceedings of Eastern Family Economics and Resource Management Association.* Available at: http://www.fermascholar.org/wp-content/uploads/2013/06/id_theft_risk_oneill1.pdf

O'Neill, B., & Xiao, J. J. (2005). Consumer practices to reduce identity theft risk: An exploratory study. *Journal of Family and Consumer Sciences, 97*(1), 33–38.

Shadel, D. P., & Pak, K. B. S. (2007). *The psychology of consumer fraud.* Unpublished Ph.D. dissertation, Tilburg University. Retrieved from http://taos.publishpath.com/Websites/taos/Images/ProgramsTaosTilburgDissertations/Pak.ShadelDissertationFINAL.pdf

Sirgy, M. J. (1996). Strategic marketing planning guided by the quality-of-life (QOL) concept. *Journal of Business Ethics, 15*(March), 241–259.

Sullivan, B. (2004). *Your evil twin: Behind the identity theft epidemic.* Hoboken, NJ: John Wiley & Sons.

Sullivan, B. (2007). *Gotcha capitalism: How hidden fees rip you off every day and what you can do about it.* New York: Ballantine Books.

Vander Nat, P. J., & Keep, W. W. (2002). Marketing fraud: An approach for differentiating multilevel marketing from pyramid schemes. *Journal of Public Policy & Marketing, 21*(1), 139–151.

Varey, R. J. (2010). Marketing means and ends for a sustainable society: A welfare agenda for transformative change. *Journal of Macromarketing, 30*(2), 112.

Yosifon, D. G. (2009). The consumer interest in corporate law. *UC Davis Law Review, 43*, 253–313.

Chapter 6
Media and Consumer Economic Wellbeing

Abstract This chapter discusses potential effects of mass media on consumer economic wellbeing. Two categories of media, news media and advertisement, are examined. News media companies in the USA are privately owned and their major motivations are profit seeking. Some behavioral patterns described in the business chapter can also be found in news media companies. Among news media professionals, a group of people, labeled consumer journalists, serve as consumer advocates. In many circumstances, they promote consumer economic wellbeing even at the expenses of business interests sometimes. Advertisements are criticized by social science researchers as harmful to consumers in several aspects. However, in the advertisement industry, a concept of Advertisement Social Responsibility is proposed that have potential to improve consumer wellbeing and societal wellbeing. Advertisements can be categorized in many ways in different dimensions. This chapter reviews some of these types of ads and their effects on consumer behavior and wellbeing.

6.1 Role of News Media

6.1.1 Effects of Media

News media may affect many aspects of consumer wellbeing through its impact on consumer behavior, sales, markets, and the economy as a whole.

On Sales. Media reviews may influence sales of consumer products, which may be considered as an indirect guidance for consumer buying. A researcher explores if journalist review affect wine sales and if these reviews are consistent in opinions in Norwegian newspapers. The results show that wine sales are significantly influenced by the judgments of wine critics; a 10 % rise in newspapers' scores in Norway is accompanied by an average increase of 16–18 % in sales figures for table wines. The effects of wine reviews vary somewhat from newspaper to newspaper. The journalists give no unanimous recommendation of good wine buys to consumers. However, a majority of the reviewers seem to agree in the ranking of most wines (Horverak 2009).

J.J. Xiao, *Consumer Economic Wellbeing*, International Series on Consumer Science, DOI 10.1007/978-1-4939-2821-7_6

On Consumer Behavior. Research shows that news reports encourage consumer action for self-protection. Researchers assemble a data set to gauge the impact of news reports on consumer sign-ups with the US Do Not Call (DNC) Registry and find that news reports increase consumer registrations. The impact increases with mention of the toll-free telephone number and URL, but decreases with the length of the headline and main text. Furthermore, they find evidence that reports affect behavior through persuasion as well as information. The impact on registration is higher for reports that mention the number of other people registering. Finally, the impact of news reports on consumer registration is stronger in national than local newspapers and in politically neutral and Democratic than in Republican newspapers (Goh et al. 2011).

Consumer perception for news media may help explain consumption behavior. A researcher tests whether sentiment in TV news can be used as a proxy for consumer sentiment in order to explain changes in private consumption growth in the USA. The University of Michigan Index of Consumer Sentiment (ICS) is taken to compare its explanatory power with TV sentiment in classical consumer behavior models. He finds that TV sentiment can be used at least as good a proxy for consumer sentiment as the ICS, while TV sentiment can best explain private consumption behavior with personal income and savings (Uhl 2012).

On Financial Market. Consumer sentiment news may affect stock markets. Researchers examine the equity market reaction to the monthly release of Australian consumer sentiment news. Research indicates that consumer sentiment has valuable information. Further, they document the "negativity effect" in which, upon announcement of bad sentiment news, the equity market experiences a significant negative announcement day effect (Akhtar et al. 2011).

Research indicates expert recommendations through the news media may be informative for individual investors. Researchers analyze both the market reaction and long-term returns of stock picks mentioned on the Consumer News and Business Channel (CNBC) program "Mad Money," hosted by former hedge fund manager Jim Cramer. They find that Cramer's stock-picking style is consistent with a positive-feedback trading strategy, favoring stocks which have outperformed over an interval prior to the pick date. Subsequent to a pick, Cramer's immediate effect on a stock appears inversely proportional to the corresponding firm's market capitalization. The returns over a 6-month horizon provide some evidence in favor of Cramer's stock-picking ability. In particular, his recommendations on small-cap stocks accurately predict the long-run trends (Lim and Rosario 2010).

On the Economy. Policy makers believe that news media affects politics and regulation of media ownership would enhance ideological diversities. Then it is important to understand consumer responses to media slant. Researchers construct a new index of media slant that measures the similarity of a news outlet's language to that of a congressional Republican or Democrat. They estimate a model of newspaper demand that incorporates slant explicitly, estimate the slant that would be chosen if newspapers independently maximized their own profits, and compare these profit-maximizing points with firms' actual choices. They find that readers have an economically significant preference for like-minded news (Gentzkow and Shapiro 2010).

News may affect consumer confidence that may in turn influence the economy. Researchers study associations between the real economy, consumer confidence and economic news coverage in national newspapers for the Netherlands during the period 1990–2009. Media-attention for economic developments is associated with consumer confidence, with more negative news decreasing consumer confidence; this result holds after controlling for the real economy (stock-market). The relationship differs for different business-cycles. The effect is in particular stronger for the months following the beginning of the credit-crisis (Hollanders and Vliegenthart 2011).

6.1.2 Consumer Journalism

Consumer journalism refers to practices of journalists who actively promote consumer interests in news reporting. Cron (1997) provides an overview of consumer journalism about its origin, history, and developments in the USA. Residing within journalism is a kind of reporting and writing that is designed to serve readers as "consumers." This journalism helps the reader, listener or viewer make a reasoned judgment, a choice, about a product or service in the marketplace or a course of conduct or action. That choice is then expressed in an exchange decision of some kind, a transaction that can enhance the consumer's social, economic, and physical wellbeing.

Consumer journalism roots may be detected in the nineteenth century, which was a time of great scientific, technological, and economic ferment. To meet the needs of new middle class, many "journalists of manners" came out. One of the most influential and successful of America's earliest magazines of manners was *The Saturday Evening Post* founded in 1821. In this era of rapid change, the popular women's and home magazines provided their readers with a stabilizing literature that focused on family and children, the comfort and safety of the home, and the basic social courtesies appropriate in the new American culture. The demand was enough to support as many as 2,500 magazines of one kind or another between 1850 and 1865. The latter half of the nineteenth century was a great age of retailing. During this period, a new type of consumer journalism called "muckraking" was developed. Famous examples of muckraking included the "Guard against Adulteration" editorial in *Good Housekeeping*, a long term publication founded in 1885. Joseph Pulitzer invented a new type of tabloid journalism called "yellow journalism" and published *New York World* in 1883 with a promise to expose all fraud and sham, fight all public evils and abuses and battle for the people with earnest sincerity. The most impressive work was being published in *McClure's*, which managing editor, Lincoln Steffens, serialized his *Shame of the Cities*, later publishing his articles in book form. In 1906, Upton Sinclair published *The Jungle*, a shocking look inside the meat-packing industry. The book was so influential that it helped

Congress pass two pieces of landmark consumer legislation: the Meat Inspection Act and the Pure Food and Drug Act.

The third type of consumer journalism conducting product testing and then publishing the testing results came out from the first three decades of the twentieth century. In 1909, *Good Housekeeping* started to install a modern laboratory and settled upon an oval seal with the legend, "Tested and Approved by the *Good Housekeeping* Institute conducted by *Good Housekeeping* magazine." F. J. Schlink, who worked for the National Bureau of Standards for product testing, wrote with Stuart Chase a bestseller *Your Money's Worth: A Study in the Waste of the Consumer's Dollar*. In 1929, Schlink established Consumer's Research as a product testing organization and published test result in his new advertising-free journal, *Consumer Bulletin*. In 1932, Schlink and Arthur Kallet, testing engineers in Consumer's Research, wrote *100,000,000 Guinea Pigs*, an account of government fumbling and inaction with regard to food and drugs of doubtful integrity and safety being sold to unsuspecting consumers. In 1936, Kallet left Consumers' Research because of political and labor conflicts to start Consumer Union and its own magazine, *Consumer Reports*. Since then, this magazine remains the preeminent example of pure consumer journalism: factual, objective, advisory and focused on what the consumer needs to know in order to make a reasoned judgment about a product or service in the marketplace. *Consumer Reports* is still being published today and providing unbiased information for millions of consumers to make informed shopping decisions.

After World War II, the US economy began a long and sustained economic boom. The fourth type of consumer journalism was developed that can be called "business journalism." Business journalism was directly for manufacturers and service and professional groups to write articles in which their products or services were presented to the public in a positive light. During the 1960s and 1970s, the US consumer movement was in its peak. President Kennedy proposed the concept of "Consumer Rights" and four specific consumer rights. Ralph Nader published the influential book *Unsafe at Any Speed*, which concluded that America's annual toll of 51,000 highway deaths could be significantly reduced by industry improvements to motor vehicles. Several years later, he recruited hundreds of students, called "Nader's Raiders" who researched and published reports on the failure of many government agencies and programs. In the heyday of the consumer movements, university departments of journalism began adding a "consumer reporting" elective. The National Press club in Washington, DC recognized the value of this kind of journalism by establishing an annual awards program for excellence in consumer reporting. In the 1980s, consumer reporting expanded to broader areas including many areas under the name of lifestyles. In the 1990s, consumer stories were regularly covered by reporters. One new trend was the coverage of consumer issues by television news magazine shows such as *60 Minutes*. More research needs to be done to document the statuses and trends of consumer journalism in recent decades.

6.2 Role of Advertisement

From the perspective of enhancing consumer economic wellbeing, commercial advertisements should provide accurate information for consumers to make informed, effective purchase decisions. Ads can be both beneficial and harmful for consumer economic wellbeing.

6.2.1 Criticism on Advertising

In the 1960s, a leading professor of consumer economics expressed a critical view on advertising. He believed that "present-day advertising is featuring the irrational and the irrelevant, and is often employed as a means of consumer manipulation" (Warne 1962, p. 10). In a paper published in *American Economic Review*, he cited "the oppressive volume and questionable standards in advertising" as one of major criticism on business practices at his time (Warne 1961, p. 534).

Advertising may hurt consumer interests at the macroeconomic level. An influential communication researcher provides a criticism on social functions of advertising in his book *The Codes of Advertising* (Jhally 1987). He believes that advertisers and media companies control capital in a free market society and control the social reality of the masses. Advertisers achieve this goal by manipulating the meanings that give value to products consumers use and advertising supplies meanings of consumer products. Consumers take cues from everything they experience including advertisements. Ads, consequently, help to give symbolic meaning to products and to the use of those products.

Researchers argue that discussing vagueness in pricing claims is a step toward evaluating deception. Consumers are frequently presented with a higher reference price to compare with a lower advertised selling price. The research on reference prices has traditionally been conducted based on the implicit assumption that consumers' interpretations of a given semantic phrase, e.g., "Regular Price/Sale Price," are consistent across all consumers, but this fundamental assumption has never been tested. Guidelines issued by the Federal Trade Commission and the Council of Better Business Bureaus, as well as regulations enacted by approximately half of all states, appear to be based on a similar assumption. However, given the variability among consumers' perceptions found in other areas of consumer research, it is reasonable to expect that consumer interpretations of semantic phrases may vary. Given the potential variability, a pricing claim may be deemed informative or deceptive depending on the meaning the particular consumer attaches to the claim (Compeau et al. 2004).

Advertisements may be harmful for children if they are designed and delivered less socially responsibly. A marketing professor argues that while younger children do appear to be vulnerable to advertising messages, the thrust of anti-advertising criticism is bound to a mistaken view that advertising *is* marketing, and an anti-materialist perspective bound to the economic demands of children upon their parents. There is also the issue of advertising that has seemingly not been overtly targeted at children, yet which is received by them (Preston 2005).

6.2.2 Advertisement Social Responsibility

Advertisement social responsibility is an extension of corporate social responsibility that applies in advertisement. Practices related to advertisement social responsibility can be considered as an ethic business behavior. A scholar of ad regulation discusses the interaction of law and ethics in matters of advertisers' responsibility for protecting consumers. According to him, ethic business behaviors can be expected but not depended. A better way to protect consumers is to strengthen law instead of promoting business ethic behaviors (Preston 2010). As consumer professionals who care about consumer wellbeing, ethic business behaviors should be encouraged and fully used for the consumer interest.

Usage of Socially Responsible Advertisement. Corporate social responsibility (CSR) advertisements may benefit both issuing companies and receiving consumers. Researchers investigate how companies use CSR advertisements to legitimize their ethical positions and how CSR advertisements vary across countries. They find that companies use different strategies for publicizing CSR. There are campaigns that appeal to consumer rationality as well as campaigns that appeal to emotions. There is also evidence that companies use their advertisements to respond to public pressure and thus create or maintain their legitimacy in the eyes of society (Farache and Perks 2010).

Many advertisement companies engage in CSR activities. Researchers analyze the annual reports of the top six holding companies in the global advertising industry. They observe which advertising companies disclose their CSR activities and what activities they undertake as well as the development of a CSR disclosure index for advertising agencies. The results indicate that some advertising companies do engage in CSR activities and disclose them in their annual report but the level of these CSR disclosures is different between the organizations (Waller and Lanis 2009).

CSR advertising may help companies be more competitive in the marketplace. Researchers review corporate image advertising, the tool investigated for informing about the firm's CSR record, discusses the skepticism construct and theoretical explanations of why this communication approach might induce skepticism, considers extant empirical findings that lend support to these theories. They also describe several elements of CSR advertising claims considered to be diagnostic and capable of inhibiting skepticism responses to CSR image advertisements among consumers (Pomering and Johnson 2009a).

Special strategies can be used to enhance effectiveness of CSR ads. Researchers discuss issues related to the CSR-based corporate image advertising and propose a research agenda to investigate the ability of two message variables, social topic information and social impact claim specificity, to influence attitudinal development and cognitive responses (Pomering and Johnson 2009b). They focus on the potentially corrosive cognitive response of skepticism and suggest that these message variables are possibly able to inhibit the development of consumer skepticism and build a positive reputation.

Effectiveness of CSR Ads. CSR ads can be more effective if appropriate formats are used. Using four types of public service announcement (PSA) print advertisements sponsored by Mothers Against Drunk Driving (MADD), researchers examine participants' differences in emotional response to the ads, overall attitude toward the ads, perceived social responsibility of the sponsor, and intent to donate. They find that the use of real victims in print ad PSAs garners the strongest emotional response, the most positive attitude toward the advertisement, the strongest perceived social responsibility, and the highest proclivity to donate to the nonprofit. Conversely, the use of deceptive advertising is not significantly different from using an actor portrayal disclosure as regards perceived social responsibility and emotional response to the ad. They conclude that the use of real victims in PSAs demonstrates socially responsible behavior by the nonprofit organization (Shanahan and Hopkins 2007).

Brand familiarity may alter effects of CRS ads on consumer behavior. For example, there are numerous retailers in the specialty coffee market that sell Fair Trade Coffee, a socially responsible product. Some retailers sell it to meet the demand of socially responsible consumers, some are motivated by their own concern for small coffee producers and others sell it because of the taste profile of a particular grower's coffee. Researchers find that for fair trade coffee ads, consumers are more likely to choose a brand after watching its ad with social responsibility appeal if the brand is well-known. Otherwise, consumers are more likely to choose a brand with a taste appeal (Obermiller et al. 2009).

Ethical Ads Perceived by Business Professionals. As business insiders, advertising and marketing practitioners' perception of ethical ads is informative. Researchers have conducted an experimental study to examine ethical judgments of ads among advertising and marketing practitioners. The results indicate that respondents generally rate ads targeting individuals who are not autonomous as less ethical than ads targeting those who are perceived as autonomous. Similarly, ads target at those with low sovereignty are perceived as less ethical than ads aiming at consumers perceived to have high sovereignty. Finally, ads for harmful products are perceived to be less ethical than ads for nonharmful products (Nwachukwu et al. 1997).

6.2.3 Types of Ads

Direct-to-consumer ads. The direct-to-consumer advertising (DTCA) phenomenon has received attention because of its attempt to reach out to consumers by bypassing important gatekeepers such as physicians. The emergence of new information platforms and the introduction of genetic tests directly to the consumer have heightened the concern with DTCA and its potential consequences. Based on a critical review on cancer-related direct-to-consumer drug advertising, researchers argue that the effects of DTCA are particularly important given the communication inequalities among social groups, with class, race, and ethnicity influencing how people access, seek, process and act on information. To benefit all groups of consumers, DTCA should develop strategies to reach those who are less likely to be benefited but need the message conveyed by the ad (Kontos and Viswanath 2011).

Researchers review the existing perspectives on direct-to-consumer pharmaceutical advertising and find that, despite the outcry of consumer groups and criticism from Congress, the escalating practice has remained largely unaltered. They suggest that changes are eminent, but to effect that change, academic research must seek out and answer questions with relevant policy implications (Royne and Myers 2008).

Additionally, researchers examine consumer attitudes toward two potential direct-to-consumer (DTC) advertising regulatory options, prior approval of DTC ads and a total ban, and how those attitudes are influenced by perceived DTC ad effects and receiver-specific characteristics within the context of the third-person effect framework. Results suggest that consumers support the prevetting of DTC ads, but not the banning of DTC ads. Their support for prior approval is unaffected by demographic, predispositional, and ad-effect perceptual differences. Their support for a ban is associated with age, attitude toward DTC advertising, and perceptions of negative effects on self and others (Huh et al. 2006).

Financial Ads. The mutual fund industry has experienced tremendous growth in recent years. During this time period mutual funds have become somewhat of a commodity with many funds using advertising to attract investors. Based on a content analysis to determine the informational content of fund advertising, researchers find that while the average number of informational cues increased during the time period 1979–1989, there was no significant increase in the information content of mutual fund advertising between 1989 and 1999. Relatively few funds include information such as loads, 12b-1 fees, and expense ratios in their advertisements, and fund ads rarely discuss risk (Jones and Smythe 2003). Future research needs to estimate how informative of these ads for consumer financial decision making.

Based on a content analysis of a total of 1,430 retirement financial service advertisements in six national US business-finance magazines from 2006 to 2009, researchers find that several changes in this type of ad. Since the Pension Protection Act of 2006 and the subsequent economic crisis occurred, these ads have increasingly included financial product-focused information, including *risk–return information*, *transaction cost* and *composition of product* in advertisements. Regardless of significant changes in regulation and the economy, these ads constantly included *transaction cost* and *composition of product* information in advertising. However, researchers suggest that the increase in the use of financial information in these ads might also lead to information overload for average consumers, especially those who have low financial literacy (Lee et al. 2011).

Comparative Price Ads. Based on over two decades of research, researchers conclude that advertised references prices do indeed enhance consumers' perceptions of the value of a deal. The higher the advertised reference price in relation to the offering prices (i.e., size of discount), the higher the perceived value of a deal. Researchers find that increasing a reference price while holding the selling price constant improves the perceptions of the value of the deal even for less believable reference prices. However, decreasing the selling price while holding an exaggerated reference price constant does not improve the perception of the value of a deal (Compeau et al. 2002).

Subliminal ads. Subliminal means "below threshold." Subliminal ads refer to ads that use techniques to convey message to consumers without consumers' knowing. Every 20 years, subliminal advertising pops back into popular culture. Based on a review of nearly 50 years of research on subliminal advertising, a journalism researcher concludes that the literature repeatedly shows that most effects of subliminal ads are only obtained in highly artificial situations, and no research has shown an effect that changed attitudes or impacted purchasing behavior, contrary to popular culture (Broyles 2006). Implications of subliminal ads on consumer wellbeing need to be examined in future research.

Puffery ads. Consumer responses to ad puffery differ in media contests and consumer knowledge levels. Ads often contain puffery—product descriptions that purport to be important but actually provide little if any meaningful information. Experiment results show that consumers' reactions to these descriptions depend on whether they perceive themselves to be more or less knowledgeable about the product than others whom the ad is specifically intended to influence. When an ad appears in a professional magazine that is read primarily by experts in the product domain, puffery generally increases the ad's effectiveness. This is also true when the ad appears in a popular magazine but readers perceive themselves to know less about the product than consumers at large. If consumers believe they know as much as or more than general consumers, however, puffery decreases the ad's effectiveness (Xu and Wyer 2010). Future research may examine implications of puffery ads on consumer economic wellbeing.

6.2.4 Ad Effects on Consumer Behavior

On consumer understanding of ads. Consumers with low-literacy may have difficulty understanding misleading ads. Researchers study picture–text incongruity in print advertisements among low- and high-literacy consumers and find that while low-literacy consumers rely heavily on pictorial information when making market-based decisions, they also do attempt to read relevant information. When the advertisement picture and text are aligned, so too should be the conclusions low-literacy consumers draw. They ask what happens when the pictures and accompanying text are incongruent. Results of an experiment indicate that low-literacy consumers misinterpret an advertisement with text-picture incongruity more regularly than do high-literacy consumers. Furthermore, low-literacy consumers demonstrate errors in comprehension that reflect picture-based processing (Jae et al. 2008).

On consumer health behavior. Consumers may not be able to consider the future consequences of their behaviors and are prone to discount future health risks. Researchers conduct two experiments to test the effectiveness of framing techniques designed to persuade consumers who typically do not consider the future consequences of their behaviors to make better health decisions. Results show that present-oriented consumers can be more strongly persuaded by messages that emphasize proximal rather than distal consequences of unhealthy food choices. The findings also suggest that messages focused on promotion strategies (vs. prevention strategies) result in higher behavioral intentions for present-oriented consumers (Kees 2011).

On youth health behavior. A significant consumer issue today concerns tobacco advertising, youth smoking behavior, and how to reduce youth smoking. Research of an intervention program demonstrates significant changes in students' understanding of the role of tobacco advertising among youth. Students have a basic grasp of the role of tobacco advertising and its persuasive intent. Students can identify the advertising strategies of trying to convey the image of *looking cool* and *being popular* (Beltramini and Bridge 2001).

Antismoking advertisements directed to adolescents appear to reduce the prevalence of smoking among youth. Researchers use a longitudinal design to test the influence of individual factors on the effectiveness of two types of message content in antismoking advertisements. As expected, effectiveness is influenced by individual factors. Long-term health content is more effective among nonwhites, males, and high school students, while short-term content appear to work better among junior high males (Smith and Stutts 2006).

Researchers also study advertising effects on adolescent tobacco and alcohol consumption. Exploring the simultaneous effects of key variables on the unhealthy consumption behavior of adolescents, researchers focus on the relative effects of advertising, parental and peer influence, and self-efficacy on adolescent tobacco use and alcohol consumption. The results suggest that advertising effects are largely neutralized by parental and peer influence; peer and parental influence strongly predict adolescent tobacco use and alcohol consumption; and self-efficacy is a weak predictor of both adolescent risk behaviors (Kinard and Webster 2010).

On child attitude toward ads. There have been numerous discussions regarding what factors influence children's obesity level and their attitude toward advertising. Among many possible factors, parental influence cannot be ignored, because children (7–12 years old) generally spend more time with their parents than any other individuals. A researcher investigates the possible influences of parental communication styles/patterns while watching TV with their children on their children's obesity level (body mass index) as well as parental influence's effect on children's attitudes toward TV snack/fast-food ads. The results reveal that parental communication styles/patterns significantly influence children's attitude toward TV snack/ fast-food ads (Yu 2011).

6.3 Summary

Two major components of mass media include news media and advertisement. News media can help improve consumer economic wellbeing by providing unbiased and prompt information through news stories and reviews. Future research could systematically examine effects of news stories on consumer economic wellbeing. In addition, more research on consumer journalism should be conducted and consumer journalists in modern society need to be identified, evaluated, and awarded.

Advertising is criticized by some social scientists on the ground that ads are misleading consumers to make decisions against their interests. However, advertising with social responsibility should be encouraged since it has potential to promote both consumer and business interests. Ads can be categorized in various ways such as topic, technique, style, etc. Consumers need to know these types to get information they need to make informed decisions. Special attention is needs to be paid for ads targeting youth. Furthermore, the unintentional negative impact of ads targeting adults on children and youth must be considered, as oftentimes children and youth are exposed to such advertisements. More ads with an intention to protect children and youth should be encouraged to help guide the development of healthy behaviors.

References

Akhtar, S., Faff, R., Oliver, B., & Subrahmanyam, A. (2011). The power of bad: The negativity bias in Australian consumer sentiment announcements on stock returns. *Journal of Banking & Finance, 35*(5), 1239.

Beltramini, R. F., & Bridge, P. D. (2001). Relationship between tobacco advertising and youth smoking: Assessing the effectiveness of a school-based, antismoking intervention program. *The Journal of Consumer Affairs, 35*(2), 263–277.

Broyles, S. J. (2006). Subliminal advertising and the perpetual popularity of playing to peoples paranoia. *The Journal of Consumer Affairs, 40*(2), 392–406.

Compeau, L. D., Grewal, D., & Chandrashekaran, R. (2002). Bits, briefs, and applications: Comparative price advertising: Believe it or not. *The Journal of Consumer Affairs, 36*(2), 284–294.

Compeau, L. D., Lindsey-Mullikin, J., Grewal, D., & Petty, R. D. (2004). Consumers interpretations of the semantic phrases found in reference price advertisements. *The Journal of Consumer Affairs, 38*(1), 178–187.

Cron, T. O. (1997). Consumer journalism. In S. Brobeck (Ed.), *Encyclopedia of the consumer movement* (pp. 342–350). Santa Barbara, CA: ABC-CLIO.

Farache, F., & Perks, K. J. (2010). CSR advertisements: A legitimacy tool? *Corporate Communications, 15*(3), 235–248.

Gentzkow, M., & Shapiro, J. M. (2010). What drives media slant? Evidence from U.S. daily newspapers. *Econometrica, 78*(1), 35.

Goh, K., Hui, K., & Png, I. P. L. (2011). Newspaper reports and consumer choice: Evidence from the Do Not Call Registry. *Management Science, 57*(9), 1640–1654.

Hollanders, D., & Vliegenthart, R. (2011). The influence of negative newspaper coverage on consumer confidence: The Dutch case. *Journal of Economic Psychology, 32*(3), 367.

Horverak, Ø. (2009). Wine journalism-marketing or consumers' guide? *Marketing Science, 28*(3), 573–579.

Huh, J., DeLorme, D. E., & Reid, L. N. (2006). Perceived third-person effects and consumer attitudes on prevetting and banning DTC advertising. *Journal of Consumer Affairs, 40*(1), 90–116.

Jae, H., Delvecchio, D. S., & Cowles, D. (2008). Picture-text incongruency in print advertisements among low- and high-literacy consumers. *The Journal of Consumer Affairs, 42*(3), 439–451.

Jhally, S. (1987). *The codes of advertising: Fetishism and the political economy of meaning in the consumer society*. New York: St. Martin's Press.

Jones, M. A., & Smythe, T. (2003). The information content of mutual fund print advertising. *The Journal of Consumer Affairs, 37*(1), 22–41.

Kees, J. (2011). Advertising framing effects and consideration of future consequences. *The Journal of Consumer Affairs, 45*(1), 7.

Kinard, B. R., & Webster, C. (2010). The effects of advertising, social influences, and self-efficacy on adolescent tobacco use and alcohol consumption. *The Journal of Consumer Affairs, 44*(1), 24.

Kontos, E. Z., & Viswanath, K. (2011). Cancer-related direct-to-consumer advertising: A critical review. *Nature Reviews Cancer, 11*(2), 142–150.

Lee, T. D., Haley, E., Yun, T. W., & Chung, W. (2011). US retirement financial services advertising's financial information provisions, communication strategies and judgmental heuristic cues. *Journal of Consumer Affairs, 45*(3), 391–418.

Lim, B., & Rosario, J. (2010). The performance and impact of stock picks mentioned on mad money. *Applied Financial Economics, 20*(14), 1113.

Nwachukwu, S. L. S., Vitell, S. J., Gilbert, F. W., & Barnes, J. H. (1997). Ethics and social responsibility in marketing: An examination of the ethical evaluation of advertising strategies. *Journal of Business Research, 39*(2), 107–118.

Obermiller, C., Burke, C., Talbott, E., & Green, G. P. (2009). Taste great or more fulfilling: The effect of brand reputation on consumer social responsibility advertising for fair trade coffee. *Corporate Reputation Review, 12*(2), 159–176.

Pomering, A., & Johnson, L. W. (2009a). Advertising corporate social responsibility initiatives to communicate corporate image. *Corporate Communications, 14*(4), 420–439.

Pomering, A., & Johnson, L. W. (2009b). Constructing a corporate social responsibility reputation using corporate image advertising. *Australasian Marketing Journal, 17*(2), 106–114.

Preston, C. (2005). Advertising to children and social responsibility. *Young Consumers, 6*(4), 61–67.

Preston, I. L. (2010). Interaction of law and ethics in matters of advertisers responsibility for protecting consumers. *The Journal of Consumer Affairs, 44*(1), 259.

Royne, M. B., & Myers, S. D. (2008). Recognizing consumer issues in DTC pharmaceutical advertising. *The Journal of Consumer Affairs, 42*(1), 60–80.

Shanahan, K. J., & Hopkins, C. D. (2007). Truths, half-truths, and deception: Perceived social responsibility and intent to donate for a nonprofit using implicature, truth, and duplicity in print advertising. *Journal of Advertising, 36*(2), 33–48.

Smith, K. H., & Stutts, M. A. (2006). The influence of individual factors on the effectiveness of message content in antismoking advertisements aimed at adolescents. *The Journal of Consumer Affairs, 40*(2), 261–293.

Uhl, M. W. (2012). And action: TV sentiment and the US consumer. *Applied Economics Letters, 19*(11), 1029.

Waller, D. S., & Lanis, R. (2009). Corporate social responsibility (csr) disclosure of advertising agencies. *Journal of Advertising, 38*(1), 109–121.

Warne, C. E. (1961). The influence of ethical and social responsibilities on advertising and selling practices. *American Economic Review, 51*(2), 527–539.

Warne, C. E. (1962). Advertising. A critic's view. *The Journal of Marketing, 26*, 10–14.

Xu, A. J., & Wyer, R. S., Jr. (2010). Puffery in advertisements: The effects of media context, communication norms, and consumer knowledge. *Journal of Consumer Research, 37*(2), 329–343.

Yu, H. (2011). Parental communication styles impact on children's attitudes toward obesity and food advertising. *Journal of Consumer Affairs, 45*(1), 87.

Chapter 7
Internet and Consumer Economic Wellbeing

Abstract Advances in technology affect consumer economic wellbeing in multiple ways. In recent decades, developments of information technology have changed many aspects of consumption. Dholakia (Technology and consumption: Understanding consumer choices & behaviors, Springer, New York, 2012) provides a comprehensive account on associations between technology and consumption. In this chapter, we focus on two relevant topics, online shopping and online banking. Online shopping is relevant to consumer spending. Online banking is a specific aspect of online shopping, purchase banking services online. Compared to the traditional shopping mode, online shopping has potential to improve consumer economic wellbeing by conducting extensive information search on the internet to locate the lowest priced and most needed products or services without traveling to the store. However, online shopping has risks of information insecurity and privacy invasion that have potential to harm consumer economic wellbeing.

7.1 Online Shopping

7.1.1 Online Shopping and Consumer Economic Wellbeing

Cai and Cude (2008) provide a comprehensive review on online shopping research. Based on their definition, online shopping covers several shopping related activities that include finding retailers and products, searching for product information, selecting payment options, communicating with other consumers and retailers, and purchasing products or services. Compared to off line shopping, online shopping provides opportunities for consumers to search for information extensively and save resources (time, energy, and money) regarding purchases, which has potential to improve consumer economic wellbeing. However, online shoppers also face risks of information insecurity and privacy invasion. Most online shopping research projects are conducted by business researchers who are interested in creating attractive online stores to attract consumers to stay there longer and spend more on their products or services. Much existing research also focuses on what consumer characteristics are more important for online shopping. Little research is found to examine how online shopping improves consumer economic wellbeing.

J.J. Xiao, *Consumer Economic Wellbeing*, International Series on Consumer Science, DOI 10.1007/978-1-4939-2821-7_7

7.1.2 Theories of Online Shopping

Several psychological theories have been applied and expanded to explain consumer behavior in online shopping. Researchers have used the Theory of Planned Behavior (TPB) (Azjen 1991) as the basis for studies of online shopping behavior. For example, consumers' experiences, their concerns about privacy, and their perceptions of the trustworthiness of the internet are found to be associated with their internet shopping behaviors (George 2002). The theory is also used to develop a model of intention to search online incorporated consumers' shopping attitudes, consumers' perceptions of the extent to which significant referents approve of internet use for shopping, consumers' perceived behavioral control, and consumers' past internet purchase experiences as predictors for consumers' intentions to search (Shim et al. 2001). Research based on this theory suggests that consumers may link personal values to attitude toward online grocery buying—but also that this relation may be moderated by whether the consumer previously has carried out an online purchase or an online grocery purchase (Hansen 2008).

The Technology Acceptance Model (TAM) is used to explain the linkage between consumers' perceptions of the usefulness of the Internet and its ease of use with their acceptance and usage of online shopping (Davis 1993; O'Cass and Fenech 2003). Based on an integrated model of initial trust and TAM, research shows that initial trust beliefs are significantly influenced by initial trust bases such as company reputation, structural assurance, and trusting stance. Initial trust beliefs indirectly influenced the first purchase intention through consumer attitude (Kim 2012).

Online shopping seems reducing consumer transaction costs but research finds that it reduces some costs but increases other costs. Coase's (1937) transaction cost economics argues that transaction costs are the major concern for coordinating the exchange of goods and services between suppliers and buyers. In the context of online shopping, researchers have decomposed the transaction costs into seven categories: search cost, comparison cost, examination cost, negotiation cost, payment cost, delivery cost, and post-service cost and find that internet shopping lowers the search cost but raises the examination, payment, and post-service transaction costs (Liang and Huang 1998).

The media choice theory proposes that selection of media for a specific task is a function of the characteristics of the medium and the task (Fulk et al. 1987). According to the theory, media can be differentiated by the degree of interactivity, communication richness, social presence, and vividness. Researchers have evaluated those characteristics and applied them to the choice of online shopping (Hoffman and Novak 1996; Palmer 1997).

7.1.3 Consumer Behavior in Online Shopping

Empirical studies have indicated that consumers' demographic and socio-economic characteristics are influential in their use of online shopping. Researchers have found consistently that consumers who are male, more educated, and with higher income are more likely to buy online than are those who are female, less educated, and with lower income (Forsythe and Shi 2003; Kau et al. 2003; Swinyard and Smith 2003).

Researchers also find that consumers' internet usage, such as internet experience in years and frequency of Internet use, and access to high-speed Internet connections, have a positive effect on online buying and are highly correlated with socio-economic characteristics such as income, education, and marital status (Swinyard and Smith 2003). A generation gap is identified for all but one experience good. Web shopping experience is not a significant factor for search goods but is for experience and credence goods (Wan et al. 2012).

Gender differences in online shopping have also been noted. A study on gender differences in online shopping shows that utilitarian and hedonic values have indirect positive effects on consumer online patronage intention through their associated online counterparts. Additionally, both utilitarian and hedonic values are found to influence their associated online counterparts more strongly for men than for women (Lin 2011). Another study finds that when evaluated across different purchasing situations, perceived difficulty in selecting items is an important action barrier only for women. Less fun significantly affects online clothing purchases for men purchasing clothing for themselves, but not for women doing the same (Hansen and Jensen 2009). Research based on a college student sample shows that male and female participants show significant differences in their shopping orientations, online information searches and purchase experiences (Seock and Bailey 2008).

Consumer lifestyles and personalities influence online shopping propensities. For example, "time-starved" people tend to shop online more compared to people with an active "get-up-and-go" lifestyle and adventurous inclinations who tend to shop offline (Casas et al. 2001). Consumers' attitudes toward online shopping, their shopping experience, and their shopping durations also can affect their adoption and use of online shopping although the relationships are not straightforward (Bellman et al. 1999; Golob 2003; Swinyard and Smith 2003). Study results demonstrate that individuals high on empathic concern feel greater satisfaction with the service provider, and display a greater propensity to help other online shoppers (Anaza 2014). In a study of fashion consumers who shop from private sale sites, the respondents are divided into four groups, fashion followers, fashion opinion leaders, fashion innovators and innovative communicators. The results show that innovative communicators have significantly higher levels of visit frequency and purchase intention (Kim and Martinez 2013). A study of online auction finds that there are distinct auction shopper segments based on adventure and gratification shopping motivations. Four cluster groups show significant differences in demographic characteristics of age and gender, and psychographic characteristics of impulsiveness, variety-seeking tendency, and price sensitivity (Lee et al. 2013).

Situational factors may influence consumer decisions in online shopping. A study on online grocery shopping indicates the importance of situational factors, such as having a baby or developing health problems as triggers for starting to buy groceries online. Many shoppers are found to discontinue online grocery shopping after the initial trigger has disappeared or they have experienced a problem with the service

(Hand et al. 2009). Consumers living in rural areas may behave differently than their urban counterparts. A research on rural consumers shows that prior dissatisfaction with local retailing is a powerful driver of outshopping, beliefs about online shopping, and online shopping. Outshopping, the purchasing of good outside of one self's local trading area, is positively related to online shopping at both points in time, suggesting that variables found to affect outshopping in the literature may affect online shopping in a similar way (Lennon et al. 2009).

Furthermore, cultural differences are found in online shopping. Adopting the Technology Acceptance Model (TAM), researchers examine the role of culture in influencing online shopping, comparing differences across three countries: Germany, Norway, and the United States. Findings show that the full TAM model does not hold for the European samples. In addition, cognitive involvement influences perceived usefulness and perceived ease of use in all countries, but the relationship between affective involvement and behavioral intention does not hold in Germany (Smith et al. 2013). Based on a sample of Chinese consumers, "Openness to change orientation" and "self-enhancement orientation" are found to have positive effects on respondents' online shopping behavior (Wu et al. 2011). A study conducted in Israel finds that online shoppers are experienced internet users who valued online information searching. They are also more likely to shop over the phone, but do not especially like to go shopping (Liebermann and Stashevsky 2009).

Several studies examine consumer behavior regarding online apparel shopping. A study shows that retail brand trust, off-line patronage, clothing involvement and two factors of website quality (usability and information quality, visual appeal and image) are found to significantly influence online apparel shopping intention. Off-line patronage is the strongest predictor of online shopping intention (Jones and Kim 2010). Another study of garment purchase shows that two of the concerns with fit and size of garment dimensions (concerns with overall appearance and concerns with imagining fit/size in online shopping) are negatively related to online purchase intentions (Kim and Damhorst 2010). Clothing consumer research indicates that online consumers perceived visual, tactile, and trial risks of product performance based on the evaluation of product attributes through virtual product experience (Yu et al. 2012).

The process of online shopping is also examined by researchers. Researchers investigate consumers' motivations for placing items in an online shopping cart with or without buying, termed virtual cart use. Beyond current purchase intentions, researchers investigate reasons for why consumers place items in their carts include: securing online price promotions, obtaining more information on certain products, organizing shopping items, and entertainment (Close and Kukar-Kinney 2010). They identify key drivers to online cart abandonment and suggest cognitive and behavioral reasons for this non-buyer behavior. They show that the factors influencing consumer online search, consideration, and evaluation play a larger role in cart abandonment than factors at the purchase decision stage. In particular, many consumers use online carts for entertainment or as a shopping research and organizational tool, which may induce them to buy at a later session or via another channel (Kukar-Kinney and Close 2010).

Consumer satisfaction in online shopping is negatively affected by business deception. A researcher investigates the negative influence of consumer's perceptions of online retailer's deceptive practices (perceived deception) on consumer's relational variables (satisfaction and loyalty intentions to the online retailer). The results show that satisfaction has totally mediated the influence of deception on loyalty. A direct effect of deception on loyalty is found among more educated consumers, consumers who have a more positive attitude toward the internet and consumers who have purchased a physical product (Román 2010). A longitudinal study shows that the relationship between attribute-level evaluations and satisfaction is dynamic and changes over time (Ha 2012).

Because more consumers use phones to make purchases, differences in user preferences between electronic and mobile commerce in consumer shopping are examined in research. Researchers conclude that m-commerce should be a shopping medium complementary to classic e-commerce rather than a direct alternative to it (Ozok and Wei 2010).

7.1.4 Effective Online Shopping Sites

Many studies explore factors associated with effective online store sites. Researchers examine how two dimensions of web aesthetics, aesthetic formality and aesthetic appeal, influence online consumers' psychological reactions and online purchase intention. The research indicates that consumers' cognitive, affective, and conative outcomes can be significantly evoked by aesthetic stimuli; the two dimensions of web aesthetics exhibit dissimilar patterns of influences (Wang et al. 2011).

Researchers examine the effects of image interactivity technology (IIT) features and experimenting with appearance (EA) on consumer online shopping behavior. The results show that the level of IIT and EA positively affect shopping enjoyment as well as decrease perceived risk toward the online retailer. In turn, shopping enjoyment and perceived risk significantly influence the consumers' attitude toward the online retailer (Lee et al. 2010).

Researchers examine website features on consumer online shopping behavior and find that website's 3Es (entertainment, escapist and aesthetic experiences) influence pleasure and/or arousal. Pleasure, arousal, entertainment, and aesthetic experiences have direct effects on the website patronage intention (Jeong et al. 2009). Research suggests that utilitarian flow elements that facilitate shopping may indeed increase purchasing. However, hedonic elements of flow are found to be unrelated to online buying, although they are positively related to outcomes associated with pathological Internet use (Bridges and Florsheim 2008).

Researchers investigate how order effects and other market competitive factors work together to attract consumers' attention to online vendors and find that the effect of serial position of a vendor in a list is mediated by consumers' attention which in turn affects the probability of the vendor being accepted (Xu and Kim 2008).

A researcher tests whether organizing the same number of products in different ways on an online store's website influences attitudes toward the store. The research reveals that when the products are sorted into more subcategories (9 as opposed to 3), such that more subcategory options appear in the selection menu, participants perceive that the website offers a greater variety of products and experience greater ease of navigation and shopping pleasure, which improve their attitudes toward the online store (Chang 2011).

Researchers have also tested the hypothesis that background music tempo positively affects consumer arousal. The result suggests that product category moderates the influence of arousal on pleasure such that a positive effect occurs when shopping online for hedonic products but not for utilitarian products. In addition, consumer trust mediates the positive influence of pleasure on purchase intention (Ding and Lin 2012).

Researchers have repeatedly tested an integrated model in diverse purchasing situations with different Web presentation styles and product categories. The findings indicate that perceived risk toward the website/product influences purchasing intention through cognition- and affect-based attitudes (Chang and Wu 2012).

A study provides support for perceived usefulness and perceived entertainment value as strong predictors of consumer attitude toward using all three of the sensory enabling technologies (SETs)—2D larger view and alternative views, 3D rotation views, and virtual try-on. The impact of perceived ease-of-use is significant only for 3D rotation views, suggesting that the impact of perceived ease-of-use differs by technology (Kim and Forsythe 2009).

Researchers test a gestalt model of consumer perceptions of online shopping environments and confirm the importance of the three main categories investigated in the literature, ease of understanding, informativeness, and involving qualities (Demangeot and Broderick 2010).

7.1.5 Information Search in Online Shopping

According to Stigler's (1961) economics of information theory, a dominant paradigm in consumer information search research, consumers search until the perceived marginal benefits of search are equal to the perceived marginal costs. The theory assumes that consumers use an implicit cost-benefit analysis to choose a search strategy — what, when, where, and how much to search. Researchers also have incorporated other constructs, such as ability to search and motivation to search, into this cost-benefit framework (Schmidt and Spreng 1996). Many factors can affect consumers' perceptions of search benefits and costs; the factors can be categorized into individual difference variables (e.g., demographic and socioeconomic characteristics), product type and product attributes, types of information sources used, and order of access (Srinivasan and Ratchford 1991).

Information technology has brought the potential to influence almost all dimensions of consumers' information search behaviors, ranging from the amount of search, number and types of sources searched, and timing of search to the distribution and weighting of information gathered (Bakos and Brynjolfsson 2000). One of the most important benefits of the internet is the quantity and quality of information that the internet can provide with minimal effort and cost. Empirical evidence indicates that consumers search more for information online than offline when they shop online (Ratchford et al. 2003) and substitute online information sources for offline ones (Klein and Ford 2003). Consumers perceive higher transaction value when an online seller adopts another online retailer's sale price as advertised reference price (ARP) than when the online seller uses an offline competitor's sale price as the ARP (Lo et al. 2013). Research also shows that consumers' perceived value and each cost component (information searching cost, moral hazard cost, and specific asset investment) are positively related to repurchase intention. Importantly, information searching cost exerts the most significant influence on repurchase intentions among the four relational factors (Wu et al. 2014).

Research shows that both information load and search tools transform the way in which consumers form their consideration sets, resulting in smaller, more stable, and more homogenous sets, integrated by more equally preferred alternatives. Furthermore, interaction effects show that search tools enhance their effectiveness in high information load settings (Parra and Ruiz 2009).

Researchers also examine the role of online comparison shopping tools and find that perceived usefulness of comparison shopping tools is influenced by comparison shopping proneness as well as directly by some of the online decision-making style dimensions (Park and Gretzel 2010).

7.1.6 Online Consumer Reviews

Online consumer reviews have become an important source of information to consumers, especially as a complement to or even a substitute for other forms of business-to-consumer and offline word-of-mouth communication about product characteristics (McWilliam 2000). However, online consumer reviews might not be a good strategy for gathering product information because consumers' incentives to provide reviews are not clear; online venders can control the information displayed; and reviews may have a bias toward the product evaluations (Chevalier and Mayzlin 2002).

Furthermore, a study of blogs shows that perceived usefulness of bloggers' recommendations and trust have significant influential effect on blog users' attitude toward and intention to shop online. Moreover, different determinants affect the users of perceived-high-reputation and perceived-low-reputation blogs (Hsu et al. 2013).

Researchers have studied the entire market of Amazon Shorts e-books, which are digital microproducts sold at a low and uniform price. With the minimal role of price in the buying decision, social discussion via eWOM becomes a collective signal of reputation, and ultimately a significant demand driver. The result suggests that eWOM can be used to convey the reputation of the product (e.g., the book), the reputation of the brand (i.e., the author), and the reputation of complementary goods (e.g., books in the same category) (Amblee and Bui 2011). Researchers also examine the influence of online consumer reviews (OCRs) on the purchase intention. The results show that the greater the perceived credibility of OCRs among potential consumers, the higher is the purchase intention (Lee et al. 2011).

7.2 Online Banking

7.2.1 Online Banking and Consumer Economic Wellbeing

Online banking and e-banking are used in an exchangeable way in the literature. Online banking refers to that consumers do banking businesses on the internet without visiting a physical location. Assuming that online banking services charge the same service fees for consumers online or offline, online banking services provide additional benefits such as convenience and time saving for consumers that have potential to improve consumer economic wellbeing. Like online shopping, online banking also brings new risks of information insecurity and privacy invasion for consumers. Much current research on online banking focuses on consumer behavior in adopting online banking technologies such as ATM, debit card, direct deposit and direct payment, and overall online banking from business and public policy perspectives. Research motivated to improve consumer economic wellbeing needs to be increased in the future.

7.2.2 Theories on Adoption of E-Banking Technologies

Lee et al. (2008) provide a comprehensive review on consumer adoption of e-banking technologies. Researchers have applied two psychological theories to understand consumer adoption of e-banking technologies. The first is the theory of diffusion of innovation (DI) (Rogers 1965). DI posits that innovations spread through society in an S-curve, as early adopters select the innovation first, followed by the majority, until a technology or innovation becomes common. DI is a cumulative model in that the total number of people who accept innovation only increases over time. DI is further refined by conceptualizing the adoption of an innovation as the probability of adopting an innovation at any point in time (Bass 1969). Thus, Bass' model recognizes the existence of non-adopters, even at the maturity stage of a new technology, while Rogers' model assumes that all consumers will eventually adopt the innovation as it moves through its product life cycle. The DI model includes five characteristics of innovation that influence consumer acceptance that are: relative advantage (i.e., the benefit of an innovation is greater than what it is replacing), compatibility (i.e., an innovation fits into a specific society), simplicity (i.e., an innovation is easy to understand and use), communicability (i.e., the benefit of using an innovation is visible and communicated), and trialability (i.e., an innovation can be tried before purchase). The extent to which innovation satisfies these five qualities determines the likelihood and also the speed of innovation. The DI is used to understand consumer bank technology acceptance (e.g., Dabholkar 1996; Daniel 1999; Howcroft et al. 2002; Lockett and Littler 1997; Lee and Lee 2000).

Another commonly used theory is the technology acceptance model (TAM). The TAM extends the theory of planned behavior to the adoption of computers in the workplace (Davis 1989). Based on this model, a prospective user's overall feelings or attitudes toward using a given technology-based system or procedure represents major determinants as to whether or not he/she will ultimately use the system. This model assumes that ease of use and perceived technology usefulness are critical constructs that influence an individual's attitude toward using the innovative technology.

7.2.3 Consumer Characteristics Associated with Adoption of E-Banking Technologies

Based on the theory of diffusion of innovation, those who adopt technologies in the early stage of the life cycle differ from those who adopt it in its maturity stage in certain distinctive characteristics. For instance, those who adopt innovation in its introduction stage tend to be venturesome, gregarious, and have a high propensity for risk (Lassar et al. 2005). These individuals also tend to have multiple sources of information. Further, non-adopters of banking technology are less likely to have communication with professional information providers and to communicate with friends and family (Lee and Lee 2000).

Demographics such as income and education are also related to technology adoption. High income and education increase the likelihood of technology adoption (Daniel 1999; Jayawardhena and Foley 2000; Karjaluoto et al. 2002; Kolodinsky et al. 2004; Lee and Lee 2000; Lee et al. 2002). Specifically, with regards to banking technologies, consumers with above average income and at least some high school education are more likely to use e-banking services than those with below average income and less than a high school education (Kennickell and Kwast 1997; Klee 2006; Stavins 2002; Taube 1988). This pattern is also supported by international evidence. In Finland, household income and education predict whether or not consumers adopt Internet banking (Mattilia et al. 2003). Educated and wealthy consumers are among those most likely to adopt Internet banking in Australia (Sathye 1999).

Age is also related to innovation adoption, as younger persons are generally more likely to adopt (Karjaluoto et al. 2002; Lee et al. 2002; Zeithaml and Gilly 1987). However, the effect of age appears to vary across different types of banking technologies. For instance, respondents over the age of 65 are the least likely to adopt phone banking and PC banking. Those in their middle age are less likely to adopt PC banking, versus the youngest group of consumers, aged 35 and below. Studies also report that while elderly consumers were less likely to adopt ATM usage (Gilly and Zeithaml 1985; Lee and Lee 2000; Taube 1988), they are more likely than younger consumers to use electronic fund transfer (EFT) (Lee and Lee 2000).

A few studies report that men tend to adopt computer-related technologies more often than women (Gefen and Straub 1997). Since many married couples have jointly held banking accounts, e-banking adoption may be related to the combination of marital status and gender, with married couples more likely to adopt these innovations than either single males or single females (Kolodinsky et al. 2004).

The opposite descriptions of innovators delineate the general profile of non-adopters, or laggards. Specifically, laggards tend to be less educated and have lower incomes; they are rather isolated in terms of social networks and are less likely to communicate with professional information providers than innovators, such as reading magazines and/or third party experts that are expected to provide consumers with exposure to innovations (Dickerson and Gentry 1983; Gatignon and Robertson 1985; Gilly and Zeithaml 1985; Kennedy 1983; Lee and Lee 2000; Midgley and Dowling 1978; Zeithaml and Gilly 1987). Based on the 1995 and 2004 Surveys of Consumer Finance (SCF), e-banking laggards tend to be older, less educated, have less income, and divorced/separated than adopters of e-banking (Lee et al. 2008).

7.2.4 Consumer Characteristics on E-Banking Adoption

Research is also conducted to understand consumer behavior in using online banking. Using data from Jordan and the technology acceptance model (TAM), a researcher finds that perceived ease of use, perceived usefulness, subjective norms, security and trust, Internet experience and enjoyment are the important factors that affect customers' adoption of e-banking in Jordan (Abbad 2013). Research in Malaysia indicates that perceived usefulness, perceived case of use, convenience, computer efficacy, device features and security influence the adoption of e-banking (Tan et al. 2010). Research in Romania shows that perceived usefulness, compatibility, and technical resources, security and cost have significant effects on adoption of e-Banking services (Nor et al. 2011).

Researchers examine factors contributing to consumer satisfaction of e-banking and find the relationship between the predictors (accessibility, trust, ease of use and usefulness) and satisfaction with electronic banking (Liébana-Cabanillas et al. 2013). Another research finds that the influence of online satisfaction on commitment is significantly stronger for highly involved users; conversely, the effect of satisfaction on trust is weaker (Sanchez-Franco 2009).

E-banks must focus on service quality to increase customer satisfaction and trust and to obtain customer loyalty, suggested by a research in Taiwan (Chu et al. 2012). Researchers in Spain show that efficiency of a website and responsiveness to complaints have positive influences on loyalty of e-banking (Marimon et al. 2012). Personal factors significantly influence technology readiness and customer relationship management. Technology readiness has a significant impact on customer relation management and relationship quality, indicated by another research in Taiwan (Kuo 2011). Research indicates that both perceived usefulness and perceived ease of use have significant impacts on customer interactions with Internet e-banking services (Liao and Wong 2008).

7.2.5 *Other Research Topics on E-Banking*

Researchers also examine diverse topics on e-banking. Research indicates that the positive effect of corporate social responsibility (CSR) on users' attitudes toward green e-banking services is moderated by perceived ease of use, perceived usefulness, and perceived self-efficacy with technology (Lekakos et al. 2014). Researchers examine the e-banking distribution channels in Serbia and find the dependence of the selected channels against the socio-economic factors: employment rate and average monthly income per capita (Rankovic et al. 2013).

Introducing information systems into organizations initiates a change in human behaviors, which is often perceived as obtrusive and distracting. End-user training may help manage this challenge by getting the users familiar with the system and its functionality. For this purpose, researchers describe a qualitative case study of how the end-user training on an e-Bank was organized, and how the training was delivered to its elderly customers (Oinas-Kukkonen et al. 2010).

Privacy and security are the major sources of dissatisfaction of e-banking, which have momentously impacted users' satisfaction, reflected in research in Malaysia. Meanwhile, accessibility, convenience, design and content are sources of satisfaction. Besides, the speed, product features availability, and reasonable service fees and charges, as well as the bank's operations management factor are critical to the success of the e-banks (Poon 2007).

To prevent social engineering attacks is an important consumer protection issue in e-banking. Researchers conduct different kinds of phishing experiment case studies to shed some light into social engineering attacks, such as phone phishing and phishing website attacks for designing effective countermeasures and analyzing the efficiency of performing security awareness about phishing threats. Results show the importance of conducting phishing training awareness for all users and doubling the efforts in developing phishing prevention techniques (Aburrous et al. 2010).

7.3 Summary

Internet provides opportunities for consumers to shop online more conveniently and efficiently. Research shows that internet helps consumers reduce some transaction costs such as search and comparison but also increase other costs such as review, evaluation, and post purchase services. In addition, the development of online shopping brings potential risks and hazards to consumers, especially to vulnerable consumers such as children, youth, and elderly. Much current research focuses on how consumers behave in the online shopping environment and how online companies provide better environments for consumers to buy more. More future research also needs to evaluate the effect of online shopping on consumer economic wellbeing.

Internet also brings opportunities for consumers to do banking online. Consumer adoptions to online baking technologies vary. Online banking also brings serious issues of financial security and privacy that may hurt consumer economic wellbeing and need more future research. Future research also needs to further examine strategies to help vulnerable consumers in online banking environment and provide them satisfactory services by taking advantage of the internet technology.

Both online shopping and online banking are relevant to consumer spending, one aspect of consumer economic wellbeing. More future research also needs to examine effects of internet technology on consumer behavior in earning, borrowing, and saving and their impacts on consumer economic wellbeing.

References

Abbad, M. M. (2013). E-banking in Jordan. *Behaviour & Information Technology, 32*(7), 681–694.

Aburrous, M., Hossain, M. A., Dahal, K., & Thabtah, F. (2010). Experimental case studies for investigating e-banking phishing techniques and attack strategies. *Cognitive Computation, 2*(3), 242–253.

Amblee, N., & Bui, T. (2011). Harnessing the influence of social proof in online shopping: The effect of electronic word of mouth on sales of digital microproducts. *International Journal of Electronic Commerce, 16*(2), 91–113.

Anaza, N. A. (2014). Personality antecedents of customer citizenship behaviors in online shopping situations. *Psychology & Marketing, 31*(4), 251–263.

Azjen, I. (1991). The theory of planned behavior. *Organizational Behavior and Human Decision Processes, 50*, 179–211.

Bakos, J. Y., & Brynjolfsson, E. (2000). Bundling and competition on the Internet. *Marketing Science, 19*(1), 63–82.

Bass, F. M. (1969). A new product growth for model consumer durables. *Management Science, 15*(5), 215–227.

Bellman, S., Lohse, G. L., & Johnson, E. J. (1999). Predictors of online buying behavior. *Communications of the Association for Computing Machinery, 42*, 32–38.

Bridges, E., & Florsheim, R. (2008). Hedonic and utilitarian shopping goals: The online experience. *Journal of Business Research, 61*(4), 309–314.

Cai, Y., & Cude, B. J. (2008). Online shopping. In J. J. Xiao (Ed.), *Handbook of consumer finance research* (pp. 137–159). New York: Springer.

Casas, J., Zmud, J., & Bricka, S. (2001, January). *Impact of shopping via Internet on travel for shopping purpose*. Paper presented at the 80th Annual Meeting of the Transportation Research Board, Washington, DC.

Chang, C. (2011). The effect of the number of product subcategories on perceived variety and shopping experience in an online store. *Journal of Interactive Marketing, 25*(3), 159–168.

Chang, M. L., & Wu, W. Y. (2012). Revisiting perceived risk in the context of online shopping: An alternative perspective of decision-making styles. *Psychology & Marketing, 29*(5), 378–400.

Chevalier, J. A., & Mayzlin, D. (2002). The effect of word of mouth on sales: Online book reviews. *Journal of Marketing Research, 39*, 345–354.

Chu, P. Y., Lee, G. Y., & Chao, Y. (2012). Service quality, customer satisfaction, customer trust, and loyalty in an e-banking context. *Social Behavior and Personality: An International Journal, 40*(8), 1271–1283.

Close, A. G., & Kukar-Kinney, M. (2010). Beyond buying: Motivations behind consumers' online shopping cart use. *Journal of Business Research, 63*(9), 986–992.

Coase, R. H. (1937). The nature of the firm. *Economica, 4*, 386–405.

Dabholkar, P. A. (1996). Consumer evaluations of new technology-based self service options: An investigation of alternative models of service quality. *International Journal of Research in Marketing, 13*, 29–51.

Daniel, E. (1999). Provision of electronic banking in the UK and the republic of Ireland. *International Journal of Bank Marketing, 17*(2), 72–82.

Davis, F. D. (1989). Perceived usefulness, perceived ease of use, and user acceptance of information technology. *MIS Quarterly, 13*(3), 319–339.

Davis, F. D. (1993). User acceptance of information technology: System characteristics, user perceptions and behavioral impacts. *International Journal of Man-Machine Studies, 38*, 475–487.

Demangeot, C., & Broderick, A. J. (2010). Consumer perceptions of online shopping environments: A gestalt approach. *Psychology & Marketing, 27*(2), 117–140.

Dholakia, R. (2012). *Technology and consumption: Understanding consumer choices & behaviors*. New York: Springer.

Dickerson, M. D., & Gentry, J. W. (1983). Characteristics of adopters and non-adopters of home computers. *Journal of Consumer Research, 10*(2), 225–235.

Ding, C. G., & Lin, C. H. (2012). How does background music tempo work for online shopping? *Electronic Commerce Research and Applications, 11*(3), 299–307.

Forsythe, S., & Shi, B. (2003). Consumer patronage and risk perceptions in Internet shopping. *Journal of Business Research, 56*, 867–875.

Fulk, J., Steinfeld, C. W., Schmitz, J., & Power, G. J. (1987). A social information processing model of media use in organizations. *Communications Research, 14*, 520–552.

Gatignon, H., & Robertson, T. R. (1985). A Propositional inventory for new diffusion research. *Journal of Consumer Research, 11*(4), 849–867.

Gefen, D., & Straub, D. W. (1997). Gender differences in the perception and use of E-mail: An extension to the technology acceptance model. *MIS Quarterly, 21*(4), 389–399.

George, J. F. (2002). Influences on the intent to make Internet purchases. *Internet Research: Electronic Networking Applications and Policy, 12*(2), 165–180.

Gilly, M. C., & Zeithaml, V. (1985). The elderly consumer and adoption of technologies. *Journal of Consumer Research, 12*(3), 353–357.

Golob, T. F. (2003). Structural equation modeling for travel behavior research. *Transportation Research Part B, 37*, 1–25.

Ha, H. Y. (2012). The effects of online shopping attributes on satisfaction-purchase intention link: A longitudinal study. *International Journal of Consumer Studies, 36*(3), 327–334.

Hand, C., Riley, F. D., Harris, P., Singh, J., & Rettie, R. (2009). Online grocery shopping: The influence of situational factors. *European Journal of Marketing, 43*(9/10), 1205–1219.

Hansen, T. (2008). Consumer values, the theory of planned behaviour and online grocery shopping. *International Journal of Consumer Studies, 32*(2), 128–137.

Hansen, T., & Jensen, J. M. (2009). Shopping orientation and online clothing purchases: The role of gender and purchase situation. *European Journal of Marketing, 43*(9/10), 1154–1170.

Hoffman, D. L., & Novak, T. P. (1996). Marketing in the hypermedia computer-mediated environments: Conceptual foundations. *Journal of Marketing, 60*(3), 50–68.

Howcroft, B., Hamilton, R., & Hewer, P. (2002). Consumer attitude and the usage and adoption of home-based banking in the United Kingdom. *International Journal of Bank Marketing, 20*(3), 111–121.

Hsu, C. L., Lin, J. C. C., & Chiang, H. S. (2013). The effects of blogger recommendations on customers' online shopping intentions. *Internet Research, 23*(1), 69–88.

Jayawardhena, C., & Foley, P. (2000). Changes in the banking sector - The case of internet banking in the UK. *Internet Research, 10*(1), 19–31.

Jeong, S. W., Fiore, A. M., Niehm, L. S., & Lorenz, F. O. (2009). The role of experiential value in online shopping: The impacts of product presentation on consumer responses towards an apparel web site. *Internet Research, 19*(1), 105–124.

Jones, C., & Kim, S. (2010). Influences of retail brand trust, off-line patronage, clothing involvement and website quality on online apparel shopping intention. *International Journal of Consumer Studies, 34*(6), 627–637.

Karjaluoto, H., Mattila, M., & Pento, T. (2002). Factors underlying attitude formation towards online banking in Finland. *International Journal of Bank Marketing, 20*(6), 261–272.

Kau, A. K., Tang, Y. E., & Ghose, S. (2003). Typology of online shoppers. *The Journal of Consumer Marketing, 20*(2/3), 139–156.

Kennedy, A. (1983). Development, adoption and diffusion of new industrial products. *European Journal of Marketing, 17*(3), 31–87.

Kennickell, A. B., & Kwast, M. L. (1997). *Who uses electronic banking? Results from the 1995 Survey of Consumer Finances*. Paper presented at the Annual Meeting of the Western Economic Association, Seattle, WA.

Kim, J. B. (2012). An empirical study on consumer first purchase intention in online shopping: Integrating initial trust and TAM. *Electronic Commerce Research, 12*(2), 125–150.

Kim, H., & Damhorst, M. L. (2010). The relationship of body-related self-discrepancy to body dissatisfaction, apparel involvement, concerns with fit and size of garments, and purchase intentions in online apparel shopping. *Clothing and Textiles Research Journal, 28*(4), 239–254.

Kim, J., & Forsythe, S. (2009). Adoption of sensory enabling technology for online apparel shopping. *European Journal of Marketing, 43*(9/10), 1101–1120.

Kim, S., & Martinez, B. (2013). Fashion consumer groups and online shopping at private sale sites. *International Journal of Consumer Studies, 37*(4), 367–372.

Klee, E. (2006). *Families' use of payment instruments during a decade of change in the U.S. payment system*. Working Paper, Board of Governors of the Federal Reserve System, Washington, DC.

Klein, L. R., & Ford, G. (2003). Consumer search for information in the digital age: An empirical study of prepurchase search for automobiles. *Journal of Interactive Marketing, 17*(3), 29–49.

Kolodinsky, J. M., Hogarth, J. M., & Hilgert, M. A. (2004). The adoption of electronic banking technologies by US consumers. *International Journal of Bank Marketing, 22*(4), 238–249.

Kukar-Kinney, M., & Close, A. G. (2010). The determinants of consumers' online shopping cart abandonment. *Journal of the Academy of Marketing Science, 38*(2), 240–250.

Kuo, T. (2011). The antecedents of customer relationship in e-banking industry. *Journal of Computer Information Systems, 51*(3), 57–66.

Lassar, W. M., Manolis, C., & Lassar, S. S. (2005). The relationship between consumer innovativeness, personal characteristics, and online banking adoption. *International Journal of Bank Marketing, 23*(2), 176–200.

Lee, J., Cho, J. E., & Abdul-Rahman, F. (2008). E-banking. In J. J. Xiao (Ed.), *Handbook of consumer finance research* (pp. 104–123). New York: Springer.

Lee, H.-H., Kim, J., & Fiore, A. M. (2010). Affective and cognitive online shopping experience effects of image interactivity technology and experimenting with appearance. *Clothing and Textiles Research Journal, 28*(2), 140–154.

Lee, M. Y., Kim, Y. K., & Lee, H. J. (2013). Adventure versus gratification: Emotional shopping in online auctions. *European Journal of Marketing, 47*(1-2), 49–70.

Lee, E., & Lee, J. (2000). Haven't adopted electronic financial services yet? The acceptance and diffusion of electronic banking technologies. *Financial Counseling and Planning, 11*(1), 49–61.

Lee, E., Lee, J., & Schumann, D. W. (2002). The influence of communication source and mode on consumer adoption of technological innovations. *Journal of Consumer Affairs, 36*(1), 1–27.

Lee, J., Park, D.-H., & Han, I. (2011). The different effects of online consumer reviews on consumers' purchase intentions depending on trust in online shopping malls: An advertising perspective. *Internet Research, 21*(2), 187–206.

Lekakos, G., Vlachos, P., & Koritos, C. (2014). Green is good but is usability better? Consumer reactions to environmental initiatives in e-banking services. *Ethics and Information Technology, 16*(2), 103–117.

Lennon, S. J., Ha, Y., Johnson, K. K., Jasper, C. R., Damhorst, M. L., & Lyons, N. (2009). Rural consumers' online shopping for food and fiber products as a form of outshopping. *Clothing and Textiles Research Journal, 27*(1), 3–30.

Liang, T. P., & Huang, J. S. (1998). An empirical study on consumer acceptance of products in electronic markets: A transaction cost model. *Decision Support Systems, 24*, 29–43.

Liao, Z., & Wong, W. K. (2008). The determinants of customer interactions with internet-enabled e-banking services. *Journal of the Operational Research Society, 59*(9), 1201–1210.

Liébana-Cabanillas, F., Muñoz-Leiva, F., & Rejón-Guardia, F. (2013). The determinants of satisfaction with e-banking. *Industrial Management & Data Systems, 113*(5), 750–767.

Liebermann, Y., & Stashevsky, S. (2009). Determinants of online shopping: Examination of an early-stage online market. *Canadian Journal of Administrative Sciences, 26*(4), 316–331.

Lin, H. H. (2011). Gender differences in the linkage of online patronage behavior with TV-and-online shopping values. *Service Business, 5*(4), 295–312.

Lo, S. K., Chou, Y. J., & Teng, C. I. (2013). Source effect of advertised reference price influences on transaction value in online shopping environments. *Electronic Commerce Research, 13*(4), 411–421.

Lockett, A., & Littler, D. (1997). The adoption of direct banking services. *Journal of Marketing Management, 13*(8), 791–811.

Marimon, F., Petnji Yaya, L. H., & Casadesus Fa, M. (2012). Impact of e-Quality and service recovery on loyalty: A study of e-banking in Spain. *Total Quality Management & Business Excellence, 23*(7-8), 769–787.

Mattilia, M., Karjaluoto, H., & Pento, T. (2003). Internet banking adoption among mature customers: Early majority or laggards? *Journal of Services Marketing, 17*(5), 514–528.

McWilliam, G. (2000). Building strong brands through online communities. *MIT Sloan Management Review, 41*(3), 43–54.

Midgley, D. F., & Dowling, G. R. (1978). Innovativeness: The concept and its measurement. *Journal of Consumer Research, 4*(4), 229–242.

Nor, K. M., Barbuta-Misu, N., & Stroe, R. (2011). A model for analyzing the determinant factors of adoption e-banking services by Romanian customers. *Economic Computation and Economic Cybernetics Studies and Research, 45*(4), 53–70.

O'Cass, A., & Fenech, T. (2003). Web retailing adoption: Exploring the nature of Internet users Web retailing behavior. *Journal of Retailing and Consumer Services, 10*, 81–94.

Oinas-Kukkonen, H., Hohtari, S., & Pekkola, S. (2010). Organizing end-user training: A case study of an e-bank and its elderly customers. *Journal of Organizational and End User Computing (JOEUC), 22*(4), 95–112.

Ozok, A. A., & Wei, J. (2010). An empirical comparison of consumer usability preferences in online shopping using stationary and mobile devices: Results from a college student population. *Electronic Commerce Research, 10*(2), 111–137.

Palmer, J. W. (1997). Electronic commerce in retailing: Differences across retail formats. *The Information Society, 13*, 75–91.

Park, Y. A., & Gretzel, U. (2010). Influence of consumers' online decision-making style on comparison shopping proneness and perceived usefulness of comparison shopping tools. *Journal of Electronic Commerce Research, 11*(4), 342–354.

Parra, J. F., & Ruiz, S. (2009). Consideration sets in online shopping environments: The effects of search tool and information load. *Electronic Commerce Research and Applications, 8*(5), 252–262.

Poon, W. C. (2007). Users' adoption of e-banking services: The Malaysian perspective. *Journal of Business & Industrial Marketing, 23*(1), 59–69.

Rankovic, M., Simovic, V., Vaskovic, V., & Novakovic, N. (2013). Research on the e-banking payment distribution channels - Case study: Serbia. *Metalurgia International, 18*(1), 163–168.

Ratchford, B., Lee, M. S., & Talukdar, D. (2003). The impact of the Internet on information search for automobiles. *Journal of Marketing Research, 40*, 193–209.

Rogers, E. M. (1965). *Diffusion of Innovations*. New York: The Free Press.

Román, S. (2010). Relational consequences of perceived deception in online shopping: The moderating roles of type of product, consumer's attitude toward the internet and consumer's demographics. *Journal of Business Ethics, 95*(3), 373–391.

Sanchez-Franco, M. J. (2009). The moderating effects of involvement on the relationships between satisfaction, trust and commitment in e-banking. *Journal of Interactive Marketing, 23*(3), 247–258.

Sathye, M. (1999). Adoption of internet banking by Australian consumers: An empirical investigation. *International Journal of Bank Marketing, 17*(7), 324–334.

Schmidt, J. B., & Spreng, R. A. (1996). A proposed model of external consumer information search. *Journal of Academy of Marketing Science, 24*, 246–256.

Seock, Y.-K., & Bailey, L. R. (2008). The influence of college students' shopping orientations and gender differences on online information searches and purchase behaviours. *International Journal of Consumer Studies, 32*(2), 113–121.

Shim, S., Eastlick, M. A., Lotz, S. L., & Warrington, P. (2001). An online prepurchase intentions model: The role of intention to search. *Journal of Retailing, 77*, 397–416.

Smith, R., Deitz, G., Royne, M. B., Hansen, J. D., Grunhagen, M., & Witte, C. (2013). Cross-cultural examination of online shopping behavior: A comparison of Norway, Germany, and the United States. *Journal of Business Research, 66*(3), 328–335.

Srinivasan, N., & Ratchford, B. (1991). An empirical test of a model of external search for automobiles. *Journal of Consumer Research, 18*(2), 233–242.

Stavins, J. (2002). Effect of consumer characteristics on the use of payment instruments. *New England Economic Review, Q3*, 19–31.

Stigler, G. J. (1961). The economics of information. *Journal of Political Economics, 29*, 213–225.

Swinyard, W. R., & Smith, S. M. (2003). Why people (don't) shop online: A lifestyle study of the Internet consumer. *Psychology & Marketing, 20*, 567–597.

Tan, K. S., Chong, S. C., Loh, P. L., & Lin, B. (2010). An evaluation of e-banking and m-banking adoption factors and preference in Malaysia: A case study. *International Journal of Mobile Communications, 8*(5), 507–527.

Taube, P. M. (1988). The influence of selected factors on the frequency of atm usage. *Journal of Retail Banking, 10*(1), 47–52.

Wan, Y., Nakayama, M., & Sutcliffe, N. (2012). The impact of age and shopping experiences on the classification of search, experience, and credence goods in online shopping. *Information Systems and E-Business Management, 10*(1), 135–148.

Wang, Y. J., Minor, M. S., & Wei, J. (2011). Aesthetics and the online shopping environment: Understanding consumer responses. *Journal of Retailing, 87*(1), 46–58.

Wu, L., Cai, Y., & Liu, D. (2011). Online shopping among Chinese consumers: An exploratory investigation of demographics and value orientation. *International Journal of Consumer Studies, 35*(4), 458–469.

Wu, L.-Y., Chen, K. Y., Chen, P.-Y., & Cheng, S.-L. (2014). Perceived value, transaction cost, and repurchase-intention in online shopping: A relational exchange perspective. *Journal of Business Research, 67*(1), 2768–2776.

Xu, Y., & Kim, H.-W. (2008). Order effect and vendor inspection in online comparison shopping. *Journal of Retailing, 84*(4), 477–486.

Yu, U. J., Lee, H. H., & Damhorst, M. L. (2012). Exploring multidimensions of product performance risk in the online apparel shopping context: Visual, tactile, and trial risks. *Clothing and Textiles Research Journal, 30*(4), 251–266.

Zeithaml, V. A., & Gilly, M. C. (1987). Characteristics affecting the acceptance of retailing technologies: A comparison of elderly and non-elderly consumers. *Journal of Retailing, 63*(1), 49–68.

Part III
Components of Consumer Economic Wellbeing

Chapter 8
Consumer Income

Abstract Income is the most commonly used measure of consumer economic wellbeing. This chapter discusses income and related concepts. The chapter first presents descriptive statistics of consumer income in the USA. Then the research literature on topics such as earning determinants, income inequality, intergenerational transfer, poverty, and top 1 % income share are described.

8.1 Income Overview and Group Differences

Income can be defined in various ways for different purposes. The US Census Bureau has been compiling income estimates since 1947 (Weinberg et al. 1999). Based on the report of the US Census Bureau, in 2012, the median household income is $51,017 (DeNavas-Walt et al. 2013).

Using the national average median income as a norm in 2012, couple households fare best (median income $75,694), whereas male headed households are close to the average ($48,634). Other household types have lower than average median incomes: female nonfamily households ($26,016) and male nonfamily households ($36,989).

Racial and ethnic differences are found in household income. Asian and white households have above average income ($68,636 and $57,009, respectively) while Hispanic and black households have below average income ($39,005 and $33,321, respectively). This pattern has lasted for the last 40 years (1967–2012) (DeNavas-Walt et al. 2013, Fig. 1).

Age has a hump shape pattern in terms of income. The youngest group (age 15–24) has the lowest median income ($30,604), the late middle age group (age 45–54) has the highest ($66,411), and the oldest age group (age 65 or older) has the second lowest median income ($33,848).

Gender differences of income exist in the last 50 years and women always earn less than men. In 2012, median earning for male workers is $48,398 and that for female workers is $37,791 with a female-to-male earning ratio of 77 %, which has increased from 60 % in 1960 (DeNavas-Walt et al. 2013, Fig. 2).

Rich and not-so-rich consumers have different income sources evidenced by various levels of net worth. According to the 2010 Survey of Consumer Finance, top three income sources among American families are wages (68.1 %), business, farm,

J.J. Xiao, *Consumer Economic Wellbeing*, International Series on Consumer Science, DOI 10.1007/978-1-4939-2821-7_8

self-employment (12.2 %), and social security or retirement (12.0 %). Compared to net worth groups, top two income sources for families at the bottom 25 % net worth are wages (75.9 %) and transfers or other income (11.1 %). Top two income sources for families at the top 10 % net worth are wages (55.8 %) and business, farm, self-employment (23.9 %). For families at middle level (25–90 %) net worth, top two income sources are wages (80.7–69.7 %) and social security or retirement incomes (9.6–20.1 %) (Bricker et al. 2012, Table 2).

8.2 Determinants of Earning

8.2.1 Earning Puzzles

This section reviews the research literature on determinants of labor income. Labor income may not be closely related to schooling and cognitive functioning that is suggested by a literature review (Bowles et al. 2001). Researchers find several puzzles that cannot be explained by the standard labor economic theory: individuals with similar characteristics receive quite different earnings; advantages of children of successful parents receive additional benefits besides superior education, the inheritance of wealth, or the genetic inheritance of cognitive ability; and seemingly irrelevant personal characteristics, including beauty, height, obesity, and even whether one keeps a clean house, are often robust predictors of earnings.

8.2.2 Conceptual Models of Earning

Bowles et al. (2001) describe conceptual models that explain determinants of earning. The Walrasian model suggests that services provided by an employee to the production process is an exogenously determined attribute of the worker. Productively identical individuals will receive the same wage in all employments. This model can be considered as the standard labor economic theory that ignores behavioral characteristics of parties to an exchange. The Schumpeterian model contends that, at any given moment, factor payments typically include what may be termed "disequilibrium rents." These rents are attributed to technical change, product innovation, changes in business organization, and other shocks. People differ in their ability to identify and capture these rents, and personal dispositions and capacities contributing to success in this may correspond only weakly to productive skills. The Coasean model identifies that individual traits may be relevant to attenuating the incentive problems when labor effort is endogenous. These *incentive-enhancing preferences* may bear a competitive return even if they do not contribute directly to production. After reviewing these conceptual models, Bowles et al. (2001) then provide their own model, the model of incentive enhancing preferences. Three examples of incentive enhancing preferences include time preference, sense of self-efficacy, and increase of marginal utility of income.

Using data from the Panel Study of Income Dynamics, researchers study adult males whose motivational and behavioral traits were measured 15–25 years prior to the observations of their current earnings. The motivational traits measured are preference for challenge over affiliation, fear of failure, sense of personal efficacy, and degree of trust. Behavioral measures include church attendance, participation in social clubs, television viewing, newspaper reading, and an interviewer's assessment of the cleanliness of the respondent's home. They find that these trait and behavioral variables are good predictors of earnings years later taking account of a wide range of more conventional educational, cognitive, and demographic influences (Duncan and Dunifon 1998). Another study using national longitudinal data finds that behavioral traits have a significant influence on the earnings of women, controlling for standard human capital variables (Osborne 2000). Reasoning and evidence suggest that incentive-enhancing preferences and other earnings-relevant behavioral traits may be influenced by schooling, and may explain some of the economic returns to schooling, as well as other individual differences in earnings (Bowles et al. 2001).

8.2.3 The Role of Schooling

Bowles et al. (2001) suggest that while both cognitive functioning and schooling are important determinants of earnings, the economic return of schooling is not accounted for primarily by its contribution to enhanced cognitive scores. Instead, differences in cognitive scores account for very little of the residual earnings variance and these data provide no support for the hypothesis that the effect of cognitive scores on earnings has increased secularly over the four decades covered by their estimates. However, schooling types may make differences in human capital investment. In the last four decades, average colleges in the USA are less selective but students who attend more selective colleges receive higher return on the investment (Hoxby 2009).

Even though the role of school is limited in a consumer's earning, consumers with higher educational levels still are more likely to find a job and making more money. Based on statistics provided by the US Bureau of Labor Statistics (2013), the unemployment rate for a high school graduate is 7.5 % while that of a bachelor degree holder is only 4 %. The median weekly earning for a bachelor holder is $1,108 while for a high school graduate, it is only $651.

8.3 Income Inequality

8.3.1 Definition and Trends

Income inequality can be considered an indicator of economic ill-being at a collective level. From a consumer perspective, research on income inequality may provide policy implications that can be used to improve consumer economic wellbeing.

Consistent with this perspective, consumer advocates are concerned about trends of income inequality to lobby for pro-consumer public policies. The Census Bureau has traditionally used two methods to measure income inequality—the shares of aggregate household income received by quintiles and the Gini index (a common measure of income inequality). In 2012, the top quintile of households receive 51.0 % of total income in which top 5 % receive 22.3 % of total income, while lowest quintile of households receive 3.2 % of total income. Another measure of income inequality, the Gini index is 0.477 (0 refers to perfect equality and 1 refers to perfect inequality) (DeNavas-Walt et al. 2013).

Researchers analyze distributional changes over the last quarter of the twentieth century. Both male wage rate inequality and family income inequality have accelerated during the early 1980s, increased at a slower rate through the early 1990s and then stabilized at a high level through the early 2000s. The similarity in the timing of changes in these two distributions has been used as evidence that increased family income inequality primarily reflects increased inequality of wage rates (Gottschalk and Danziger 2005).

Another study examines the level and distribution of economic wellbeing in the USA during the 1980s and 1990s based on the standard measure of money income and a measure of imputed income. Over the 1982–2000 period, median wellbeing increases faster when these adjustments are made than when standard money income is used. This adjustment widens the income gap between African-Americans and whites but increases the relative wellbeing of the elderly. Adding imputed rent and annuities from household wealth to household income considerably increases measured inequality and the share of income from wealth in inequality. However, both measures show about the same rise in inequality over the period (Wolff and Zacharias 2009).

A research review on income inequality concludes that inequality in wages, earnings, and total family incomes in the USA has increased markedly since 1980, with some trends beginning as early as the late 1960s. The level of inequality today, for both market income and disposable income, is greater than at any point in the past 40 years or longer and may be as high as in the late 1910s or 1920s (McCall and Percheski 2010).

Researchers investigate the distribution of wellbeing among world citizens during the last two centuries. The estimates show that inequality of world distribution of income worsened from the beginning of the nineteenth century to World War II and after that seemed to have stabilized or to have grown more slowly. In the early nineteenth century most inequality was due to differences within countries; later, it was due to differences between countries (Bourguignon and Morrisson 2002). Other researchers review key studies on global interpersonal inequality and conclude that there is no change in global interpersonal inequality over 1970–2000 (Anand and Segal 2008).

8.3.2 Determinants of Income Inequality

Rising income inequality from the mid-1990s to the present is characterized by rapid income growth among top earners and new patterns of employment and income pooling across families and households, suggested by a literature review. Research on economic inequality has expanded from a more narrow focus on wage inequalities and labor markets to other domains including incentive pay, corporate governance, income pooling and family formation, social and economic policy, and political institutions (McCall and Percheski 2010).

Income instability, work skill, and occupation may affect income inequality. Based on data from the Panel Study of Income Dynamics, researchers find that income instability should be considered as a major cause for income inequality (Gottschalk and Moffitt 2009). The increase in inequality reflects an absolute as well as a relative decline in the earnings of less skilled workers. In fact, the decline in wages for less skilled workers canceled out the impact of the rising wages for more skilled workers, so little or no change in mean wages has occurred (Gottschalk 1997). Researchers examine the rise of intra-occupational wage inequality in the USA from 1983 to 2002 with data from the Current Population Survey. They find that the direct association between occupations and wage inequality declined over this period as within-occupational inequality grew faster than between-occupational inequality (Kim and Sakamoto 2008).

Technology may cause income inequality. A researcher examines associations between technology change and income inequality and concludes that the behavior of wages and returns to schooling in the USA indicates that technical change has been skill-biased during the past 60 years, and probably for most of the twentieth century (Acemoglu 2002). After studying the impact of internet use on the earnings of US workers with data from the Current Population Survey, researchers find robustly significant positive associations between web use and earnings growth, indicating that some skills and behaviors associated with internet use are rewarded by the labor market (DiMaggio and Bonikowski 2008). Analyzing data from the Current Population Survey for 1963–2005, researchers find that the growth of overall wage inequality in the 1990s is slowing down. However, two different paths exist. Upper-tail inequality existing between the 90th percentile and 50th percentile increased steadily since 1980 even adjusting for changes in labor force composition, while lower-tail inequality existing between the 50th percentile and 10th percentile rose sharply in the first half of the 1980s and plateaued or contracted thereafter. These patterns are potentially reconciled by a modified version of the skill-biased technical change hypothesis that emphasizes the role of information technology in complementing abstract tasks required by higher education and substituting for routine tasks required by lower education (Autor et al. 2008).

It is also possible that income inequality has resulted from family demographic and structure changes. Researchers examine inequality among American families with children and find that from 1975 to 2005, the variance in incomes of American families with children has increased by two-thirds. Disparities in education and single parenthood contribute to income inequality, but rising educational attainment and women's employment offset these effects. Most of the increase in family income inequality is due to increasing within-group inequality, which is widely shared across family types and levels of schooling (Western et al. 2008). A study documents the trends of family structure and income inequality during 1976–2000 and argues that single mother families are always at the bottom of the income distribution, contributing to their greater income inequality within the group (Martin 2006). A researcher uses matched data for parents and siblings in Israel to decompose the sibling correlation in schooling and earnings. Findings suggest that sibling interaction plays a more important role than child-parent interaction in explaining sibling correlation in schooling and earning. Sibling size is negatively associated with schooling and earning. Thus, decreasing sibling size is one possible way to reduce income inequality (Beenstock 2008). A study examines income inequality among retired households and finds that inequality of investment income has contributed most to for retired singles and couples (Xiao et al. 1999).

Skill mismatch may be another important reason of income inequality. Research indicates that skill mismatch is a significant source of inequality in real earnings in the USA and that a substantial fraction of the increase in wage dispersion during the period 1973–2002 was due to the increase in mismatch rates and mismatch premia. In 2000–2002, surplus and deficit qualifications taken together accounted for 4.3–4.6 % of the variance of log earnings, or around 15 % of the total explained variance. The dramatic increase in over-education rates and premia accounts for around 20–48 % of the increase in the Gini coefficient during the 30 years under analysis for males and females respectively (Slonimczyk 2013).

Income inequality may become more serious and last forever if no systematic reform of the global economic system occurs. In 2014, a book entitled *Capital in the Twenty-first Century* describing the root reason of income inequality from a global perspective became a *New York Times* bestseller. The author, Thomas Piketty, is a French economist. Based on his long term rigid research of tax records of many countries, he asserts that when the rate of return on capital is greater than the rate of economic growth over the long term, the result is concentration of wealth, and this unequal distribution of wealth causes social and economic instability. Piketty proposes a global system of progressive wealth taxes to help reduce inequality and avoid the vast majority of wealth coming under the control of a tiny minority (Piketty 2014).

8.4 Intergenerational Transfer of Economic Status

8.4.1 Definition and Trends

Intergenerational transfers refer to resource transfers from one generation to the other that may affect consumer economic wellbeing. Such transfers are categorized to two types: private transfers and public transfers. In the current world, private transfers are from the old generation to the young generation in most countries.

But in the field of public transfers, there is evidence showing that the transfer direction is from the young to the old in many developed countries. In the aging society, this raises a question of whether this pattern can be sustainable (Lee 2013).

Intergenerational transfer is relevant to redistribution economic policies. Early research on the statistical relationship between parents' and their children's economic status after becoming adults found only a weak connection and thus seemed to confirm that the USA was indeed the "land of opportunity." But more recent research shows that the estimates of high levels of intergenerational mobility are artifacts of two types of measurement errors: mistakes in reporting income, particularly when individuals are asked to recall the income of their parents, and transitory components in current income uncorrelated with underlying permanent income. When corrected, the intergenerational correlations for economic status appear to be substantial, many of them three times the average of the US studies surveyed by Becker and Tomes (1986).

8.4.2 Relevant Factors

On the basis of these and other empirical regularities, researchers conclude that the intergenerational transmission of economic status is accounted for by a heterogeneous collection of mechanisms, including the genetic and cultural transmission of cognitive skills and noncognitive personality traits in demand by employers, the inheritance of wealth and income-enhancing group memberships, such as race, and the superior education and health status enjoyed by the children of higher status families. Researchers find that the combined inheritance processes operating through superior cognitive performance and educational attainments of those with well-off parents, while important, explain at most three-fifths of the intergenerational transmission of economic status. Moreover, while genetic transmission of earnings-enhancing traits appears to play a role, the genetic transmission of IQ appears to be relatively unimportant. Most economic models treat one's income as the sum of the returns to the factors of production one brings to the market, like skills, or capital goods. But *any* individual trait that affects income and for which parent-offspring similarity is strong will contribute to the intergenerational transmission of economic success, including race, geographical location, height, beauty or other aspects of physical appearance, health status and personality (Bowles and Gintis 2002).

8.4.3 Reasons and Motivations

The major cause for intergenerational transfer of earning may be the intergenerational transmission of ability. Researchers present a simple model of investment and intergenerational decision making that can be interpreted as a conceptual aggregation of many more detailed economic models. From the model they derive one class of predictions about the role of endowments and credit markets in determining intergenerational correlations. The theory asserts that intergenerational earnings mobility is determined by the transmission of ability. Parents can transfer consumption between generations and among siblings using bequests. When credit constraints are considered, middle-earning families may be most susceptible to credit constraints; earnings mobility then would be least prevalent among families in the middle of the parent earnings distribution (Grawe and Mulligan 2002).

A researcher provides a theoretical analysis by modeling the dynamics of the earnings distribution among successive generations of workers as a stochastic process. The process arises from the random assignment of abilities to individuals by nature, together with the utility maximizing bequest decisions of their parents. The model assumes that parents cannot borrow to make human capital investments in their offspring. Consequently the allocation of training resources among the young people of any generation depends upon the distribution of earnings among their parents. This implies in turn that the often noted conflict between egalitarian redistributive policies and economic efficiency is mitigated (Loury 1981).

Four possible reasons for intergenerational transfer are proposed based on a literature review. The first reason is altruistic concern for one's children. The second reason is that parents and children form an incomplete annuities market. The third reason is that individuals may simply strike it rich in their professions and investments or save too much in working years and find themselves unable to consume all their resources. The fourth reason is that the transfer from parents to children is the implicit payment by parents to their children for providing in kind services, such as assisting with chores, trips to the doctor, and so on (Kotlikoff 1988).

Researchers also examine the motivations of private transfers, focusing on whether it is for altruism or exchange purposes. They analyze data from the National Survey of Families and Households and find that empirical patterns for inter-vivos transfers (i.e., transfers between living persons) are more consistent with the exchange than altruism purpose (Cox and Rank 1992).

Evidence from some developing countries shows that private transfers of money and times are motivated by exchange purposes. Using data from Indonesia, researchers show that the extent of exchange and underlying motivations differ across families but substantial evidence supports the theory that transfers within families serve as insurance for family members. The results also suggest that between some parents and children money is exchanged for time. Additionally, some evidence is consistent with the idea that parents pay for their children's education partly as a loan that is later repaid. Compared to results obtained previously for Malaysia using similar data and methods, the findings regarding motivations for transfers are remarkably similar across the two countries (Frankenberg et al. 2002).

8.4.4 International Comparison

Evidence shows variations of intergenerational transfer of earnings between countries. Based on a research review, most US studies that used multiyear measures of father's earnings and measured son's earnings after his first few years in the labor market estimated the intergenerational earnings elasticity at about 0.4 or higher. After comparing international studies on this topic, the researcher concludes that the USA and the UK appear to be less mobile societies than Canada, Finland, and Sweden (Solon 2002). By making more efficient use of the available information in the Panel Study of Income Dynamics (PSID), researchers generate reliable estimates of the recent time series variation in intergenerational mobility. Their results, which pertain to the cohorts born between 1952 and 1975, do not reveal major changes in intergenerational mobility (Lee and Solon 2009).

8.4.5 Effects of Private Transfer of Wealth on Health

Inheritance is considered as private transfer of wealth. Evidence shows that inheritance may have beneficial effects on health. Using data from PSID, a researcher examines the relationship between inheritance and health, finding that when all groups are pooled together, there are no causal effects of the amount or the receipt of an inheritance on health. However, when effects are allowed to differ across gender or whether individuals expected to receive a bequest, causal effects of inheritances are found. The health of men is worse after the receipt of an inheritance relative to that of women. Furthermore, those who expect to receive an inheritance are better off after receiving an inheritance (Carman 2013).

8.4.6 Effects of Intergenerational Transfer on Wealth

Economists disagree regarding the major source of wealth accumulation; some argue wealth accumulates from life cycle savings while others argue the accumulation is a result of international transfers. Modigliani (1988) examines evidence from seven studies largely relying on independent methods but using broadly similar, customary definitions and concludes that the share of wealth received by transfer does not exceed one-fourth, which is used to defend his life-cycle model.

However, more economists find evidence that wealth accumulation is mainly from intergenerational transfers. Using historical US data to directly estimate the contribution of intergenerational transfers to aggregate capital accumulation, research indicates that intergenerational transfers account for the vast majority of aggregate US capital formation; only a negligible fraction of actual capital accumulation can be traced to life-cycle or "hump" savings. They believe that life-cycle models of savings that emphasize savings for retirement as the dominant form of capital accumulation should give way to models that illuminate the determinants of intergenerational transfers (Kotlikoff and Summers 1981).

Using data from the 1983–1986 Survey of Consumer Finance, researchers find that intended transfers, such as gifts from parents to adult children living in a separate household, are the source of at least 20 % of aggregate wealth. Actual wealth due to intended transfers is likely to be higher, and possibly much higher. Bequests, setting aside the question of whether they are intended, account for an additional 31 % of net worth. Finally, inter-vivos transfers are about half as large as transfers that occur upon the death of the donor (Gale and Scholz 1994).

8.4.7 Effects of Social Policy on Private Transfers

Social policy intervention may alter private transfer behaviors. Researchers examine the influences of social expenditures and social services on financial support and practical help from older parents to their adult children based on data from the Survey of Health, Aging and Retirement in Europe. They find that social policy plays an important role for intergenerational transfer patterns. Particularly, the more public assistance is provided to citizens, the more likely parents are to support their adult children financially and practically, but this support is less intense in terms of money and time given. Thus, the analyses support the hypothesis that posits a division of labor between family and state for downward intergenerational transfers (Brandt and Deindl 2013).

Social welfare systems can be considered a form of public transfers. Evidence shows that international transfers of welfare receipts may occur. With data from the PSID, a researcher compares daughters from low-income families who did not receive Aid to Families with Dependent Children (AFDC) to daughters from low-income families who did receive assistance to better account for family income in the intergenerational association of AFDC. She finds that women whose families received AFDC during their childhood are more likely to receive AFDC as adults relative to those women whose families did not receive AFDC. Controlling for family income explains part but not all of the effects of childhood AFDC receipt. Among daughters from chronically poor families, parental AFDC use is not associated with additional years of AFDC participation. The findings suggest that the intergenerational transmission of financial resources does explain part of the intergenerational association of welfare use (Martin 2003).

Tax policies may influence private transfers. Researchers have used the Luxembourg Income Study data to explore the impact of taxes and transfer payments on the distribution of income across 13 countries for different years. The five-parameter generalized beta distribution and ten of its special cases are considered as models for the size distribution of income. The results identify the best-fitting two-, three-, and four-parameter models as well as describe the inter-temporal patterns of inequality corresponding to earnings, total income, and disposable income. A general pattern of increasing inequality is observed for almost all countries considered along with significantly different distributional impacts of taxes and transfer payments across countries (Dastrup et al. 2007).

8.4.8 Intergenerational Transfer: A Sociological Perspective

Economists typically focus on the intergenerational transmission of income or wealth in regard to inheritance of inequality. In contrast, sociologists are more likely to analyze intergenerational mobility between different class positions. Sociologists' results relating to the mobility regimes that operate within class structures are more complex, since it is supposed that the association between class origins and destinations may vary in strength across the component cells of the mobility table—that is, from one intergenerational transition to another. The main findings from recent sociological research are summarized as follows: (1) in all modern societies, significant associations between class of origin and class of destination prevail; (2) there is a general propensity for intergenerational class *im*mobility through the operation of class-specific inheritance effects; (3) within particular societies, mobility regimes show a high degree of constancy over time; (4) educational attainment is a major—probably *the* major—mediating factor in class mobility; (5) modern societies are not meritocracies in the sense that, once educational qualifications and other "merit" variables are controlled, class of destination is no longer dependent on class of origin; and (6) the mediating role of education varies significantly in its importance from one type of intergenerational transition to another (Erikson and Goldthorpe 2002).

8.5 Low Income Consumers

For an individual, living in poverty is an indicator of economic ill-being. A lower poverty rate is an indicator of consumer well-being at a collective level. According to a US Census report, in 2012, the official poverty rate is 15.0 % and 46.5 million people are in poverty. The poverty rate in 2012 is close to the highest since 2000. Female headed households are more likely to be in poverty than couple and male headed households (30.9 % vs. 6.3 % and 16.4 %). Black and Hispanic Americans are more likely than white non-Hispanic and Asian Americans to be in poverty (27.2 % and 25.6 % vs. 9.7 % and 12.7 %). Children under 18 are more likely than adults and elders (65 or older) to be in poverty (21.8 % vs. 13.7 % and 9.1 %) (DeNavas-Walt et al. 2013).

Having no health insurance is another indicator of economic ill-being. Based on a US Census report, in 2012, the percentage of Americans without health insurance is 15.4 % (48 million Americans). Hispanic, African, and Asian Americans are less likely than European Americans to have health insurance (rates of lack of coverage are 29.1 %, 19.0 %, 15.1 % vs. 11.1 %, respectively). Rates of lack of coverage are higher than average among young and middle aged adults, age 19–25 (27.2 %), 26–34 (27.2 %), and 35–44 (21.1 %). Lower income Americans are more likely to be uninsured. Rates of lack of coverage for Americans with household income less than $25,000 and $25,000–$49,999 are 24.9 % and 21.4 %, respectively, compared to those with household income $50,000–$74,999 and $75,000 or higher for which the rates are 15.0 % and 7.9 %, respectively (DeNavas-Walt et al. 2013). On March 23, 2010, President Obama signed the Affordable Care Act into law. The law puts in place comprehensive health insurance reforms that will roll out over four years and beyond, with most changes taking place by 2014. This new law expects to provide health insurance coverage for more Americans who are currently uninsured (About the law 2010).

8.5.1 Economic Issues Faced by Low Income Consumers

Low-income families are facing a different set of financial issues compared to their higher income counterparts, such as financial service access, asset accumulation, home ownership, credit use, and health insurance access (Garasky et al. 2008; Xiao et al. 2010). Low-income individuals often reside in high-density, low-to-moderate income (LMI) communities that often display minority and ethnic enclave characteristics or geographical isolation characteristics (such as rural communities or tribal areas). Access to affordable financial products and services becomes a function of limited income (for example, lack of auto ownership) along with geographical-spatial considerations (for example, limited or nonexistent public transportation and geographical isolation). Such limitations create barriers to conveniently accessing affordable financial services for LMI individuals and families. Payday lenders and check-cashing outlets tend to concentrate in high-density LMI communities (Graves 2003; Immergluck 2004; Praeger 2009). In addition, LMI communities can be characterized as supplier-driven, cash-oriented economies and markets (Robles 2007, 2009a).

Low-income individuals are more likely to be the unbanked (Berry 2004; Washington 2006). The bulk of the research on the unbanked has focused mainly on the recently arrived immigrant or immigrant legacy LMI individuals and families (Perry 2008). For recent immigrants, learning the host country's culture and social system would help them in effective consumer decision making (Ogden et al. 2004). In addition, research is exploring how recently arrived immigrants assimilate into host communities in the unit of '"communities"' instead of "individuals" (Hatton and Leigh 2011). In high-density immigrant and immigrant legacy communities, saving behaviors occur outside of mainstream financial institutions and often in an extended family or communal context (Chang 2010; Chung-Hevener 2006; Robles 2007, 2009a). Research indicates that the unbanked often seek out businesses that engage in predatory practices and charge excessive fees and prices, possibly leading to further economic distress (Rhine et al. 2006).

8.5.2 *Policies for Helping Low Income Consumers*

Started in the 1990s, the anti-poverty policy moved to help low-income individuals and households build assets or wealth (Blank 2002). Lifting welfare eligibility limits on the value of a vehicle resulted in the greater likelihood that low-income individuals and families could own a car (Sullivan 2006). Automobile ownership is important because it provides access to employment opportunities (Garasky et al. 2006) and affordable financial services that are rarely located in inner cities or LMI communities (Graves 2003; Praeger 2009). Partially under the rubric of asset building, government has intensified efforts to promote low-income homeownership in the early to mid-2000s prior to the housing crisis (Belsk et al. 2005). However, the targeting of subprime financial products in LMI communities—and specifically, communities of color has exacerbated the wealth divide and created uncertainty surrounding future nuclear family homeownership opportunities. The continuing high national unemployment rate has contributed to a return to 1930s-style intergenerational households with adult children moving in with elder parents in order to protect assets and minimize depletion of savings (PEW Research Center 2010). Recent lump-sum tax refund research indicates that LMI families do display future-oriented financial behaviors and asset building resiliency focused on children's educational expenditures and family communal mobility aspirations (Garcia 2009; Robles 2009b). Research also indicates that experiential knowledge contributes to cognitive ease and familiarity with financial services and products even for limited income individuals and households (Tescher et al. 2007).

8.5.3 *Earned Income Tax Credit (EITC)*

Earned Income Tax Credit (EITC), a federal tax credit for low- and moderate-income working consumers, is designed to encourage and reward work as well as to offset federal payroll and income taxes. To claim the credit, a taxpayer must have earnings from a job. The EITC is "refundable," meaning that if it exceeds a low-wage worker's federal income tax liability, the Internal Revenue Service refunds the balance to the taxpayer. The EITC's primary recipients are working parents with children, though a small portion of EITC is available to working adults without dependent children. The credit rises with earned income until it reaches a maximum (which varies by the number of qualified children) and then phases out as income rises further. In 2010, 27.5 million low income consumers used EITC (Marr et al. 2013). Caputo (2011) provides detailed accounts on the history, research and policy evaluation of earned income tax credit (EITC).

The EITC signifies, namely a move away from the idea of "income maintenance" as a primary rationale to one of employment or job readiness first. This is important for many reasons. Income maintenance, the idea behind the AFDC program, which TANF replaced in 1996 but which the expansion of the EITC program in part made possible, and behind the Social Security Act of 1935, which created the Social Security Program (OASDI), was predicated on the desire to ensure low-income families and retirees and their dependents, a stream of income to consume. The EITC program and efforts to privatize Social Security signify erosion to the commitments of income maintenance (R. Caputo, personal communication, September 2, 2014). In addition, approximately half the states and the District of Columbia also have passed EITC legislation (IRS 2014).

For 2013, the phase-outs begin at $17,530 for single filers and $22,870 for married filers, with the average size of the credit expected to be $2,828 for a family with children and $280 for a family without children. Detailed and updated information on who are qualified for EITC and how to apply for it is available from the Internal Revenue Service (IRS) website: http://www.irs.gov/Individuals/EITC-Home-Page--It%E2%80%99s-easier-than-ever-to-find-out-if-you-qualify-for-EITC.

EITC has many positive impacts on economic wellbeing for utilizing families and the society. EITC significantly increases the work effort of its recipients. This program has enhanced child wellbeing by improving the health of infants, educational outcomes for young children in low-income households, and boosting work effort and earnings extending into the next generation. For society, EITC reduces poverty and provides a short-term safety net for most of its recipients (for more details, see a research summary by Marr et al. 2013). The following are a few of such studies with more details.

EITC may have positive impacts on household economic behavior. Based on data collected from 194 black, Latino, and white parents who received EITC refunds of at least $1,000, researchers find that the majority of households (57 %) report that they plan to allocate a considerable portion of their refund to savings, and 39 % are estimated to accomplish their goal. Although 72 % of the sample plan to pay bills and debt with the refund, 84 % are found to do so. The results also suggest that households often readjust planned allocations to meet emergencies, debt, and bills. Despite setbacks, many recipients have significant asset accumulation goals, which they say are fueled by the expectation of ongoing annual tax refunds (Mendenhall et al. 2012).

EITC may improve low income consumers' subjective wellbeing. Researchers use data from the National Survey of Families and Households to study the impact of the 1990 federal EITC expansion on several outcomes related to mental health and subjective wellbeing. Results suggest that the 1990 EITC reform has generated sizeable health benefits for low-skilled mothers. Such women have experienced lower depression symptomatology, an increase in self-reported happiness, and improved self-efficacy relative to their childless counterparts. Consistent with previous research, married mothers have captured most of the health benefits, with unmarried mothers' health changing very little following the 1990 EITC reform (Boyd-Swan et al. 2013).

EITC may have positive impacts on child wellbeing for those whose families use it. Researchers estimate the causal effect of income on children's math and reading achievement based on an instrumental variable derived from EITC expansion.

The largest of these changes has increased family income by as much as 20 %, or approximately $2,100, between 1993 and 1997. The baseline estimates imply that a $1,000 increase in income raises combined math and reading test scores by 6 % of a standard deviation in the short run. Test gains are larger for children from disadvantaged families and robust to a variety of alternative specifications (Dahl and Lochner 2012). Researchers examine the impact of EITC on infant health outcomes. They find that increased EITC income reduces the incidence of low birth weight and increases mean birth weight. For single low education (<=12 years) mothers, an increase of $1,000 in EITC income is associated with 6.7–10.8 % reduction in the low birth weight rate, with larger impacts for births to African American mothers. They consider that part of the mechanism for this improvement in birth outcomes is the result of more prenatal care and less negative health behaviors (smoking). They also demonstrate EITC's potential for positive external benefits of the social safety net (Hoynes et al. 2012).

8.6 High Income Consumers: The Top 1 %

8.6.1 Trends

High income is desirable from an individual consumer's perspective. However, the concentration of high income in a small portion of a population can be an indicator of consumer economic ill-being at a collective level, signifying economic inequality. Researchers have documented trends of the top 1 % income and wealth share from international and historical perspectives. The top 1 % income share has more than doubled in the USA over the last 30 years. While other English-speaking countries have also experienced sharp increases in the top 1 % income share, many high-income countries such as Japan, France, or Germany have seen much less increase in top income shares (Alvaredo et al. 2013).

8.6.2 Influencing Factors

Researchers have identified four causing factors from the international and historical perspective: (1) Top tax rates have moved in the opposite direction from top income shares; (2) The labor pay is determined by bargaining and the reactions to top rate cuts may lead simply to a redistribution of surplus; (3) Private wealth has followed a U-shaped path over time, particularly in Europe, where inherited wealth is making a return in Europe; and (4) The correlation between earned income and capital income has substantially increased in recent decades in the USA (Alvaredo et al. 2013).

Researchers find that those in the Forbes 400 are less likely to have inherited their wealth or to have grown up wealthy. The Forbes 400 of today also are those who are able to access education while young and apply their skills to the most scalable industries: technology, finance, and mass retail. Researchers believe that the US evidence on income and wealth shares for the top 1 % is most consistent with a "superstar"-style explanation rooted in the importance of scale and skill-biased technological change. It is less consistent with an argument that the gains to the top 1 % are rooted in greater managerial power or changes in social norms about what managers should earn (Kaplan and Rauh 2013).

Household capital income may cause income inequality. Using micro-data from the Cross-National Equivalent File for three prominent panel studies in the UK, Germany, and the USA, researchers use the factor decomposition method to examine household capital income on income inequality. The factor decomposition of disposable income into single income components shows that capital income is exceedingly volatile and that its share in disposable income has risen in recent years. Moreover, capital income makes a disproportionately high contribution to overall inequality in relation to its share in disposable income, which applies to Germany and USA in particular (Fräßdorf et al. 2011).

Other researchers believe that the increase in the incomes and wages of the top 1 % over the last three decades should be interpreted as driven largely by the creation and/or redistribution of economic rents, and not simply as the outcome of well-functioning competitive markets rewarding skills or productivity based on marginal differences. This rise in rents accruing to the top 1 % could be the result of increased opportunities for rent-shifting, increased incentives for rent-shifting, or a combination of both. Consequently, this rise in incomes at the very top has been the primary impediment to having growth in living standards for low- and moderate-income households approach the growth rate of economy-wide productivity (Bivens and Mishel 2013).

Researchers have explored five possible reasons why the US political system has failed to counterbalance rising inequality. First, both Republicans and many Democrats have experienced an ideological shift towards acceptance of a form of free market capitalism that offers less support for government provision of transfers, lower marginal tax rates for those with high incomes, and deregulation of a number of industries. Second, immigration and low turnout of the poor have combined to make the distribution of voters more weighted to high incomes than reflecting the distribution of households. Third, rising real income and wealth has made a larger fraction of the population less attracted to turning to government for social insurance. Fourth, the rich have been able to use their resources to influence electoral, legislative, and regulatory processes through campaign contributions, lobbying, and revolving door employment of politicians and bureaucrats. Fifth, the political process is distorted by institutions that reduce the accountability of elected officials to the majority and hampered by institutions that combine with political polarization to create policy gridlock (Bonica et al. 2013).

8.6.3 Consequences of Top 1 %

Research indicates that countries with more inequality at one point in time also experience less earnings mobility across the generations, a relationship that has been called "The Great Gatsby Curve." The interaction between families, labor markets, and public policies all structure a child's opportunities and determine the extent to which adult earnings are related to family background—but they do so in different ways across national contexts. Both cross-country comparisons and the underlying trends suggest that these drivers are all configured most likely to lower, or at least not raise, the degree of intergenerational earnings mobility for the next generation of Americans coming of age in a more polarized labor market. This trend will likely continue unless there are changes in public policy that promote the human capital of children in a way that offers relatively greater benefits to the relatively disadvantaged (Corak 2013). An influential economics scholar believes increase of top 1 % of income may not be bad for the society and discusses what economic policies should be adopted to deal with this phenomenon (Mankiw 2013).

8.6.4 Economic Policies

Researchers believe that because the rise in top incomes is largely driven by rents, there is the potential for checking (or even reversing) this rise through policy measures with little to no adverse impact on overall economic growth. They suggest two complementary approaches for policymakers wishing to reverse the rise in the top 1 %'s share of income: dismantling the institutional sources of their increased ability to channel rents their way and reducing the return to this rent-seeking by significantly increasing marginal rates of taxation on high incomes (Bivens and Mishel 2013).

8.7 Summary

Income is an important indicator of consumer economic wellbeing. Increase in income is usually considered as improvement of economic wellbeing. Income is not only a measure of economic status and it can also be used for determining social status and social welfare use. There are variations among groups within countries. In the USA, gender, racial, and family type differences are obvious. Income sources of the poor, middle class, and rich are very different.

Research indicates that schooling and cognitive ability are important factors of earning. But there are other noncognitive factors that influence earning too. In addition, schooling not only enhances students' cognitive ability but also other abilities to increase their earning potential in labor markets. Higher education contributes to a consumer's earning ability significantly.

Income inequality is considered an indicator of economic ill-being at a collective level. The trend of income inequality is getting worse in recent years in the USA and other countries. Governments have responsibilities to curb the further increase of income inequality to avoid social and economic crises since individual persons and firms cannot help with these issues.

Intergenerational transfer is a way to transfer economic resources between generations. The trend is moving from private transfers to public transfers. Research indicates that economic wellbeing can be transferred across generations. In private transfers, research evidences support the exchange theory in which parents who help children expect children's return services for their old age care giving. The social trend is moving from private transfer to public transfer and from the old helping the young to the young helping old. If society is going to be aging, this transfer pattern may not be sustainable.

Consumers in poverty are considered to be experiencing economic ill-being. There are many unique economic issues faced by low income consumers. To help these consumers to increase income, governments develop specific policies. Earned income tax credit is such a policy, which is to encourage low income consumers to work by returning taxes more than their earnings as incentives.

Researchers have discussed the trends and consequences of the extremely high income group and impacts on social development. They also discuss causes and policy recommendations to deal with potentially negative impacts of the top 1 % income group on society.

References

About the law (2010). Retried from http://www.healthcare.gov/law/about/index.html

Acemoglu, D. (2002). Technical change, inequality, and the labor market. *Journal of Economic Literature, 40*(1), 7–72.

Alvaredo, F., Atkinson, A. B., Piketty, T., & Saez, E. (2013). The top 1 percent in international and historical perspective. *Journal of Economic Perspective, 27*(3), 3–20.

Anand, S., & Segal, P. (2008). What do we know about global income inequality? *Journal of Economic Literature, 46*(1), 57–94.

Autor, D., Katz, L., & Kearney, M. (2008). Trends in U.S. wage inequality: Revising the revisionists. *The Review of Economics and Statistics, 90*(2), 300–323.

Becker, G. S., & Tomes, N. (1986). Human capital and the rise and fall of families. *Journal of Labor Economics, 4*(3), S1–S39.

Beenstock, M. (2008). Deconstructing the sibling correlation: How families increase inequality. *Journal of Family and Economic Issues, 29*(3), 325–345.

Belsk, E., Retsinas, N., & Duda, M. (2005, September). *The financial returns to low-income home ownership.* Joint Center for Housing Studies Working Paper W05-9. Cambridge, MA: Harvard University.

Berry, C. (2004, February). *To bank or not to bank? A survey of low-income households.* Joint Center for Housing Studies Working Paper BABC 04-3. Cambridge, MA: Harvard University.

Bivens, J., & Mishel, L. (2013). The pay of corporate executives and financial professionals as evidence of rents in top 1 percent incomes. *Journal of Economic Perspective, 27*(3), 57–78.

Blank, R. (2002). Evaluating welfare reform in the United States. *Journal of Economic Literature, 40*, 1105–1166.

Bricker, J., Kennickell, A. B., Moore, K. B.. & Sabelhaus, J. (2012). Changes in US family finances from 2007 to 2010: Evidence from the Survey of Consumer Finances. Federal Reserve Bulletin, 100, 1–80.

Bonica, A., McCarty, N., Poole, K. T., & Rosenthal, H. (2013). Why hasn't democracy slowed rising inequality? *Journal of Economic Perspective, 27*(3), 103–124.

Bourguignon, F., & Morrisson, C. (2002). Inequality among world citizens: 1820-1992. *The American Economic Review, 92*(4), 727–744.

Bowles, S., & Gintis, H. (2002). The inheritance of inequality. *The Journal of Economic Perspectives, 16*(3), 3–30.

Bowles, S., Gintis, H., & Osborne, M. (2001). The determinants of earnings: A behavioural approach. *Journal of Economic Literature, 39*(4), 1137–1176.

Boyd-Swan, C., Herbst, C. M., Ifcher, J., & Zarghamee, H. (2013). *The earned income tax credit, health, and happiness. Discussion Paper Series* (Vol. 7261). Bonn: Forschungsinstitut zur Zukunft der Arbeit.

Brandt, M., & Deindl, C. (2013). Intergenerational transfers to adult children in Europe: Do social policies matter? *Journal of Marriage and Family, 75*(1), 235–251.

Caputo, R. K. (2011). *U.S. social welfare reform: Policy transitions from 1981 to the present.* New York: Springer.

Carman, K. G. (2013). Inheritances, intergenerational transfers, and the accumulation of health. *American Economic Review, 103*(3), 451–455.

Chang, M. (2010). *Lifting as we climb: Women of color, wealth, and America's future. Racial wealth divide monograph.* Oakland, CA: Insight Center for Community and Economic Development.

Chung-Hevener, C. (2006). *Alternative financial vehicles: Rotating Savings and Credit Associations (ROSCAS)*, Working Paper, Community Development Division of the Federal Reserve Bank of Philadelphia. Retrieved from http://www.philadelphiafed.org/community-development/publications/discussion-papers/discussionpaper-ROSCAs.pdf

Corak, M. (2013). Income inequality, equality of opportunity, and intergenerational mobility. *Journal of Economic Perspective, 27*(3), 79–102.

Cox, D., & Rank, M. R. (1992). Inter-vivos transfers and intergenerational exchange. *The Review of Economics and Statistics, 74*, 305–314.

Dahl, G. B., & Lochner, L. (2012). The impact of family income on child achievement: Evidence from the earned income tax credit. *The American Economic Review, 102*(5), 1927–1956.

Dastrup, S. R., Hartshorn, R., & McDonald, J. B. (2007). The impact of taxes and transfer payments on the distribution of income: A parametric comparison. *Journal of Economic Inequality, 5*(3), 353–369.

DeNavas-Walt, C., Proctor, B. D., & Smith, J. C. (2013). *Income, poverty, and health insurance coverage in the United States: 2012. U.S. Census Bureau, Current Population Reports, P60-245.* Washington, DC: U.S. Government Printing Office.

DiMaggio, P., & Bonikowski, B. (2008). Make money surfing the web? The impact of internet use on the earnings of U.S. workers. *American Sociological Review, 73*(2), 227–250.

Duncan, G. J., & Dunifon, R. (1998). Soft-skills and long-run market success. *Research in Labor Economics, 17*, 123–150.

Erikson, R., & Goldthorpe, J. H. (2002). Intergenerational inequality: A sociological perspective. *The Journal of Economic Perspectives, 16*(3), 31–44.

Frankenberg, E., Lillard, L., & Willis, R. J. (2002). Patterns of intergenerational transfers in Southeast Asia. *Journal of Marriage and Family, 64*(3), 627–641.

Fräßdorf, A., Grabka, M. M., & Schwarze, J. (2011). The impact of household capital income on income inequality—A factor decomposition analysis for the UK, Germany and the USA. *Journal of Economic Inequality, 9*(1), 35–56.

Gale, W. G., & Scholz, J. K. (1994). Intergenerational transfers and the accumulation of wealth. *The Journal of Economic Perspectives, 8*(4), 145–160.

Garasky, S., Fletcher, C. N., & Jensen, H. H. (2006). Transiting to work: The role of private transportation for low-income households. *Journal of Consumer Affairs, 40*(1), 64–89.

Garasky, S., Nielsen, R. B., & Fletcher, C. N. (2008). Consumer finances of low-income families. In J. J. Xiao (Ed.), *Handbook of consumer finance research* (pp. 223–238). New York: Springer.
Garcia, J. (2009). Preliminary findings from Demos' low-to-middle income household survey, 2008. *Demos Fact Sheet: Credit Card Debt.* Retrieved from http://www.demos.org/pubs/ccdebt_factsheet.pdf
Gottschalk, P. (1997). Inequality, income growth, and mobility: The basic facts. *The Journal of Economic Perspectives, 11*(2), 21–40.
Gottschalk, P., & Danziger, S. (2005). Inequality of wage rates, earnings and family income in the United States, 1975-2002. *The Review of Income and Wealth, 51*(2), 231–254.
Gottschalk, P., & Moffitt, R. (2009). The rising instability of US earnings. *The Journal of Economic Perspectives, 23*, 3–24.
Graves, S. (2003). Landscapes of predation, landscapes of neglect: A location analysis of payday lender and banks. *The Professional Geographer, 55*, 303–317.
Grawe, N. D., & Mulligan, C. B. (2002). Economic interpretations of intergenerational correlations. *The Journal of Economic Perspectives, 16*(3), 45–58.
Hatton, T., & Leigh, A. (2011). Immigrants assimilate as communities, not just as individuals. *Journal of Population Economics, 24*, 389. doi:10.1007/s00148-009-0277-0.
Hoxby, C. (2009). The changing selectivity of American colleges. *The Journal of Economic Perspectives, 23*(4), 95–118.
Hoynes, H. W., Miller, D. L., & Simon, D. (2012). *Income, the earned income tax credit, and infant health (No. w18206).* Cambridge, MA: National Bureau of Economic Research.
Immergluck, D. (2004). Hyper-segmentation and exclusion in financial services in the U.S. The effects on low-Income and minority neighborhoods. *The Social Policy Journal, 3*(3), 25–44.
IRS. (2014). *States and local governments with earned income tax credit.* Retried from http://www.irs.gov/Individuals/States-and-Local-Governments-with-Earned-Income-Tax-Credit
Kaplan, S. N., & Rauh, J. (2013). It's the market: The broad-based rise in the return to top talent. *Journal of Economic Perspective, 27*(3), 35–56.
Kim, C., & Sakamoto, A. (2008). The rise of intra-occupational wage inequality in the United States, 1983 to 2002. *American Sociological Review, 73*(1), 129–157.
Kotlikoff, L. J. (1988). Intergenerational transfers and savings. *The Journal of Economic Perspectives, 2*(2), 41–58.
Kotlikoff, L. J., & Summers, L. H. (1981). The role of intergenerational transfers in aggregate capital accumulation. *Journal of Political Economy, 89*(4), 706–732.
Lee, R. (2013). Intergenerational transfers, the biological life cycle, and human society. *Population and Development Review, 38*(s1), 23–35.
Lee, C., & Solon, G. (2009). Trends in intergenerational income mobility. *The Review of Economics and Statistics, 91*(4), 766–772.
Loury, G. C. (1981). Intergenerational transfers and the distribution of earnings. *Econometrica, 49*, 843–867.
Mankiw, N. G. (2013). Defending the one percent. *Journal of Economic Perspective, 27*(3), 21–34.
Marr, C., Charite, J., & Huang, C. C. (2013). *Earned Income Tax Credit promotes work, encourages children's success at school, research finds (Research Brief).* Washington, DC: Center on Budget and Policy Priorities.
Martin, M. A. (2003). The role of family income in the intergenerational association of AFDC receipt. *Journal of Marriage and Family, 65*(2), 326–340.
Martin, M. A. (2006). Family structure and income inequality in families with children, 1976 to 2000. *Demography, 43*(3), 421–445.
McCall, L., & Percheski, C. (2010). Income inequality: New trends and research directions. *Annual Review of Sociology, 36*, 329–347.
Mendenhall, R., Edin, K., Crowley, S., Sykes, J., Tach, L., Kriz, K., et al. (2012). The role of earned income tax credit in the budgets of low-income households. *Social Service Review, 86*(3), 367–400.
Modigliani, F. (1988). The role of intergenerational transfers and life cycle saving in the accumulation of wealth. *The Journal of Economic Perspectives, 2*(2), 15–40.

Ogden, D. T., Ogden, J. R., & Schau, H. J. (2004). Exploring the impact of culture and acculturation on consumer purchase decisions: Toward a microcultural perspective. *Academy of Marketing Science Review, 2004*(8), 1–22.

Osborne, M. (2000). *The power of personality: Labor market rewards and the transmission of earnings. Working paper*. Amherst, MA: University of Massachusetts.

Perry, V. G. (2008). Acculturation, microculture, and banking: An analysis of Hispanic consumers in the U.S.A. *Journal of Services Marketing, 22*(6), 423–433.

PEW Research Center. (2010). *The return of the multi-generational family household*: A social and demographic trends report.

Piketty, T. (2014). *Capital in the twenty-first century*. Boston: Harvard University Press.

Praeger, R. (2009). *Determinants of the location of payday lenders, pawnshops and check-cashing outlets. Finance and Economics Discussion Series, Working Paper No. 2009–33*. Washington, DC: Division of Research & Statistics and Monetary Affairs, Federal Reserve Board.

Rhine, S. L. W., Greene, W. H., & Toussaint-Comeau, M. (2006). The importance of check-cashing businesses to the unbanked: Racial/ethnic differences. *The Review of Economics and Statistics, 88*(1), 146–157.

Robles, B. (2007). *Financial services and product usage by Latinos in the United States*. Madison, WI: Filene Research Institute.

Robles, B. (2009a). *U.S. Latino families, heads of households, and the elderly: Emerging trends in financial services and asset-building behaviors*. Madison, WI: Filene Research Institute.

Robles, B. (2009b). A tax education and asset building campaign for low-income and limited-English worker populations: Lessons from four states, TY 2004-TY 2007. In *Recent research on tax administration and compliance: Selected papers given at the 2009 IRS Research Conference* (pp. 227–252). Retrieved from http://www.irs.gov/pub/irs-soi/09rescon.pdf

Slonimczyk, F. (2013). Earnings inequality and skill mismatch in the US: 1973–2002. *Journal of Economic Inequality, 11*(2), 163–194.

Solon, G. (2002). Cross-country differences in intergenerational earnings mobility. *The Journal of Economic Perspectives, 16*(3), 59–66.

Sullivan, J. (2006). Welfare reform, saving, and vehicle ownership: Do asset limits and vehicle exemptions matter? *Journal of Human Resources, 41*, 72–105.

Tescher, J., Sawady, E., & Kutner, S. (2007). *The power of experience in understanding the underbanked market*. Center for Financial Services Innovations. Retrieved June 27, 2010 at http://cfsinnovation.com/system/files/imported/managed_documents/keybank_paper.pdf

U.S. Bureau of Labor Statistics. (2013). *Earnings and unemployment rate by educational attainment*. Retried from http://www.bls.gov/emp/ep_chart_001.htm

Washington, E. (2006). The impact of banking and fringe banking regulation on the number of unbanked Americans. *Journal of Human Resources, 41*, 106–137.

Weinberg, D. H., Nelson, C. T., Roemer, M. I., & Welniak, E. J., Jr. (1999). Fifty years of US income data from the Current Population Survey: Alternatives, trends, and quality. *American Economic Review, 89*(2), 18–22.

Western, B., Bloome, D., & Percheski, C. (2008). Inequality among American families with children, 1975 to 2005. *American Sociological Review, 73*(6), 903–920.

Wolff, E., & Zacharias, A. (2009). Household wealth and the measurement of economic well-being in the United States. *Journal of Economic Inequality, 7*(2), 83–115.

Xiao, J. J., Collins, M., Ford, M., Keller, P., Kim, J., & Robles, B. (2010). *A review of financial behavior research: Implications for financial education*. Paper presented at the NEFE Colloquium, Denver, CO.

Xiao, J. J., Malroutu, Y. L. & Yuh, Y. (1999). Sources of income inequality among the elderly. *Financial Counseling and Planning, 10*(2), 49–59.

Chapter 9
Consumer Spending

Abstract This chapter first introduces several theories on consumption such as the life cycle hypothesis, precautionary saving model, behavioral life cycle hypothesis, hyperbolic consumption model consumption benefits and costs, and decision making styles. Then the research literature related to consumer expenditures over the life cycle and in several major expenditure categories such as housing, transportation, food, and health care is described. After introducing the topic of consumer confidence, the research literature on desirable and undesirable consumption behaviors is reviewed. Desired consumption behaviors include smart shopping, sustainable consumption, ethical consumption, and socially responsible consumption. Undesirable consumption behaviors refer to conspicuous consumption, unethical consumption, compulsive buying, impulsive buying, and overspending.

9.1 Theories of Consumption

9.1.1 Life Cycle Hypothesis

Several theories of consumption have been developed in the literature such as the absolute income hypothesis (Keynes 1936), relative income hypothesis (Duesenberry 1967), life cycle hypothesis (Modigliani 1986), and the permanent income hypothesis (Friedman 1957). The life cycle hypothesis is a dominant theory in economics on consumption and saving behavior. The theory was originally proposed by the Nobel Laureate Franco Modigliani and his colleague in the 1950s (Modigliani and Brumberg 1954). The theory was later verified with macro data (Ando and Modigliani 1964), which was wildly cited as a major reference of the life cycle hypothesis. Modigliani reiterated this theory in his Nobel Prize lecture (Modigliani 1986). According to this model, consumers maximize their intertemporal utilities over the life cycle assuming that they are fully informed about their life cycle income and wealth.

In the similar time, Friedman (1957) developed his permanent income model. Theoretically, permanent income refers to a stable income flow over the life-span and transitory income is unexpected, temporary income such as bonus or lottery prize. The model assumes that consumers act as if they know their permanent income level over their life cycle and consume mainly from their permanent income and

J.J. Xiao, *Consumer Economic Wellbeing*, International Series on Consumer Science, DOI 10.1007/978-1-4939-2821-7_9

save mainly their transitory income. Both theories are influential in the economic literature. Later economists refer the two models as the life cycle permanent income model (Attanasio and Weber 2010).

The life cycle model can be loosely defined as a framework where individuals maximize utility over time given a set of intertemporal trading opportunities. This conceptual framework treats the intertemporal allocation of resources in a way which is similar to the allocation of resources among different commodities. Decisions will then depend on the total amount of resources (in the intertemporal context: current and future income as well as current wealth), on preferences over the different commodities (in the intertemporal context: present and future consumption, and possibly bequests), and on relative prices (interest rates and intertemporal trade opportunities) (Attanasio and Weber 2010). The life cycle hypothesis assumes that consumers know their life cycle wealth and they save when they are in working years and dissave when they retire. The major implication of this theory is that the main purpose of consumer activities such as saving and borrowing is to smooth consumption over the life cycle, specifically smooth consumption before and after retirement. One major contribution to this theory was made by Hall (1978) who exploited the idea of using the first-order conditions of the intertemporal optimization problem faced by the consumer to derive testable implications of the model. This approach, known as the Euler equation approach, makes it possible to empirically analyze a problem that is analytically intractable by circumventing the need to derive closed-form solutions (Attanasio and Weber 2010).

The life cycle hypothesis became dominant in the last 60 years because the theory explains facts that cannot be explained by the then dominant Keynesian model of consumption. However, the life cycle hypothesis has its own limitations identified by many economists, demonstrated by following facts that are inconsistent with its theoretical predictions: (1) The age profile of consumption is hump shaped, apparently tracking the age profile of income for each education group; (2) consumption drops at retirement; (3) the growth rate of consumption seems "too" sensitive to predictable changes in income; and (4) consumption seems to react to changes in available resources that are fully predictable and transitory, such as tax refunds (Attanasio and Weber 2010).

The life cycle model can be viewed as a general framework and many specific models dealing with specific topics can be developed based on this framework (Browning and Crossley 2001). Numerous theoretical and empirical studies are conducted based on the life cycle framework. In the following, we review several major new theories and empirical studies on life cycle behaviors.

9.1.2 Precautionary Saving Model

When consumers face important income uncertainty, they are both "prudent" that they have a precautionary saving motive and "impatient" in the sense that if future income is known with certainty they will choose to consume more than their current income (Kimball 1990). Inspired by the previous research (Deaton 1991; Kimball 1990, Zeldes 1989), Carroll (1997) has developed a buffer-stock saving model. In the model, buffer-stock savers have a target wealth-to-permanent-income ratio such that, if wealth is below the target, the precautionary saving motive dominates impatience and the consumer saves, while if wealth is above the target, impatience dominates prudence and the consumer dissaves. The model is motivated by the fact that the majority of consumers report saving for emergencies. In the traditional life cycle/permanent income model, consumption growth is determined solely by consumer preferences; in contrast, buffer-stock consumers set average consumption growth equal to average labor income growth, regardless of preferences. The model can explain three empirical puzzles: the "consumption/income parallel"; the "consumption/income divergence"; and the temporal stability of the household age/wealth profile despite the unpredictability of idiosyncratic wealth changes (Carroll 1997).

9.1.3 Behavioral Life Cycle Hypothesis

The behavior life cycle hypothesis is proposed by Shefrin and Thaler (1988). Psychological concepts such as self-control, mental accounting, and framing are incorporated in the hypothesis. The key assumption is that consumers treat components of their wealth as nonfungible. Specifically, wealth is assumed to be divided into three mental accounts, current income, current assets, and future income. The temptations to spend vary dependent upon the type of account, with the greatest for current income and least for future income. Some predictions of this theory are supported with consumer expenditure data (Levin 1998) and financial asset data (Schooley and Worden 2008; Xiao and Anderson 1997; Xiao and Olson 1993).

9.1.4 Hyperbolic Consumption Model

The hyperbolic consumption model integrates a standard economic theory of life cycle planning with a psychological theory of self-control (Angeletos et al. 2001; Laibson 1997). This model is built on three principles. First, the model adopts the standard assumptions of modern consumption models, including the ideas that consumers have uncertain future labor income and face liquidity constraints in the sense that they have limited ability to borrow against this future labor income. Second, the model extends the consumption literature by allowing consumers to borrow on credit cards and by including a partially illiquid asset in the consumers' menu of investment options. Third, the model assumes that consumers have both a short-run preference for instantaneous gratification and a long-run preference to act patiently. The model generates empirical predictions that distinguish it from the standard model with exponential discounting. First, households with hyperbolic discount functions will hold their wealth in an illiquid form, since such illiquid assets are protected from consumption splurges. Second, households with hyperbolic discount functions are very likely to borrow on their credit cards to fund instant gratification. Third, since hyperbolic households have little liquid wealth, they are unable to smooth consumption, generating a high level of comovement between income and consumption. Fourth, this comovement between income and consumption will stand out around retirement, when labor income falls and the lack of liquid wealth generates a necessary fall in consumption (Angeletos et al. 2001).

9.1.5 Benefits and Costs of Consuming

When the costs and benefits of consuming are discussed, Csikszentmihalyi (2000) argues that consuming is defined as behavior whereby entropy is increased in exchange for existential or experiential rewards. Existential rewards are well known such as the satisfaction of Maslowian needs. Experiential rewards refer to the temporary improvement in positive mood people experience when they are acting in goal-directed, purposeful ways. Consuming is one way for obtaining such experiences. In order to evaluate the impact of consuming it is necessary to measure the entropy costs of the behavior balanced against the psychic benefits it provides.

9.1.6 Decision-Making Styles

A consumer decision-making style is defined as a mental orientation characterizing a consumer's approach to making consumer choices. Researchers conceptualize eight basic characteristics of these styles and develop a Consumer Styles Inventory to measure them empirically. The eight dimensions include perfectionism or high-quality consciousness, brand consciousness, novelty-fashion consciousness, recreational, hedonistic shopping consciousness, price and "value for money" shopping consciousness, impulsiveness, confusion from overchoice, and habitual, brand-loyal orientation toward consumption (Sprotles and Kendall 1986). Based on a sample of young adults in China, similarities and differences in dimensions of these decision-making styles are found (Fan and Xiao 1998). Another study uses data from adult consumers in China and finds three market segments that are trendy and perfectionistic consumer, traditional and pragmatic consumer, as well as confused-by-overchoice consumer (Hiu et al. 2001). The similar approach is used in Germany and researchers find that six of the original US eight factors are supported. *Variety seeking* is novel to Germany that replaces brand loyalty and price-value consciousness factors found in previous countries (Walsh et al. 2001).

9.2 Consumer Expenditure

Expenditure is considered a better measure of consumption than income. In recent years, expenditures are used to measure consumer economic well-being. According to the Consumer Expenditure Survey, in 2012, the average annual household expenditure was $51,442 (U.S. Bureau of Labor Statistics 2013). Major expenditure categories are housing (32.8 % of total annual expenditure), transportation (17.5 %), food (12.8 %), and pension and social security (10.9 %) (author calculation based on raw data provided by U.S. Bureau of Labor Statistics 2013).

Another possible indicator relevant to expenditure is Engel coefficient. Engel coefficient refers to the share of food expenditure in total expenditure. The Engel's law asserts that the poorer family would spend more on food. A researcher has done extensive research and concludes that Engel's law continues to be relevant now. Within countries at the household level, evidence supporting Engel's law is strong. According to household survey data for 46 countries from around the world tabulated by income decile, food share of household expenditure falls across adjacent income deciles within each country so consistently that few exceptions are observed, and the same consistent result is found at all development levels and in all regions. At the cross-national level, evidence supporting Engel's law is also strong. According to national food share estimates for 207 countries and territories, which represent 99 % of the world's population, food share of household expenditure falls from around 50 % on average in low-income countries to around 40 % in lower middle-income countries, around 30 % in upper middle-income countries, and around 15 % in high-income countries. Food share is significantly related to income per capita in PPP, even after specification of measurement- and behavioral-related explanatory variables (Anker 2011).

Except for expenditure levels, it is not straightforward to link expenditure categories to economic well-being. A researcher examines both demographic and spending pattern changes for young, never-married adults from 1984–1985 to 2004–2005. Young singles have experienced a decrease in real total outlays, while other singles have experienced an increase during that time period. However, young singles today allocate larger shares of total outlays to food away from home and to travel, and smaller shares to food at home and to housing. The researcher concludes that whether these changes indicate an increase or decrease in economic status is unclear (Paulin 2008).

Advances in technology may drive social norms of expenditures. For example, a researcher examines cellular phone service and residential telephone service spending patterns for all consumer units and by age group from 2001 to 2006. The results show that cellular phone expenditures have increased, while residential telephone service expenditures have decreased, over that period. Wider availability and price packages that are comparable to residential telephone packages have been the main sources of this increase. Also, cellular phone expenditures are now the majority of total telephone expenditures in three younger groups (under 25, 25–34, 35–44) of the six age groups (Creech 2008).

Expenditures differ in family types. Using data from the Consumer Expenditure Survey, researchers find that cohabiting-parent families, compared to married-parent families, spend a greater amount on two adult goods (alcohol and tobacco) and a smaller amount on education. Cohabiting-parent families also differ in their spending patterns from divorced single-parent families and from never-married single-parent families (DeLeire and Kalil 2005). Families with a nonbiological mother (a step, adoptive, or foster mother) spend less on food than other two-parent families (Case et al. 2000). Similar patterns are found for health investments (Case and Paxson 2001). Single mothers are much more likely to purchase apparel and services for children than single fathers (Paulin and Lee 2002). Single-parent families spend a significantly smaller share of their budgets than do married-parent families on children's education expenses. Conversely, single-parent families spend significantly more on tobacco and alcohol products, as well as food consumed away from home, compared to married-parent families (Ziol-Guest et al. 2004).

9.2.1 Consumer Spending Over the Life Cycle

The influential life cycle model in economics suggests that consumers would smooth life cycle consumption by borrowing and saving (Ando and Modigliani 1963; Modigliani 1986). This theory suggests that the consumption pattern over the life cycle should be fairly flat. Researchers use Consumer Expenditure Survey data and a seminonparametric statistical model to estimate life cycle profiles of consumption, controlling for demographics, cohort, and time effects. They find statistically significant, reverse U-shape patterns (humps) over the life cycle for total, nondurable, and durable expenditures. Changes in household size account for roughly half of these humps. The other half remains to be explained by factors not present in the standard complete market life cycle model of consumption. If the ratio of peak consumption to consumption at age 22 is calculated, the ratio before demographic adjustment is roughly 1.6 and 1.3 thereafter. This finding is inconsistent with the basic version of the life cycle model (Fernádez-Villaverde and Krueger 2007).

In empirical studies on financial behavior over the life cycle, researchers mainly use two key independent variables, age or life cycle stages, to explain interested dependent variables such as expenditure, debt, asset, and other economic variables. When the age approach is used with multi-year data, age, cohort, and time effects are usually considered. Using the age approach, the following topics are examined such as spending patterns (Fernádez-Villaverde and Krueger 2007; Marr and McCready 2009), housing spending (Yang 2009), medical consumption (Jung and Tran 2010), social security benefits, and spending (Wilcox 1989).

The life cycle stage can be defined in a variety of ways by using marital status, age, presence of children, and other relevant variables to construct a composite variable (see Du and Kamakura 2006; Schaninger and Danko 1993 for the life cycle stage methodology). Empirical studies use the life cycle stage as an important explanatory variable in spending behavior such as expenditure patterns

(Putler et al. 2007; Wagner and Hanna 1983; Wilkes 1995), spending and home production (Hurst and Aguiar 2004), child influence on family spending (Douthitt and Fedyk 1988), expenditures on food (Blanciforti et al. 1981), out-of-pocket healthcare (Hong and Kim 2000), and tourism (Lawson 1991).

9.2.2 *Housing Expenditure*

Housing is the single largest expenditure item in the budgets of most American consumers. The average household devotes roughly one-quarter of income to housing expenditures, while poor and near-poor households commonly devote half of their incomes to housing (Quigley and Raphael 2004).

Micro data over the life cycle show different patterns in consumption for housing and non-housing goods: The consumption profile of non-housing goods is hump shaped, while the consumption profile for housing first increases monotonically and then flattens out. These patterns hold true at each consumption quartile (Yang 2009).

Racial/ethnical differences are found in housing expenditures. The amounts households spend on housing vary depending on race or Hispanic origin. Minorities spend a larger share of total expenditures on housing than do white households. When looking at consumer units that are homeowners only, the estimated market value of owned home varies significantly with factors such as income, location of homes, family size, and age of reference person as possible major contributors to these differences. Renter households apportion the same share of total expenditures to housing as homeowners do. Renters spend, on average, about two-thirds of their total housing expenditures on rent. Proportionately more black and Hispanic households are renters, compared with Asian and white consumer units. Overall, data show that black and Asian renters seem to have different spending patterns for housing (Vendemia 2008).

To examine whether or not there are housing market bubbles, researchers have developed a formula to calculate annual cost of home ownership. The annual cost includes foregone interests if renting instead of owning is used, property taxes, maintenance costs, and risk premium, while minus mortgage interests and property-related tax benefits and capital gains. Under certain assumptions, the predicted user cost is 5.0 %, that is, for every dollar of price, the owner pays 5 cents per year in cost. Leaving aside other differences between renting and owning, people should be willing to pay up to 20 times (1/0.05) the market rent to purchase a house. Hence, for example, a two-bedroom apartment that rents for $1,000/month ($12,000/year) should sell for up to $240,000 (Himmelberg et al. 2005).

For the two-thirds of US households who own homes, there is little evidence that housing has become less affordable in recent years. For the one-third of US households who are renters, the proportion of income that the median renter devotes to housing has increased only modestly. However, pronounced increases in the typical rental burdens for poor and near-poor households are found (Quigley and Raphael 2004).

For the majority of American households—including more than two-thirds of those in the top three income quintiles—housing "affordability" refers to the terms on which dwellings can be purchased and loans to purchase these assets can be amortized. In contrast, for households of lower income, for the poor, for minority households, and for many young households, "affordability" refers to the terms for rental contracts and the relationship between these rents and their low incomes. For the owner-occupied sector, lack of affordability is a problem for younger households. Here, modest changes in institutional arrangements could greatly affect the affordability of homeownership, especially for young households whose incomes will increase over the life cycle. For low-income renters, more aggressive policy is needed. Rental housing can be made affordable to low-income households through policies that increase housing supply or those that augment the purchasing power of poor households (Quigley and Raphael 2004).

9.2.3 Transportation Expenditure

Transportation expenditure is the second largest category for American consumers. The life cycle transportation expenditures differ in cohort and age. Research on age, period, and cohort effects on household transportation expenditure ratios in the USA and Japan indicates that (1) among a total of three effects, the period effect is the smallest; (2) with the exception of the latest birth cohort, the cohort effect shows a clear upward trend; and (3) the age effect decreases in the 20s and 30s, and next increases with a peak detected in the late 50s, and finally decreases (Fukuda 2010).

Increases in fuel prices may impact other household expenses. Using data from the 2002 Consumer Expenditure Survey, results show that households adjust their food consumption, vehicular purchases, and savings rates in the short run. In the long term, adjustments are also made to housing expenses (Ferdous et al. 2010).

A researcher studies vehicle-fuel expenditure allocation in multi-vehicle households based on the Almost Ideal Demand System (AIDS) with data from surveys conducted by the Energy Information Administration in 1988, 1991, and 1994, augmented with a comprehensive set of household and vehicle characteristics. Results show that vehicle characteristics are the most significant factors in the expenditure allocation process. Own-price elasticities for all vehicles are close to 1, suggesting that vehicle expenditures change at almost the same rate as the price change rate (Oladosu 2003).

9.2.4 Food Expenditure

The third largest expenditure category is food. Food expenditures have different implications for different income groups. Using the U.S. Bureau of Labor Statistics' 1992 Consumer Expenditure Survey and Detailed Monthly Consumer Price Indices, a study obtains expenditure elasticities (ratio of percentage change of food demand quantity to percentage change of food expenditure), own-price elasticities (ratio of percentage change of food demand quantity to percentage change of food price), and subsistence quantities (minimum or committed quantities) for each income group across nine broadly aggregated food commodity groups. Elasticity estimates and subsistence quantity estimates differ across income groups, supporting the premise that policies targeted at specific income groups should be based on the target group's elasticity estimates rather than average population elasticities (Raper et al. 2002).

Family type differences are found in food expenditures. Using the Consumer Expenditure Survey Diary Component (1990–2003), researchers find that single parents, compared to married parents, allocate a greater share of their food budget to alcohol and food purchased away from home. Conversely, single parents spend a smaller share of their food budget on vegetables and fruits. Compared to married parents, single fathers spend a greater share on alcohol and food purchased away from home and a lesser share on vegetables, fruits, meat and beans, desserts and snacks, and prepared foods. Single mothers, compared to married parents, spend a greater share on grains and nonalcoholic beverages and a lesser share on vegetables and alcohol. Single mothers and fathers differ from each other in almost all categories of food and beverage expenditure (Ziol-Guest et al. 2006).

Food expenditures also differ in age cohorts. Data from 23 years of the U.S. Consumer Expenditure Survey (1982–2004) are analyzed to investigate cohort effects on food-away-from-home (FAFH) expenditures using the age, period, and cohort model. Analyses reveal that later-born cohorts spend more on FAFH, both in dollar amount and in food budget share, compared with earlier-born cohorts. Significant cohort differences in FAFH remain after additional sociodemographic and economic variables are controlled (Zan and Fan 2010).

Ethnic differences in food expenditures are found too. Hispanic households allocate significantly more of their budget to food eaten at home and significantly less to food consumed away from home, compared to non-Hispanic white households (Fan and Zuiker 1998). Hispanic households devote a higher proportion of their budget to food at home (25.8 %) than the average American household, while the Hispanic proportion spent on food away from home is only 3.6 % (Lanfranco et al. 2002). Research suggests that there are statistically significant differences in budget allocations between Hispanic Americans and African Americans. Hispanic households allocate a larger proportion of their budget to both food consumed at home and food consumed away from home than African Americans, at any level of total expenditure, but less than non-Hispanic Caucasians. On average, the difference in budget share for food away from home is about 15 % between African Americans and Hispanics (Fan and Lewis 1999).

Food away from home may have negative associations with health. Using state-level data from the Behavioral Risk Factor Surveillance System, evidence suggests that food-away-from-home expenditures are positively related to obesity, while food-at-home expenditures are negatively related to obesity. However, the magnitudes of these effects, while statistically significant, are relatively small (Cai et al. 2008). Research indicates that household fast food expenditures and children's television viewing have negative effects on children's dietary quality (You and Nayga 2005).

9.2.5 Healthcare Expenditure

Healthcare expenditure is not a major expenditure category for American consumers but has increased rapidly in recent years. Total healthcare expenditures that include consumer out-of-pocket expenditure are highly concentrated in the USA, with 5 % of the population accounting for the majority of health expenditures (Berk and Monheit 2001). This concentration has proved remarkably stable over time; however, the degree of concentration has declined over the past decade. Using data from the 1996–2003 Medical Expenditure Panel Survey (MEPS), researchers find that a rapid growth in prescription drug spending, which is diffused over a large fraction of the population, versus slower growth in spending for inpatient care largely accounts for the recent change in concentration (Zuvekas and Cohen 2007).

A researcher examines the degree of convergence in per capita healthcare expenditure and its nine components across the US states from 1980 to 2004. This research provides moderate evidence of convergence in total healthcare expenditures and the diverse performance of expenditure components regarding convergence. Hospital care is responsible for the bulk of cross-state convergence in total expenditure, whereas the expenditure on prescription drugs is the most important diverging factor (Wang 2009).

Age differences are obvious. A researcher compares healthcare expenditures between the 55–64-year-old and 65–74-year-old age groups. For both age groups, the share of average annual expenditures allocated to healthcare expenditures has risen over both decades. The increase in the share of healthcare expenditures allocated to health insurance from 1985 to 2005 mirrors a decrease in healthcare expenditures allocated to medical services over the period for both groups. Consumption of healthcare increases with age, with the 65–74-year-olds spending more overall on total health care in both decades. This age group also spends more on health insurance and drugs than the 55–64-year-old group in each of the survey years, while spending less overall on medical services and about the same on medical supplies (Duetsch 2008).

Out-of-pocket healthcare expenditure patterns of households and the financial costs over the stages of the household life cycle are examined using the 1995 Consumer Expenditure Survey. Elderly households not only spend more for health care, but also experience higher financial burdens than other households (Hong and Kim 2000). Using data from the 1980–1997 Consumer Expenditure Surveys, researchers find that the seniors who have insurance coverage in addition to Medicare, on average, spend more on health care and prescription drugs than those who have Medicare coverage only (Fan et al. 2003).

End of life expenses are also significant. Using data from the Consumer Expenditure Surveys 1980–2000, researchers examine pre-widowhood shifts in medical and funeral/burial expenditures and discuss how these changes may affect post-widowhood economic well-being. Results suggest that funeral/burial and medical expenditures, when combined, typically constitute a 63.1 % income share for recently widowed households (Fan and Zick 2004).

Healthcare expenditures differ across races/ethnicities and immigration status. Researchers estimate healthcare expenditures associated with overweight and obesity and examine the influence of age, race, and gender with data from the 1998 Medical Expenditure Panel Survey. The result shows that healthcare costs associated with overweight and obesity are substantial and vary according to race and age (Wee et al. 2005). Another study examines whether black-white and Hispanic-white disparities are evident in total healthcare expenditure. Black-white and Hispanic-white disparities diminish in the upper quartiles of expenditure, but expenditures by blacks and Hispanics remain significantly lower than by whites throughout the distribution. Blacks and Hispanics receive significantly disparate care at high expenditure levels, suggesting prioritization of improved access to quality care among minorities with critical health issues (Cook and Manning 2009). Researchers compare the healthcare expenditures of immigrants residing in the USA with healthcare expenditures of US-born persons. The results show that per capita total healthcare expenditures of immigrants are 55 % lower than those of US-born persons. Similarly, expenditures for uninsured and publicly insured immigrants are approximately half those of their US-born counterparts. Immigrant children have 74 % lower per capita health care expenditures than US-born children. However, emergency department expenditures are more than three times higher for immigrant children than for US-born children. Overall, healthcare expenditures are substantially lower for immigrants than for US-born persons (Mohanty et al. 2005).

Healthcare costs are major concerns of policy makers, healthcare providers and insurers, and consumers (Sharpe 2008). The high costs are particularly evident in two aspects of healthcare expenditures: aggregate healthcare expenditures tripled in the last five decades, rising from 5.2 % of GDP in 1960 to over 16 % in 2007 (Gruber and Levy 2009). Another concern is that healthcare share of GDP in the USA is much higher than other developed countries (Sharpe 2008). Detailed analyses reveal that this rise has virtually all been absorbed by increased insurance, with little increase in out-of pocket expenses for individuals. While individuals paid almost 70 % of their medical costs out-of-pocket in 1960, that share has fallen to 26 % today. Increased spending on health has instead manifested itself primarily in rising insurance spending, particularly for the public sector. Even as healthcare costs have been rapidly rising, private insurance has remained almost as generous as before, while public insurance has gotten much more generous. The generosity is expressed in three aspects. First, health insurance has shifted from fee-to-service contracts to other cost control approaches such as health maintenance organizations. Second, portability of employer-sponsored health insurance required by law has decreased costs of those who are between jobs. Third, because of state and federal mandates, private insurance includes benefits such as substance use and maternity costs that workers may not use (Gruber and Levy 2009).

Public insurance programs mainly cover vulnerable families. Almost 40 % of children from lower education families had public coverage in 2007, nearly twice the fraction that had it in 1989. A second implicit insurance mechanism is the provision of subsidized or free care by medical providers, also known as uncompensated care. Finally, bankruptcy offers a kind of last-ditch insurance for households, both uninsured and insured ones, with medical bills that they are unable to pay. These patterns are consistent with the overall decline in the share of health spending borne by households as out-of-pocket medical spending and the general rise in risk-bearing by the public sector (Gruber and Levy 2009).

Researchers examine the cost containment performance of health maintenance organization (HMO) plans relative to non-HMOs using data from the 2000 Medical Expenditure Panel Survey. When various compounding factors are controlled for, among the privately insured, nonelderly population, HMO enrollment is found to contain neither total healthcare spending nor total insurance payment, though it reduces total out-of-pocket expenditure. The favorable cost sharing for enrollees and the distinct reimbursement schemes in HMO plans seem to account for no significant overall cost saving (Shin and Moon 2007).

To ensure healthcare coverage to most of the population, a series of public policies are enacted. In the 1960s, for example, these concerns helped lead to the establishment of Medicare for the elderly and Medicaid for the poor. In more recent decades, similar concerns have led to the Consolidated Omnibus Budget Reconciliation Act of 1986, commonly known as COBRA, which provides displaced workers continued access to employer-sponsored health insurance. Other results are the Health Insurance Portability and Accountability Act of 1996 (HIPAA), which limits the restrictions that can be placed on insurance coverage when workers change jobs and the State Children's Health Insurance Program (SCHIP), which provides subsidized health insurance coverage for low-income children. Yet another policy change is Medicare Part D, the single largest expansion of Medicare benefits since the program's inception, which has provided drug coverage for senior citizens since 2006 (Gruber and Levy 2009). The new law covers any Americans who get health benefits through work, buy insurance themselves, are on Medicare, or don't currently have insurance. It makes insurance more affordable right away by providing small businesses with a tax credit to provide coverage and, in 2014, by providing tax credits to those who need help in buying insurance. The Affordable Care Act is projected to reduce premium costs for millions of families and small-business owners who are priced out of coverage today. This could help as many as 32 million Americans who have no health care today receive coverage (About the law 2010). Recent research indicates that taking all existing coverage expansions together, 20 million Americans have gained coverage as of May 1, 2014, under the ACA. Recent national surveys seem to confirm this presumption. The Congressional Budget Office projects that the law will decrease the number of uninsured people by 12 million this year and by 26 million by 2017. Early polling data from Gallup, RAND, and the Urban Institute indicate that the number of uninsured people may have already declined by 5–9 million and that the proportion of US adults lacking insurance has fallen from 18 % in the third quarter of 2013 to 13.4 % in May 2014 (Blumenthal and Collins 2014).

9.3 Consumer Confidence

Consumer perception about the economy is measured by consumer confidence. Consumer confidence is usually used to predict future consumption of consumers. The University of Michigan's Consumer Sentiment Index and the Conference Board's Consumer Confidence Index are the most widely followed measures of US consumer confidence. The Michigan index began as an annual survey in the late 1940s. In 1952, it was converted to a quarterly survey and in 1978 to a monthly survey. The Conference Board launched its index on a bimonthly basis in 1967 and expanded it to a monthly series in 1977 (Ludvigson 2004).

Consumer confidence is usually used to predict consumer spending at the macro level of the US economy. A researcher evaluates what is known about the relationship between consumer confidence and consumer spending (Ludvigson 2004). In summary, the results on the predictability of consumer attitudes for consumer spending are somewhat mixed. For total consumer expenditures, there is modest incremental information about the future path of spending in both the Michigan and Conference Board indexes. The inclusion of both surveys' measures of expectations delivers fairly strong predictability of expenditure growth on goods (excluding motor vehicles). For other expenditure categories, however, the results are generally weaker, and for some categories of expenditure the inclusion of confidence indicators actually weakens the statistical relation between contemporaneous indicators and future consumer spending (Ludvigson 2004; Wilcox 2007). Then consumer confidence may not be a good predictor of consumer spending in all categories. Some economists examine if precautionary motives drive consumer sentiment. If precautionary motive exists, consumption growth measured from today to tomorrow should be negatively correlated with consumer sentiment today. This result is not what is found in Ludvigson (2004), nor in Carroll et al. (1994) and Bram and Ludvigson (1998), except for one study with micro data. With data from the Michigan Survey of Consumer Attitudes and Behavior (CAB), research shows that higher confidence is correlated with less saving (lower consumption growth), consistent with precautionary motives (Souleles 2004).

Researchers propose three strategies to improve the measure of consumer confidence. First, they do not see an obvious rationale for asking consumers about distant, ambiguous phenomena such as "business conditions." Consumers may usefully be queried about well-defined macroeconomic events that are directly relevant to their personal lives. Second, they believe that the traditional qualitative questions of consumer confidence surveys should at least be complemented by, and perhaps replaced by, probabilistic questions inquiring about well-defined events. Lastly, they suggest that the producers of consumer confidence statistics should prominently report their findings for separate questions and for different subgroups of the population. They believe that the improved consumer confidence indicators may be more useful for predicting consumer spending and making economic policies (Dominitz and Manski 2004).

9.4 Desirable Consumption Behavior

9.4.1 Smart Shopping Behavior

Smart spending behavior may minimize monetary costs and improve economic well-being. A study documents the potential and actual savings that consumers realize from four particular types of purchasing behavior: purchasing on sale; buying in bulk (at a lower per unit price); buying generic brands; and choosing outlets (Griffith et al. 2009). Researchers use data collected by a marketing firm on all food purchases brought into the home for a large, nationally representative sample of UK households in 2006. The results show that households save between 0 and 21 % of their annual expenditures, with a mean of 6.5 %. This translates into a saving of up to £794 a year (in the mid-2006, £1 = US$1.85) (Todd 2010), with an average of £96 per year. The results suggest that the average household saves 16 % of its annual expenditure from buying the largest package sizes, which translates into savings of £224 per year. Households save on average 2 % of their annual expenditure by buying store economy brands, with households who buy standard store brands saving an average of 3.7 %. This translates into an average saving of £25 for economy own brands and £50 for standard own brands on average (Griffith et al. 2009).

9.4.2 Sustainable Consumption

Motivations for sustainable consumption. Why do we need sustainable consumption? Jackson (2006) provided four reasons: (1) the consumption patterns that characterize modern Western society are unsustainable since they rely too heavily on finite resources and generate unacceptable environmental impacts; (2) they are also unfair. The richest nations enjoy the benefits of material affluence, while the poorest still suffer from inadequate access even to the basic necessities of life. In addition, the poorest sometimes bear more than their fair share of environmental impacts from the consumption patterns of the richest; (3) inequities in the present are compounded by our debts to the future. In many cases, the worst impacts from activities today will only transpire later on; and (4) more possessions and consumption don't always bring happiness. After a certain point, material wealth has not delivered consistent improvements in well-being.

Defining sustainable consumption. As summarized by Jackson (2006) the broad idea of sustainable consumption has been defined around a kind of double negative. Agenda 21, the United Nations sustainable development action plan, and a great deal of other early environmental literature have identified the *unsustainability* of existing patterns of consumption and production. Sustainable consumption is, in a very broad sense, born out of the idea that this unsustainability has to be reversed. Within this broad consensus, however, a variety of different definitions have been adopted by different institutions. Several points are worth noting about this range of definitions. The first is that they each takes different positions on the extent to which sustainable consumption involves changes in consumer behaviors and lifestyles. A second, related point of variation between the definitions lies in the extent to which the different positions imply consuming more efficiently, consuming more responsibly, or quite simply consuming less.

The dominant institutional consensus has tended to settle for a position which is closer to this latter kind of definition (consume efficiently) than it is to the former (change lifestyles). Essentially, this institutional view is one in which sustainable consumption means (more) consumption of more sustainable products. This is to be achieved primarily through improvements in the efficiency with which resources are converted into economic goods (Jackson 2006).

There are several reasons for this institutional retreat from the thorny issues of consumer behavior and lifestyles. The area of lifestyle choice has often been regarded as too subjective, too ideological, too value laden, or simply too intractable to be amenable to policy intervention. In particular, addressing it appears to involve questioning some fundamental assumptions about the way modern society functions. Intervening in consumer behavior would contradict the much-vaunted "sovereignty" of consumer choice. Reducing consumption appears to threaten a variety of vested interests and undermine the key structural role that consumption plays in economic growth. Finally, arguments to reduce consumption appear to undermine legitimate efforts by poorer countries to improve their quality of life. Nonetheless, the fallback position is also problematic for a number of reasons. In particular, the focus on efficiency and productivity tends to obscure important questions about the scale of resource consumption patterns. In fact, it would be entirely possible, under this framing of the problem, to have a growing number of ethical and green consumers buying more and more "sustainable" products produced by increasingly "efficient" production processes, and yet for the absolute scale of resource consumption—and the associated environmental impacts—to continue to grow (Jackson 2006).

Sustainable consumption may contribute to happiness. A study using multiple methods demonstrates that spending on charities increases subjective wellbeing (Dunn et al. 2008). Data from Chinese consumers show that consumers who reported green purchase intention and behavior had higher scores in life satisfaction compared to other consumers after controlling for gender, age, education, and family income (Xiao and Li 2011).

Anti-consumption as a sustainable lifestyle. Researchers conduct a qualitative study to explore anti-consumption practices, motivations, and values within attempts to live a more sustainable lifestyle. Anti-consumption for sustainability is to be practiced via acts of rejection, reduction, and reuse. Also, practices of anti-consumption for sustainability are constructed through the collaboration between the needs of the individual and the needs for environmental preservation. Several motivations may be associated with anti-consumption. The first is motivated by environment concerns. Consumers who are concerned about the environment may be conscious about environment protection and even pursue green products with higher prices. The second motivation is broader, concerning about social implications of consumption. To achieve certain social goals, consumers choose to reduce or eliminate consumption. For example, consumers concerned about fair trade reject products produced by socially irresponsible businesses. Politically conscious consumers do not purchase products that do not respond to their particular political ideology. Consumers who are in the mood of anti-globalization boycott products that negatively impact society. The third motivation is to prioritize consumers' own interests and well-being. Most voluntary simplifiers are driven by a desire to live a better life. They refuse to purchase items that cannot improve their happiness and reject consumption activities that do not correspond to their self-concept (Black and Cherrier 2010).

For durable goods, consumers face two options, to repair or replace. Repairing a durable product is more in line with a sustainable lifestyle. A researcher has developed an economic model to examine consumer decisions on repair or replacement. The model includes consumer discount rate as a major factor. Data from Consumer Expenditure Survey show that the discount rate measured by saving rate is associated with the repair decision. Comparing the costs of repairs and replacements and considering decreasing supply of repair workers, he concludes that American consumers are more likely to replace durable products that results in a "throw-away society" (McCollough 2010).

Public policies for sustainable consumption. A researcher argues that for sustainable consumption to take root in the policy sphere, it is necessary to actively foster political relationships and to cast this form of knowledge of sustainable consumption challenging elite economic and political institutions that regularly appropriate and deploy consumer science to advance their own interests (Cohen 2006).

Researchers discuss sustainable consumption governance at the international level. They argue that the lack of commitment to strong sustainable consumption among international governmental organizations can be explained by their "weakness" as actors in global governance and the existence of strong opposing interests among consumers and business actors (Fuchs and Lorek 2005).

Government intervention can be utilized to reduce working time. A researcher argues that in developed countries a successful path to sustainability will entail a stabilization of consumption through reductions in hours of work, a solution that neither ecologists nor economists have addressed seriously. She argues that technological changes will be insufficient to achieve sustainable consumption patterns and that averting continued increases in the scale of consumption through trading income for time is imperative (Schor 2005).

A researcher has developed a framework based on the Culture Theory to evaluate sustainable consumption polices using the UK as an example. Cultural Theory argues that societies should develop pluralistic policies to include all perspectives. Using this framework, she examines the UK's strategy for sustainable consumption, and identifies a number of failings in current policy, including strongly biased toward individualistic, market-based, and neoliberal policies. These biases allow the UK to only respond to a small part of the problem of unsustainable consumption. Policy recommendations include measures to strengthen the input from competing cultures and to realize the potential for more collective, egalitarian, and significantly less materialistic consumption patterns (Seyfang 2004).

Canadian researchers discuss a national strategy to encourage sustainable household consumption. The strategy suggests utilizing policy tools to achieve this goal such as to integrate existing federal programs, to develop interventions, to set the price right, to engage ecological tax reform, and to develop engagement activities with partners (Timmer et al. 2009).

9.4.3 Ethical Consumption

Ethical consumers are defined as those who, when making purchase decisions, consider the effects a choice has on the world around them (Harrison et al. 2005). Consumption activities of ethical consumers can be considered ethical consumptions. However, this term is inherently limited. If ethics centers on normative values, clearly those who support industrialized agriculture, market capitalism, and convenience foods are also expressing normative values—a particular ethics. Moreover, those whose food choices are guided by the desire to maintain cultural heritage may also differ from mainstream claimed moral consumptions. Despite the limitation, the term is still used in the research literature. Ethical consumption may be related to reflexivity in sociological theory. Using this conceptual framework, researchers have conducted a qualitative study with three ethnocultural groups in two regions of Canada and explored the ways reflexivity and tradition may help explain regional differences concerning ethical consumption in relation to food (Beagan et al. 2010).

Researchers have developed an index of ethical consumption activities, applied it to samples of college students from Germany and the USA, and explored the role of national culture and other factors that theoretically determine these behaviors. Consistent with the hypotheses, both respondent idealism and social engagement behaviors are significant predictors of ethical consumption (Witkowski and Reddy 2010).

The Co-operative Bank's Ethical Consumerism Report has been produced since 1999 and acts as a barometer of ethical spending in the UK. This report uses the following categories for ethical consumption: ethical food and drink, green home, eco-travel and transport, ethical personal products, community, and ethical finance (Cooperative Bank 2011).

A researcher has developed a conceptual cost-benefit framework for understanding the spread of ethical consumption based on the work by Brekke et al. (2003), in which heterogeneous preferences and sensitivity to social norms are central features. Using data from the 2004 General Social Survey, with regressions on factors associated with tendencies to "buy ethically," she finds that people are more likely to buy ethically when others around them do too, consistent with a role of social norms in promoting ethical-consumption behaviors. In addition, buying ethically is positively associated with education and income (Starr 2009).

Voluntary simplicity. Voluntary simplicity is viewed as the generic term for a variously motivated contemporary phenomenon: the foregoing of maximum consumption and, possibly, income. Motivations for voluntary simplicity might include self-centered and/or altruistic considerations (Etzioni 1998; Shaw and Newholm 2002). Ethical simplifiers refer to behaviors of voluntary simplicity that respond mostly to ethical concerns. Researchers have conducted two qualitative studies on voluntary simplicity and find three characteristics of ethical simplifiers: (1) restraint: some form of voluntary restraint is used as part of ethical consumption; (2) diversity: a wide range of different forms of simplifying behaviors; and (3) compulsion: a strong motivation toward action arises from an internal moral compulsion toward integrity rather than, or in parallel to, a wish to change the world (Shaw and Newholm 2002).

Researchers have conducted a qualitative study on buying disposed clothing for moral identities at a charity retail store in Australia. At the center of this nexus of practices are the garments which are disposed of through donation, re-commodified by the charity organization for their specialized, immersive retail outlet, and then purchased by consumers to address their individualized moral identity projects. They find that consumers have espoused a view of anti-consumption, which encompasses anti-corporatism (Brace-Govan and Binay 2010).

9.4.4 Socially Responsible Consumption

Socially responsible consumption is similar to sustainable consumption. Researchers have developed the Socially Responsible Purchase and Disposal (SRPD) scale that includes three dimensions: (1) purchasing based on firms' corporate social responsibility (CSR) performance; (2) recycling; and (3) avoidance and use reduction of products based on their environmental impact. The SRPD provides a tool for academicians and practitioners in the development of theory and marketing strategy (Webb et al. 2008).

9.5 Undesirable Consumption Behavior

9.5.1 Conspicuous Consumption

Important theories on conspicuous consumption. The symbolic value of goods can be traced back to the US economist Veblen (1899) who has proposed the concept of "conspicuous consumption." He defines conspicuous consumption as wasteful consumption that displays consumers' wealth, power, and identity; through this behavior consumers receive honor and self-satisfaction. This conspicuous consumption, beyond the inherent utility and exchange value of good, is an important manifestation of symbolic meaning of goods.

The earliest theory of the symbolic value of goods is proposed by the French sociologist Jean Baudrillard. In his book entitled *The Consumer Society*, he states that, along with the rise of consumer society characterized by the great abundance of material goods, the symbolic value of goods has two levels: the unique symbol and the social symbol. A good's unique symbol is displayed by design, style, brand, and image to distinguish its difference and uniqueness from other commodities, while a good's social symbol refers to the good as a symbol of social status, life-style, taste, and social identity (Baudrillard 1998).

German sociologist Max Weber (1978) asserts that social stratification is based on three basic dimensions: wealth and income, power, and occupational prestige, which correspond to class, political party, and status. In Weber's view, class is based on the relationship between commodity production and acquisition, and status is based on the principle of consumption of goods. Weber stresses that the main distinguishing mark for social status groups is consumption and lifestyle, while economic status, political status, and social prestige affect class attributions through influencing personal consumption and lifestyle.

French sociologist Pierre Bourdieu (1984) in his book entitled *Distinction* provides a new perspective using consumer tastes to divide social classes. Bourdieu uses economic capital and cultural capital to divide consumer tastes to different levels. For example, people with high economic capital usually use luxury cars, villas, and commercial corridors of the right bank of Paris as their tastes; those who have more cultural capital place foreign language, avant-garde culture, and art gallery of left bank of Paris as their own tastes; and people with few economic capital and cultural capital are limited to meet the demand for their own survival and have tastes such as potatoes, regular red wine, football, and public dances. People of different social classes have different tastes, the high class typically exhibits a taste of luxury lifestyle, and low-ranking strata show a taste of the necessity lifestyle. Thus social groups in this sense become taste groups. Boudieu's theory enriches the theory of conspicuous consumption (Trigg 2001).

Theoretical models of conspicuous consumption. Researchers develop theoretical models to better understand conspicuous consumption. A theoretical analysis shows that while Veblen effects of conspicuous consumption cannot ordinarily arise when preferences satisfy a "singlecrossing property," they may emerge when this property fails. In that case, "budget" brands are priced at marginal cost, while "luxury" brands, though not intrinsically superior, are sold at higher prices to consumers seeking to advertise wealth (Bagwell and Bernheim 1996). Another theoretical analysis shows that in equilibrium, the signaling value of conspicuous consumption depends in an identifiable way on the number of consumers, and consumer behavior is characterized by either snobbism or conformism. The market demand curve for the conspicuous good may exhibit a positive slope if consumers are conformist (Corneo and Jeanne 1997). Some researchers believe that although consuming more today would improve one's relative consumption now, it would worsen one's relative consumption in the future. Based on a theoretical model, researchers identify the structure of felicity (current utility) functions for which the two effects offset each other exactly. The results show that while household surveys suggest that relative consumption matters, the consumption behavior of household cannot explain to the presence of relative consumption effects (Arrow and Dasgupta 2009).

Functions of conspicuous consumption. Research shows that conspicuous consumption such as luxury products can function to boost self-esteem, express identity, and signal status. Researchers also find that luxury products have important signaling functions in relationships. Experimental research shows that women's luxury products function as a signaling system directed at other women who pose threats to their romantic relationships. Activating a motive to guard one's mate triggered women to seek and display lavish possessions. Women use pricey possessions to signal that their romantic partner is especially devoted to them. In turn, flaunting designer handbags and shoes is effective at deterring other women from poaching a relationship partner (Wang and Griskevicius 2014). However, conspicuous consumption may decrease happiness among consumers. A study is conducted in the context of luxury car consumption in Switzerland. Results from detailed panel data suggest that the prevalence of luxury cars in the area has a negative impact on individuals' happiness, with the biggest impacts arising for the poor (Winkelmann 2010).

Factors associated with conspicuous consumption. The relationship of equality and conspicuous consumptions is studied by researchers. Research shows that greater equality reduces consumption when consumers focus on the narrower possession gap, but it increases consumption when they focus on the greater position gains (i.e., when consumption is conspicuous, social competition goals are primed, and the environment is competitive) (Ordabayeva and Chandon 2011). Researchers examine associations between social stratification and conspicuous consumption in a context of a less industrialized country. Using data collected from consumers in two representative cities in China, results from structural equation modeling suggest that social class is associated with conspicuous consumption. In addition, advertisement attention is associated with one measure of conspicuous consumption, the symbol of wealth (Sun et al. 2012).

Comparative studies of conspicuous consumption. A researcher has developed a model of conspicuous consumption to empirically measure the importance of peer beliefs of Americans and Chinese consumers. According to model estimates, a Chinese consumer cares 20 % more than an American consumer about peer beliefs. The absolute size of the conspicuous consumption motive in both countries is relatively small. He uses the estimated model to evaluate the welfare effect of the 1990–2002 American luxury tax on automobiles. Results suggest that the luxury tax benefits nearly all Americans a small amount, but hurts the small fraction of consumers who love automobiles the most (Jinkins 2014). Researchers have compared young adult consumers aged 18–35 in urban China and the USA and find that Chinese young adults score higher in both materialism and conspicuous consumption (Podoshen et al. 2011). Using nationally representative data on consumption, researchers show that blacks and Hispanics devote larger shares of their expenditure bundles to visible goods (clothing, jewelry, and cars) than do comparable whites. These differences exist among virtually all subpopulations, are relatively constant over time, and are economically large (Charles et al. 2009).

9.5.2 Unethical Consumption

Several research reports describe factors associated with consumer acceptance of unethical consumption activities. Researchers study the influence of consumer cultural identification and Machiavellianism (a personality characteristic) on acceptance of unethical clothing consumption activities. Examples of unethical clothing behaviors include keeping the belt when returning a pair of pants, returning an evening dress after wearing it for a special event, etc. Based on a survey of a sample of Chinese and US students, researchers find that those more closely identifying with US culture tend to be more accepting of unethical clothing consumption activities than those identifying with Chinese culture. Those who are more Machiavellian accept more unethical behaviors than those who are less Machiavellian (Shen and Dickson 2001). Based on a sample of college students in Malaysia, researchers examine potential effects of gender and ethic course on ethic shopping behavior. The consumer ethic construct includes four dimensions such as "actively benefiting from an illegal activity," "passively benefiting at the expense of others," "actively benefiting from questionable action," and "no harm/no foul." The researchers find that female students are more ethical in two of the four dimensions of consumer ethical beliefs. Furthermore those who have not taken ethics course are found to be more ethical in at least two of the dimensions of the consumer ethical scale, consistent with previous research and calling for more effective ethic courses offered at universities (Lau and Choe 2009).

Researchers examine antecedents and consequences of unethical consumption. At a national consumer research conference, researchers have presented four research reports to explore these issues. The first report shows that in order to protect consumers from emotionally laden trade-offs between ethical attributes and other desirable product attributes (e.g., price and quality), consumers misremember negative ethical attribute information at a greater rate than they do positive ethical attribute information. The second report examines a variety of unethical behaviors, including plagiarizing, cheating, stealing, buying stolen goods, and lying and shows that consumers are likely to engage in these behaviors when they feel a lack of personal control and are exposed to information indicating that engaging in these unethical behaviors is the norm. Researchers in the third report explores how a difference in short-term versus long-term focus influences the decision to behave unethically. In psychology, priming is an implicit memory effect in which exposure to one stimulus influences a response to another stimulus. The researchers show that priming money leads individuals to focus on the present, thereby increasing the likelihood of cheating on a task, while priming time leads them to focus on the future, thereby decreasing the likelihood of cheating. Researchers in the fourth report examine the impact of the specific emotions that stem from moral violations on subsequent spending decisions (e.g., donating to charities, spending on the self vs. others) (Naylor and McGraw 2011).

Researchers also attempt to understand unethical consumption from a theoretical perspective. Neutralization is a defense mechanism through which people downplay the repercussions of their behavior. McGregor (2008) demonstrates the ability of neutralization theory (especially 13 neutralization techniques) to contribute theoretical understandings to how consumers justify the negative impacts of their purchasing behavior, and how they can continually or periodically rationalize their less than moral and ethical consumption decisions.

9.5.3 Compulsive Buying

Compulsive buying is defined as "chronic, repetitive purchasing that becomes a primary response to negative events or feelings" (O'Guinn and Faber 1989, p. 155). Compulsive buyers feel obligated to purchase things, often beyond their economic means. They do not necessarily require material acquisition, but they need to alleviate their anxiety or tension through buying.

Although compulsive buying gives an individual short-term positive reward, it results in long-term negative consequences. Compulsive buyers face great difficulty in controlling their buying and cannot stop engaging in their spending patterns despite recognizing and realizing its detrimental effects (Hirschman 1992; O'Guinn and Faber 1989). That is, compulsive buyers may dislike their behaviors, but they are compelled to repeat their behaviors.

Some research has linked compulsive buying with consumer financial attitudes and behaviors. Compulsive buyers are likely to have more credit cards and use credit cards more irrationally than normal consumers (O'Guinn and Faber 1989; Roberts 1998). They treat money as a status tool and enhance their self-esteem with purchases (Hanley and Wilhelm 1992). Paradoxically, compulsive buyers feel "a sense of conflict" over their spending (Hanley and Wilhelm 1992, p. 17). Based on a sample of college students, researchers find that students with a tendency of compulsive buying are more likely to hold credit card debts (Wang and Xiao 2009).

9.5.4 Impulsive Buying

"Impulse buying occurs when a consumer experiences a sudden, often powerful, and persistent urge to buy something immediately. The impulse to buy is hedonically complex and may stimulate emotional conflict. Also, impulse buying is prone to occur with diminished regard for its consequences" (Rook 1987, p. 191). Impulse buying is an immediate experience, often concurrent with a feeling of excitement and urgency. It compels a consumer to buy a product at that moment instead of cautiously contemplating a purchase. It is different from unplanned buying because it involves an experiential urge to buy. Therefore, impulse buying usually occurs "without pre-shopping intentions to buy the specific product category or to fulfill a specific buying task" (Beatty and Ferrell 1998, p. 170).

Impulse buying is a common experience for American consumers. Some press articles report that almost 90 % of shoppers occasionally make purchases on impulse (Welles 1986). While nationally representative research on impulse buying is lacking, several studies find that a large portion of consumers, ranging from 30 to 50 %, engage in impulsive purchases frequently in their shopping trips (e.g., Beatty and Ferrell 1998; Rook 1987).

An impulse comes on as a sudden urge that drives a person to a certain behavior, such as buying an item instantly without thought and without delay. The desire to have the item is alleviated by the purchase. "When individuals act on impulse, they tend to do so quickly and nonreflectively, which increases the likelihood of unintended and undesirable outcomes" (Rook and Fisher 1995, p. 306). One characteristic of impulse buying is that people tend to succumb to their buying impulses even though they are aware of the potentially negative consequences (Rook 1987). Impulsive buyers are driven by emotions such as excitement and pleasure whereas less impulsive buyers largely rely on utilitarian considerations. The urge to buy impulsively can be resisted if a person goes through full rationalization. Compared to compulsive buying, impulse buying comes from an acute loss of control when shopping and is a less severe problem for consumers. Impulse buying may result from transient self-control failure (Baumeister 2002) while compulsive buying is chronic loss of control despite realizations by consumers. Both buying patterns involve mixed emotions during and after the purchase.

Impulse buying can cause negative consequences for consumers. For example, impulsive individuals are more likely to misuse their credit cards. Researchers find credit cards useful in abetting spontaneous desire for things. Credit cards may even accelerate the process and speed up the gratification of buying because there is no need to count cash or write a check. Also, the financial consequences are delayed due to the payment schedules (Pirog and Roberts 2007).

9.5.5 Overspending

A minority of consumers overspend. The 2010 Survey of Consumer Finance shows that 6.0 % of families reported that their spending usually exceeds their income (Bricker et al. 2012). The 2012 National Financial Capability Study shows that 19 % of American families are spending more than their incomes (FINRAIEF 2013). Based on data from the Consumer Expenditure Survey, multivariate analyses show that income is positively and education is negatively associated with overspending (Bae et al. 1993). Overspending may be caused by debt-financed consumption sprees that may be socially costly. Easy access to credit can push economic activity above sustainable levels, eventually requiring cutbacks in spending, lay-offs from overgrown sectors, and write-downs of bad debts. From the perspective of institutional economics, tendencies toward over-borrowing have roots in consumers' predispositions to conform to rising consumption norms. Regulation should be confined to public problems not better solved via private means (Starr 2010).

9.6 Summary

Consumer spending is the most important measure of consumer economic well-being. To understand consumption behavior, economists have developed theoretical models such as the life cycle hypothesis and its variations such as the precautionary saving model. In recent years, economists have integrated psychological advances to the standard utility function models and developed behavioral models such as the behavioral life cycle hypothesis and hyperbolic consumption model to better understand consumption behavior. Consumption has both existential and experiential benefits and costs. Consumers have various decision making styles.

Consumption activities are tracked by national statistical agencies such as the U.S. Bureau of Labor Statistics that publishes statistics of consumer expenditures every year. Based on research, consumer expenditure over the life cycle shows a hump shape and consumer unit with a middle-aged head has the largest expenditure compared to consumer unit with younger or older heads. Housing, transportation, and food are three major expenditure categories for American consumers. Pension and insurance is the fourth major spending category. Healthcare expenditure is becoming important especially among older populations. Previous studies have examined group differences in consumer expenditures in various expenditure categories.

Consumer confidence is currently used to predict consumer expenditure and general economy. In fact, it may be better used to measure consumer economic well-being directly. Future research could explore how to use this concept to measure consumer subjective economic well-being.

Desirable consumption behaviors include smart shopping, sustainable consumption, ethical consumption, and socially responsible consumption behaviors. These behaviors not only help increase values of individual consumers' purchasing powers but also contribute to social welfare through individual actions. Undesirable consumption behaviors include conspicuous consumption, unethical consumption, compulsive buying, impulsive buying, and overspending behaviors. These behaviors would not only hurt consumers' short-term economic well-being but also affect their long-term welfare. In addition, these behaviors could hurt sustainable economic development by transferring unnecessary social costs to other consumers and other sectors in the society.

References

About the law. (2010). Retried November 21, 2010, from http://www.healthcare.gov/law/about/index.html

Ando, A., & Modigliani, F. (1963). The life cycle hypothesis of saving: Aggregate implications and tests. *American Economic Review, 53*(March), 55–84.

Ando, A., & Modigliani, F. (1964). The "life-cycle" hypothesis of saving: A correction. *The American Economic Review, 54*(2), 111–113.

Angeletos, G., Laibson, D., Repetto, A., Tobacman, J., & Weinberg, S. (2001). The hyperbolic consumption model: Calibration, simulation, and empirical evaluation. *Journal of Economic Perspectives, 15*(3), 47–68.

Anker, R. (2011). Engel's law around the world 150 years later. In *Political Economy Research Institute Working Paper No. 247*. Amherst, MA: University of Massachusetts at Amherst.

Arrow, K. J., & Dasgupta, P. S. (2009). Conspicuous consumption, inconspicuous leisure. *The Economic Journal, 119*(541), F497–F516.

Attanasio, O. P., & Weber, G. (2010). Consumption and saving: Models of intertemporal allocation and their implications for public policy. *Journal of Economic Literature, 48*(3), 693–751.

Bae, M., Hanna, S., & Lindamood, S. (1993). Patterns of overspending in US households. *Financial Counseling and Planning, 4*(1), 1–30.

Bagwell, L. S., & Bernheim, B. D. (1996). Veblen effects in a theory of conspicuous consumption. *The American Economic Review, 86*, 349–373.

Baudrillard, J. (1998), *The consumer society: Myths and structures*. English Translation (Original work in French published 1970). Thousand Oaks, CA: Sage.

Baumeister, R. F. (2002). Yielding to temptation: Self-control failure, impulsive purchasing, and consumer behavior. *Journal of Consumer Research, 28*(March), 670–676.

Beagan, B. L., Ristovski-Slijepcevic, S., & Chapman, G. E. (2010). "People are just becoming more conscious of how everything's connected": "Ethical" food consumption in two regions of Canada. *Sociology, 44*(4), 751–769.

Beatty, S. E., & Ferrell, M. E. (1998). Impulse buying: Modeling its precursors. *Journal of Retailing, 74*(2), 169–191.

Berk, M. L., & Monheit, A. C. (2001). The concentration of health care expenditures, revisited. *Health Affairs, 20*(2), 9–18.

Black, I. R., & Cherrier, H. (2010). Anti-consumption as part of living a sustainable lifestyle: Daily practices, contextual motivations and subjective values. *Journal of Consumer Behaviour, 9*(6), 437–453.

Blanciforti, L., Green, R., & Lane, S. (1981). Income and expenditure for relatively more versus relatively less nutritious food over the life cycle. *American Journal of Agricultural Economics, 63*, 255–260.

Blumenthal, D., & Collins, S. R. (2014). Health care coverage under the Affordable Care Act—A progress report. *New England Journal of Medicine, 371*(3), 275–281.

Bourdieu, P. (1984), *Distinction: A social critique of the judgment of taste*. English Translation by Richard Nice (Original work in French published in 1979). Cambridge, MA: Harvard University Press.

Brace-Govan, J., & Binay, J. (2010). Consumption of disposed goods for moral identities: A nexus of organization, place, things and consumers. *Journal of Consumer Behaviour, 9*(1), 69–82.

Bram, J., & Ludvigson, S. C. (1998). Does consumer confidence forecast household expenditure? A sentiment index horse race. *Federal Reserve Bank of New York: Economic Policy Review, 4*(2), 59–78.

Brekke, K. A., Kverndokk, S., & Nyborg, K. (2003, September 9–10). An economic model of moral motivation. *Journal of Public Economics, 87*, 1967–1983.

Bricker, J., Kennickell, A. B., Moore, K. B., & Sabelhaus, J. (2012). Changes in U.S. family finances from 2007 to 2010: Evidence from the survey of consumer finances. *Federal Reserve Bulletin, 98*(2), 1–80.

Browning, M., & Crossley, T. F. (2001). The life-cycle model of consumption and saving. *Journal of Economic Perspectives, 15*, 3–22.

Cai, Y., Alviola, P., Nayga, R., & Wu, X. (2008). The effect of food-away-from-home and food-at-home expenditures on obesity rates: A state-level analysis. *Journal of Agricultural and Applied Economics, 40*(2), 507–521.

Carroll, C. D. (1997). Buffer-stock saving and the life cycle/permanent income hypothesis. *The Quarterly Journal of Economics, 112*(February), 1–55.

Carroll, C. D., Fuhrer, J. C., & Wilcox, D. W. (1994). Does consumer sentiment forecast household spending? If so, why? *American Economic Review, 84*(5), 1397–1408.

Case, A., Lin, I., & McLanahan, S. (2000). How hungry is the selfish gene? *The Economic Journal, 110*, 781–804.

Case, A., & Paxson, C. (2001). Mothers and others: Who invests in children's health? *Journal of Health Economics, 20*, 301–328.

Charles, K. K., Hurst, E., & Roussanov, N. (2009). Conspicuous consumption and race. *The Quarterly Journal of Economics, 124*(2), 425–467.

Cohen, M. J. (2006). Sustainable consumption research as democratic expertise. *Journal of Consumer Policy, 29*(1), 67–77.

Cook, B., & Manning, W. (2009). Measuring racial/ethnic disparities across the distribution of health care expenditures. *Health Services Research, 44*(5p1), 1603–1621.

Cooperative Bank. (2011). *Ethical consumerism report 2011* (p. 6). Manchester, UK: The Co-operative Bank.

Corneo, G., & Jeanne, O. (1997). Conspicuous consumption, snobbism and conformism. *Journal of Public Economics, 66*(1), 55–71.

Creech, B. (2008). *Spending on telephone service. Consumer Expenditure Survey Anthology, 2008. Report 1009* (pp. 74–77). Washington, DC: U.S. Bureau of Labor Statistics.

Csikszentmihalyi, M. (2000). The costs and benefits of consuming. *Journal of Consumer Research, 27*(2), 267–272.

Deaton, A. (1991). Saving and liquidity constraints. *Econometrica, LIX*(1991), 1221–1248.

DeLeire, T., & Kalil, A. (2005). How do cohabiting couples with children spend their money? *Journal of Marriage and Family, 67*, 286–295.

Dominitz, J., & Manski, C. F. (2004). How should we measure consumer confidence? *The Journal of Economic Perspectives, 18*(2), 51–66.

Douthitt, R. A., & Fedyk, J. M. (1988). The influence of children on family life cycle spending behavior: Theory and applications. *Journal of Consumer Affairs, 22*(2), 220–248.

Du, R. Y., & Kamakura, W. A. (2006). Household life cycles and lifestyles in the United States. *Journal of Marketing Research, 43*(1), 121–132.

Duesenberry, J. (1967). *Income, saving, and the theory of consumer behavior*. New York: Oxford University Press.

Duetsch, M. (2008). Out-of-pocket health care spending patterns of older Americans, as measured by the Consumer Expenditure Survey. In *Consumer Expenditure Survey Anthology, 2008* (pp. 46–51). Report 1009. Washington, DC: U.S. Bureau of Labor Statistics.

Dunn, E. W., Aknin, L. B., & Norton, M. I. (2008). Spending money on others promotes happiness. *Science, 319*(5870), 1687–1688.

Etzioni, A. (1998). Voluntary simplicity characterization, select psychological implications, and societal consequences. *Journal of Economic Psychology, 19*, 619–643.

Fan, J. X., & Lewis, J. K. (1999). Budget allocation patterns of African Americans. *Journal of Consumer Affairs, 33*(1), 134–164.

Fan, J. X., Sharpe, D. L., & Hong, G. S. (2003). Health care and prescription drug spending by seniors. *Monthly Labor Review, 126*, 16–26.

Fan, J. X., & Xiao, J. J. (1998). Decision making styles of young Chinese adults. *Journal of Consumer Affairs, 32*(2), 275–293.

Fan, J. X., & Zick, C. D. (2004). The economic burden of health care, funeral, and burial expenditures at the end of life. *Journal of Consumer Affairs, 38*(1), 35–55.

Fan, J. X., & Zuiker, V. S. (1998). A comparison of household budget allocation patterns between Hispanic Americans and non-Hispanic White Americans. *Journal of Family and Economic Issues, 19*(2), 151–174.

Ferdous, N., Pinjari, A., Bhat, C., & Pendyala, R. (2010). A comprehensive analysis of household transportation expenditures relative to other goods and services: An application to United States consumer expenditure data. *Transportation, 37*(3), 363–390.

Fernádez-Villaverde, J., & Krueger, D. (2007). Consumption over the life cycle: Facts from Consumer Expenditure Survey data. *Review of Economics and Statistics, 89*(3), 552–565.

FINRAIEF. (2013). *Financial capability in the United States: Report of findings from the 2012 National Financial Capability Study*. Washington, DC: FINRA Investor Education Foundation.

Friedman, M. (1957). *A theory of the consumption function*. Princeton, NJ: Princeton University Press.

Fuchs, D. A., & Lorek, S. (2005). Sustainable consumption governance: A history of promises and failures. *Journal of Consumer Policy, 28*(3), 261–288.

Fukuda, K. (2010). A cohort analysis of household vehicle expenditure in the U.S. and Japan: A possibility of generational marketing. *Marketing Letters, 21*(1), 53–64.

Griffith, R., Leibtag, E., Leicester, A., & Nevo, A. (2009). Consumer shopping behavior: How much do consumers save? *Journal of Economic Perspectives, 23*(2), 99–120.

Gruber, J., & Levy, H. (2009). The evolution of medical spending risk. *Journal of Economic Perspectives, 23*(4), 25–48.

Hall, R. E. (1978). Stochastic implications of the life cycle-permanent income hypothesis: Theory and evidence. *Journal of Political Economy, 86*(6), 971–987.

Hanley, A., & Wilhelm, M. S. (1992). Compulsive buying: An exploration into self-esteem and money attitudes. *Journal of Economic Psychology, 13*, 5–18.

Harrison, R., Newholm, T., & Shaw, D. (Eds.). (2005). *The ethical consumer*. London: Sage.

Himmelberg, C., Mayer, C., & Sinai, T. (2005). Assessing high house prices: Bubbles, fundamentals and misperceptions. *Journal of Economic Perspectives, 19*(4), 67–92.

Hirschman, E. C. (1992). The consciousness of addiction: Toward a general theory of compulsive consumption. *Journal of Consumer Research, 19*(September), 155–179.

Hiu, A. S., Siu, N. Y., Wang, C. C., & Chang, L. M. (2001). An investigation of decision-making styles of consumers in China. *Journal of Consumer Affairs, 35*(2), 326–345.

Hong, G.-S., & Kim, S. Y. (2000). Out-of-pocket health care expenditure patterns and financial burden across the life cycle stages. *Journal of Consumer Affairs, 34*(2), 291–313.

Hurst, E., & Aguiar, M. (2004). *Consumption, expenditure and home production over the life cycle. Working paper*. Chicago: University of Chicago.

Jackson, T. (2006). Readings in sustainable consumption. In *The Earthscan reader in sustainable consumption* (pp. 1–27). London: Earthscan.

Jinkins, D. C. (2014). *Conspicuous consumption in the United States and China*. Working paper. Retrieved from ftp://ftp.iza.org/RePEc/Discussionpaper/dp8323.pdf

Jung, J., & Tran, C. (2010). Medical consumption over the life cycle: Facts from a U.S. medical expenditure panel survey. Retrieved January 15, 2011, from SSRN.

Keynes, N. M. (1936). *The general theory of employment, interest, and money*. London: Macmillan.

Kimball, M. S. (1990). Precautionary saving in the small and in the large. *Econometrica, 38*(January), 53–73.

Laibson, D. I. (1997). Golden eggs and hyperbolic discounting. *Quarterly Journal of Economics, 62*(2), 443–478.

Lanfranco, B. A., Ames, G. C. W., & Huang, C. L. (2002). Food expenditure patterns of the Hispanic population in the United States. *Agribusiness, 18*(2), 197–211.

Lau, T.-C., & Choe, K.-L. (2009). Consumers' acceptance of unethical consumption activities: Implications for the youth market. *International Journal of Marketing Studies, 1*(2), 56–61.

Lawson, R. (1991). Patterns of tourist expenditure and types of vacation across the family life cycle. *Journal of Travel Research, 29*(4), 12–18.

Levin, L. (1998). Are assets fungible? Testing the behavioral theory of life-cycle savings. *Journal of Economic Behavior & Organization, 36*(1), 59–83.

Ludvigson, S. C. (2004). Consumer confidence and consumer spending. *The Journal of Economic Perspectives, 18*(2), 29–50.

Marr, B., & McCready, D. (2009). The application of household life cycle variables to spending patterns using Canadian data. *Canadian Studies in Population, 23*(1), 23–47.

McCollough, J. (2010). Consumer discount rates and the decision to repair or replace a durable product: A sustainable consumption issue. *Journal of Economic Issues, 44*(1), 183–204.

McGregor, S. L. (2008). Conceptualizing immoral and unethical consumption using neutralization theory. *Family and Consumer Sciences Research Journal, 36*(3), 261–276.

Modigliani, F. (1986). Life cycle, thrift, and the wealth of nations. *American Economic Review, 76*, 297–313.

Modigliani, F., & Brumberg, R. (1954). Utility analysis and the consumption function: An interpretation of cross-section data. In K. K. Kurihara (Ed.), *Post Keynesian economics* (pp. 388–436). New Brunswick, NJ: Rutgers University Press.

Mohanty, S. A., Woolhandler, S., Himmelstein, D. U., Pati, S., Carrasquillo, O., & Bor, D. H. (2005). Health care expenditures of immigrants in the United States: A nationally representative analysis. *American Journal of Public Health, 95*(8), 1431–1438.

Naylor, R. W., & McGraw, P. (2011). Harming, stealing, lying, and cheating: Exploring the antecedents and consequences of unethical consumption behavior (A Panel Summary). *Building Connections: Proceedings of Association for Consumer Research, 39*, 230–234.

O'Guinn, T. C., & Faber, R. J. (1989). Compulsive buying: A phenomenological exploration. *Journal of Consumer Research, 16*(2), 147–157.

Oladosu, G. (2003). An almost ideal demand system model of household vehicle fuel expenditure allocation in the United States. *Energy Journal, 24*(1), 1–21.

Ordabayeva, N., & Chandon, P. (2011). Getting ahead of the Joneses: When equality increases conspicuous consumption among bottom-tier consumers. *Journal of Consumer Research, 38*(1), 27–41.

Paulin, G. (2008). Examining expenditure patterns of young, single adults in a historical context: Two recent generations compared. In *Consumer Expenditure Survey Anthology, 2008* (pp. 52–73). Report 1009. Washington, DC: U.S. Bureau of Labor Statistics.

Paulin, G., & Lee, Y. (2002, July). Expenditures of single parents: How does gender figure in? *Monthly Labor Review, 125*, 16–37.

Pirog, S. F., & Roberts, J. A. (2007). Personality and credit card misuse among college students: The mediating role of impulsiveness. *Journal of Marketing Theory and Practice, 15*(1), 65–77.

Podoshen, J. S., Li, L., & Zhang, J. (2011). Materialism and conspicuous consumption in China: A cross-cultural examination. *International Journal of Consumer Studies, 35*(1), 17–25.

Putler, D., Li, T., & Liu, Y. (2007). The value of household life cycle variables in consumer expenditure research: An empirical examination. *Canadian Journal of Administrative Sciences, 24*(4), 284–299.

Quigley, J. M., & Raphael, S. (2004). Is housing unaffordable? Why isn't it more affordable? *Journal of Economic Perspectives, 18*(1), 191–214.

Raper, K. C., Wanzala, M. N., & Nayaga, R. M., Jr. (2002). Food expenditures and household demographic composition in the US: A demand systems approach. *Applied Economics, 34*(8), 981–992.

Roberts, J. A. (1998). Compulsive buying among college students: An investigation of its antecedents, consequences, and implications for public policy. *Journal of Consumer Affairs, 32*(2), 295–319.

Rook, D. W. (1987). The buying impulse. *Journal of Consumer Research, 14*(September), 189–199.

Rook, D. W., & Fisher, R. J. (1995). Normative influences on impulsive buying behavior. *Journal of Consumer Research, 22*(December), 305–313.

Schaninger, C. M., & Danko, W. D. (1993). A conceptual and empirical comparison of alternative household lifecycle models. *Journal of Consumer Research, 19*(March), 580–594.

Schooley, D., & Worden, D. (2008). A behavioral life-cycle approach to understanding the wealth effect. *Business Economics, 43*(2), 7–15.

Schor, J. B. (2005). Sustainable consumption and work time reduction. *Journal of Industrial Ecology, 9*(1-2), 37–50.

Seyfang, G. (2004). Consuming values and contested cultures: A critical analysis of the UK strategy for sustainable consumption and production. *Review of Social Economy, 62*(3), 323–338.

Sharpe, D. L. (2008). Consumer financial issues in health care. In J. J. Xiao (Ed.), *Handbook of consumer finance research* (pp. 319–336). New York: Springer.

Shaw, D., & Newholm, T. (2002). Voluntary simplicity and the ethics of consumption. *Psychology & Marketing, 19*(2), 167–185.

Shefrin, H. M., & Thaler, R. H. (1988). The behavioral life-cycle hypothesis. *Economic Inquiry, 26*(September), 609–643.

Shen, D., & Dickson, M. A. (2001). Consumers' acceptance of unethical clothing consumption activities: Influence of cultural identification, ethnicity, and Machiavellianism. *Clothing and Textiles Research Journal, 19*(2), 76–87.

Shin, J., & Moon, S. (2007). Do HMO plans reduce health care expenditure in the private sector? *Economic Inquiry, 45*(1), 82–99.

Souleles, N. S. (2004). Expectations, heterogeneous forecast errors, and consumption: Micro evidence from the Michigan consumer sentiment surveys. *Journal of Money, Credit and Banking, 36*(1), 39–72.

Sprotles, G. B., & Kendall, E. L. (1986). A methodology for profiling consumers' decision-making styles. *Journal of Consumer Affairs, 20*(2), 267–279.

Starr, M. A. (2009). The social economics of ethical consumption: Theoretical considerations and empirical evidence. *The Journal of Socio-Economics, 38*(6), 916–925.

Starr, M. A. (2010). Debt-financed consumption sprees: Regulation, freedom and habits of thought. *Journal of Economic Issues, 44*(2), 459–470.

Sun, F., Xiao, J. J., & Zhang, Y. X. (2012). Social stratification and status consumption in China. *American Review of China Studies, 13*(1), 1–16.

Timmer, V., Prinet, E., & Timmer, D. (2009). *Sustainable household consumption: Key considerations and elements for a Canadian strategy*. Toronto, ON: Consumer Council of Canada.

Todd, M. (2010). *A graphical history of the dollar exchange rate*. Retrieved November 21, 2010, from http://www.miketodd.net/encyc/dollhist-graph3.htm

Trigg, A. B. (2001). Veblen, Bourdieu, and conspicuous consumption. *Journal of Economic Issues, 35*, 99–115.

U.S. Bureau of Labor Statistics. (2013). *Consumer expenditures - 2012*. News release. Washington, DC: Author. Retrieved from http://www.bls.gov/news.release/pdf/cesan.pdf

Veblen, T. B. (1899). *The theory of the leisure class*. Boston: Houghton Mifflin.

Vendemia, M. (2008). Housing expenditures by race and Hispanic or Latino origin. In *Consumer Expenditure Survey Anthology, 2008* (pp. 78–86). Report 1009. Washington, DC: U.S. Bureau of Labor Statistics.

Wagner, J., & Hanna, S. (1983). The effectiveness of family life cycle variables in consumer expenditure research. *Journal of Consumer Research, 10*(3), 281–291.

Walsh, G., Mitchell, V. W., & Hennig-Thurau, T. (2001). German consumer decision-making styles. *Journal of Consumer Affairs, 35*(1), 73–95.

Wang, Z. (2009). The convergence of health care expenditure in the US states. *Health Economics, 18*(1), 55–70.

Wang, Y., & Griskevicius, V. (2014). Conspicuous consumption, relationships, and rivals: Women's luxury products as signals to other women. *Journal of Consumer Research, 40*(5), 834–854.

Wang, J., & Xiao, J. J. (2009). Buying behavior, social support, and credit card indebtedness of college students. *International Journal of Consumer Studies, 33*, 2–10.

Webb, D. J., Mohr, L. A., & Harris, K. E. (2008). A re-examination of socially responsible consumption and its measurement. *Journal of Business Research, 61*(2), 91–98.

Weber, M. (1978), *Economy and society*. English Transition. (Original work in German published 1956). Berkley, CA: University of California Press.

Wee, C. C., Phillips, R. S., Legedza, A. T. R., Davis, R. B., Soukup, J. R., Colditz, G. A., et al. (2005). Health care expenditures associated with overweight and obesity among us adults: Importance of age and race. *American Journal of Public Health, 95*(1), 159–165.

Welles, G. (1986, May 21). We're in the habit of impulsive buying. *USA Today*, p. 1.

Wilcox, D. W. (1989). Social security benefits, consumption expenditure, and the Life Cycle Hypothesis. *Journal of Political Economy, 97*(2), 288–304.

Wilcox, J. (2007). Forecasting components of consumption with components of consumer sentiment. *Business Economics, 42*(4), 22–32.

Wilkes, R. E. (1995). Household lifecycle stages, transitions and product expenditures. *Journal of Consumer Research, 22*(June), 27–42.

Winkelmann, R. (2010). Conspicuous consumption and happiness. *Zurich, Socioeconomic Institute Working Paper.*

Witkowski, T. H., & Reddy, S. (2010). Antecedents of ethical consumption activities in Germany and the United States. *Australasian Marketing Journal, 18*(1), 8–14.

Xiao, J. J., & Anderson, J. G. (1997). Hierarchical financial needs reflected by household financial asset shares. *Journal of Family and Economic Issues, 18*(4), 333–356.

Xiao, J. J., & Li, H. (2011). Sustainable consumption and life satisfaction. *Social Indicators Research, 104*(2), 323–329.

Xiao, J. J., & Olson, G. I. (1993). Mental accounting and saving behavior. *Home Economics Research Journal, 22*(1), 92–109.

Yang, F. (2009). Consumption over the life cycle: How different is housing? *Review of Economic Dynamics, 12*(3), 423–443.

You, W., & Nayga, R. M., Jr. (2005). Household fast food expenditures and children's television viewing: Can they really significantly influence children's dietary quality? *Journal of Agricultural and Resource Economics, 30*(2), 302–314.

Zan, H., & Fan, J. (2010). Cohort effects of household expenditures on food away from home. *Journal of Consumer Affairs, 44*(1), 213–233.

Zeldes, S. P. (1989). Consumption and liquidity constraints: An empirical investigation. *Journal of Political Economy, 97*(2), 305–346.

Ziol-Guest, K. M., DeLeire, T., & Kalil, A. (2006). The allocation of food expenditure in married- and single-parent families. *Journal of Consumer Affairs, 40*(2), 347–371.

Ziol-Guest, K., Kalil, A., & DeLeire, T. (2004). Expenditure decisions in single-parent households. In A. Kalil & T. DeLeire (Eds.), *Family investments in children: Resources and parenting behaviors that promote success* (pp. 181–208). Mahwah, NJ: Erlbaum.

Zuvekas, S. H., & Cohen, J. W. (2007). Prescription drugs and the changing concentration of health care expenditures. *Health Affairs, 26*(1), 249–257.

Chapter 10
Consumer Borrowing

Abstract This chapter first presents an overview of consumer debt and its relevance to consumer economic wellbeing. And then the research literature on several debt categories such as mortgage, vehicle, education, credit card, and payday loans is described. Finally, the chapter reviews the research literature on consumer bankruptcy.

10.1 Overview of Consumer Debts

Debt is also called borrowing, credit, loan, and liability in different contexts. Consumer debt has potential to help consumers smooth consumption flow over life cycle stages. Without consumer debt, many consumers could not afford to own a home, go to college, and buy a car and other expensive consumer products and services. Thus, consumer debt improves the consumer wellbeing under the condition that consumers have control of it.

If consumers cannot make payments for consumer loans on time, they accumulate debts and are responsible for paying both principles and interests. Debt is an objective measure of economic status but it is not straightforward to be used for measuring economic wellbeing. Credit access can be considered an indicator of economic wellbeing since it provides opportunities for consumers to borrow from future resources to pay for current consumption. However, heaving debt out of control that results in bankruptcy is considered a situation of economic ill-being. Debts need to be managed to help consumers achieve economic wellbeing. Consumer economists believe that appropriate borrowing is a rational behavior that is necessary to smooth life cycle consumption. Dynan (2009) discusses advantages and disadvantages of consumer debts. Based on her research, although debt has positive and negative aspects, greater access to credit has mainly hurt household economic wellbeing in the last three decades.

Consumer debt has increased greatly in recent years. Using the US aggregate data, researchers show that the ratio of total household debt to aggregate personal income rose from 0.6 to 1.0 during 1980–2006. Changes in tastes, interest rates, and households' expected incomes do not increase household borrowing, but demographic shifts can explain part of the debt increase. The increase in house prices appears to have played the central role. House prices can be linked to household

J.J. Xiao, *Consumer Economic Wellbeing*, International Series on Consumer Science, DOI 10.1007/978-1-4939-2821-7_10

borrowing through several different channels. Financial innovations by financial institutions also seem to have boosted debt in both debt holdings and sizes (Dynan and Kohn 2007).

Debt may also influence consumer life such as marriage satisfaction. A researcher examines the relationship between debt and marital satisfaction using data from the National Survey of Families and Households and finds that changes in consumer debt predict changes in the marital satisfaction of married couples. Changes in consumer debt negatively predict couples' time together and positively predict arguments over money, which, in turn, are both associated with declines in marital satisfaction (Dew 2008).

Debt sizes and holding rates vary in different debt categories. In 2013, 74.5 % of American families held any debts, among which, 42.9 % held mortgages for their primary residences, 20.0 % had education loans, 30.9 % had vehicle loans, 10.1 % had other installment loans, and 38.1 % kept credit card balances. The median value for those holding any debts was $60,400. Median values for primary residence mortgages and other residential property debts were $115,000 and $90,000, respectively. Median values for education, vehicle, other installment, and credit card loans were $16,000, $11,900, $3,300, and $2,300, respectively (Bricker et al. 2014).

Several debt-based financial ratios are used to measure debt burdens. These measures are negatively associated with economic wellbeing. A commonly used one is the leverage ratio that is the ratio of total debts to total assets. In 2013, the aggregate leverage ratio of American families was 14.6 % and the median leverage ratio for debtors was 38.6 %, which increased from 12.0 % to 29.4 %, respectively, in 2001 (Bricker et al. 2014).

Another commonly used financial ratio is the debt-to-income ratio. In 2013, the aggregate debt-to-income ratio was 104.6 % and the median debt-to-income ratio for debtors was 107.4 %, which increased from 80.1 % to 76.7 %, respectively, in 2001. The aggregate payment-to-income ratio was 12.0 % and the median payment-to-income ratio for debtors was 15.9 %, which decreased a little from those in 2001. The fraction of payment-to-income ratio greater than 40 % in American families was 8.2 %, compared to 8.8 % in 2001 (Bricker et al. 2014).

Using data from 1992 to 2005 Surveys of Consumer Expenditures, researchers examine the relationship between debt service ratio (DSR) and find that a high DSR alone does not indicate higher sensitivity of consumption to a change in income. However, the DSR may help identify borrowing constrained households. In particular, the consumption of households with low liquid assets and high DSRs is more sensitive to income changes than the consumption of other low liquid asset households (Johnson and Li 2007).

Being late on debt payment is another indicator of economic ill-being since it signifies financial difficulties. In 2013, 14.9 % of American families were late on debt payment and 6.9 % were late on payment for 60 or more days; the comparable statistics were 14.0 % and 5.3 %, respectively, in 2001 (Bricker et al. 2014). Researchers examine the life cycle pattern of delinquency behavior with data from multiple Surveys of Consumer Finances. They find that among the 15 household life cycle categories, the top three most likely to be delinquent for 60 or more days are young couples with children aged 7 or older, middle-aged singles with children aged 15 or older, and middle-aged singles with children under 15. Younger households are more financially distressed than their older counterparts. Presence of children increases the probability of debt delinquency (Xiao and Yao 2014).

10.2 Mortgage

Home mortgages have become increasingly important for American households. For many consumers, without mortgage, the dream of becoming a homeowner would not be realized. Mortgage debt was 15 % of household assets in 1949, but rose to 28 % of household assets by 1979 and 41 % of household assets by 2001 (Green and Wachter 2005). An environment of rising house prices and declining interest rates existed in the USA during the 1990s and early 2000s and presented opportunities for refinancing homeowners to extract home equity by increasing their mortgage balances. Several factors were associated with mortgage refinancing boom such as the increasing home ownership rate, increasing home value, historically low interest rate, increasing refinances, increasing use of home equity loans, more relaxed credit limits, and more investment company participation (Lander 2008). To the extent that homeowners have present-biased preferences, refinancing is a dangerous temptation that reduces saving (Khandani et al. 2013).

The structure of the modern American mortgage has evolved over time. The US mortgage before the 1930s would be nearly unrecognizable today: it featured variable interest rates, high down payments, and short maturities. Before the Great Depression, homeowners typically renegotiated their loans every year as common practices. However, the modern US mortgage provides many more options to borrowers than are commonly provided in other countries: choosing whether to pay a fixed or floating rate of interest; locking in their interest rate in between the time they apply for the mortgage and the time they purchase their house; choosing the time at which the mortgage rate resets; choosing the term and the amortization period; prepaying freely; and generally borrowing against home equity freely. They can also obtain home mortgages at attractive terms with very low down payments (Green and Wachter 2005).

The menu of choices for the overwhelming majority of borrowers is possible because the US mortgage system—with the implicit government guarantee for Fannie Mae and Freddie Mac—has solved the problem of how to persuade low-risk borrowers to join with higher risk borrowers in broad mortgage pools. These mortgage pools provide the basis for mortgage-backed securities, which can then be sliced up in financial markets. But the benefits to mortgage borrowers come with their own set of risks: namely, the risk that Fannie Mae and Freddie Mac will malfunction in a way that will either cost the federal government a lot of money or lead to a systematic crisis in US financial markets, or both (Green and Wachter 2005). Unfortunately, this worry became a reality in 2008.

The first hints of trouble in the mortgage market surfaced in mid-2005, and conditions subsequently began to deteriorate rapidly. According to data from the Mortgage Bankers Association, the share of mortgage loans that were "seriously delinquent" (90 days or more past due or in the process of foreclosure) averaged 1.7 % from 1979 to 2006. But by the third quarter of 2008, the share of seriously delinquent mortgages had surged to 5.2 %. These delinquencies foreshadowed a sharp rise in foreclosures: roughly 1.7 million foreclosures were started in the first three quarters of 2008, an increase of 62 % from the 1.1 million in the first three quarters of 2007 (Mayer et al. 2009).

Mortgage default and delinquencies are considered indicators of consumer economic ill-being. Mortgage defaults and delinquencies are particularly concentrated among borrowers whose mortgages are classified as "subprime" or "near-prime." Some key players in the mortgage market typically group these two into a single category, which is called "nonprime" lending. Although the categories are not rigidly defined, subprime loans are generally targeted borrowers who have tarnished credit histories and little savings available for down payments. Near-prime mortgages are made to borrowers having more minor credit quality issues or borrowers who are unable or unwilling to provide full documentation of assets or income. Some of these borrowers are investing in real estate rather than occupying the properties they purchase (Mayer et al. 2009).

Slackened underwriting standards—manifested most dramatically by lenders allowing borrowers to forego down payments entirely—combined with stagnant to falling house prices in many parts of the country appear to be the most immediate contributors to the rise in mortgage defaults. The surge in early payment defaults and the rise in the share of mortgages with low or no documentation suggest that underwriting also deteriorated along other dimensions. Unorthodox mortgage features such as rate resets, prepayment penalties, or negative amortization provisions do not appear to be significant contributors to date to the defaults because borrowers who experienced problems with these provisions could refinance into other mortgages. However, as markets realized the extent of the poor underwriting and house prices began to fall, refinancing opportunities became more limited. Borrowers may not be able to resolve their problems with these products through refinancing going forward and thus may be forced to default (Mayer et al. 2009).

Foreclosure is an indicator of consumer economic ill-being. It may also have negative spillover effects on the neighborhood. Researchers use data on house transactions in the state of Massachusetts over the last 20 years to show that houses sold after foreclosure (or close in time to the death or bankruptcy of at least one seller) are sold at lower prices than other houses. Foreclosure discounts are particularly large on average at 27 % of the value of a house. Foreclosure discounts appear to be related to the threat of vandalism in low-priced neighborhoods. They also estimate that a foreclosure at a distance of 0.05 miles lowers the price of a house by about 1 % (Campbell et al. 2009).

One possible reason for many foreclosures and defaults may be because of consumer incompetence. Consumers may have difficulties to understand professional terms relevant to mortgage and make unwise mortgage decisions. Research indicates that in the late 1990s and early 2000s, many households paid higher mortgage rates than they needed to, particularly less educated and less wealthy households (Campbell 2006). American families usually face choosing between a fixed-rate (FRM) and an adjustable-rate mortgage (ARM). Theoretical research indicates that an ARM is generally attractive, but less so for a risk-averse household with a large mortgage, risky income, high default cost, or low moving probability (Campbell and Cocco 2003). In reality, many consumers may not know the differences between FRM and ARM, which has caused misuses of mortgage products. Researchers assess whether borrowers know their mortgage terms by comparing the distributions of these variables in the household-reported Survey of Consumer Finances to the distributions in lender reported data. Although most borrowers seem to know basic mortgage terms, borrowers with ARM appear likely to underestimate or not to know how much their interest rates could change. Borrowers who could experience large payment changes if interest rates rose are more likely to report not knowing these contract terms. Difficulties with gathering and processing information appear to be a factor in borrowers' lack of knowledge (Bucks and Pence 2008).

Government regulations are needed to better inform families who would like to use a mortgage to purchase houses. Research shows that households pay lower mortgage fees when all fees are rolled into the interest rate, simplifying the task of cost comparison (Woodward 2003). Some researchers have advocated mortgages with principal balances that automatically adjust to the regional level of house prices (Shiller 2008). Other researchers propose to require that mortgage terms be made available electronically in standardized form to permit the development of online sites for comparison shopping (Thaler and Sunstein 2008).

10.3 Vehicle Loans

Automobiles including cars and light trucks are the most commonly held nonfinancial asset among American consumers. In 2001, the share of families that owned automobiles was over 84 %—higher than the share that owned primary residences at 68 %. Roughly three-quarters of automobile purchases are financed through credit, and loans for automobile purchases are one of the most common forms of household borrowing (Agarwal et al. 2008).

Auto loans may help smooth consumption and reduce borrowing constraints. By examining the consumption reaction to predictable increases in discretionary income following the final payment of a vehicle loan with data from the Consumer Expenditure Survey, the results show that a 10 % increase in discretionary income due to a loan repayment leads to a 2–3 % increase in nondurable consumption (Stephens 2008).

Consumer demands for auto loans differ in terms of maturity and interest rates. Using data from the Consumer Expenditure Survey on auto loan contracts, researchers estimate the elasticities of loan demand with respect to interest rate and maturity. They find that, with the exception of high-income households, consumers are very responsive to maturity and less responsive to interest rate changes. Both elasticities vary with household income, with the maturity elasticity decreasing and the interest rate elasticity increasing with income (Attanasio et al. 2008).

Factors associated with auto loan prepayments are identified in research. When a framework of competing risks is used to analyze the prepayment and default options on auto loans with a large sample of such loans, researchers find that a decrease in the credit risk of an auto loan holder, as measured by the Fair Isaac Corp score, lowers the probability of default and raises the probability of prepayment. An increase in the loan-to-value ratio also increases the probability of default and lowers the probability of prepayment (Agarwal et al. 2008). A study to estimate a model of competing risks of default and prepayment on subprime automobile loans finds that prepayment rates increase rapidly with loan age but are not affected by prevailing market interest rates. Default rates are much more sensitive to aggregate shocks than are prepayment rates. Increases in unemployment tend to precede increases in default rates, suggesting that defaults on subprime automobile loans are driven largely by shocks to household liquidity (Heitfield and Sabarwal 2004).

Low-income consumers may be more likely to receive auto loans through community-based credit unions than from community banks. A study examines the role of relationship lending in the automobile loan market at a community development credit union and at a traditional community bank with data collected from actual car loan applications. Researchers find that the community bank relies on credit scoring, not relationship lending. Relationship lending is, however, a critical factor in the loan decision at the credit union. Low-income households with strong ties to the credit union are likely to receive loans, despite poor credit histories (Holmes et al. 2007).

10.4 Educational Loans

Educational loans provide important resources for consumers to invest in their children's or their own human capital. In the recent decades, education loan holding rates and sizes have increased among American families, especially young families (families with a head 40 years or younger). From 2001 to 2013 among young families, the education loan holding rate increased from 22.4 to 38.8 %, and the median education loan debt went up from $10,500 to $16,800 (Bricker et al. 2014).

Researchers examine the question whether students have borrowed too much for their university investments using national statistics. Based on three decades of national data, they find that college graduates have much higher lifetime earnings than high school graduates. The differential advantage of attending college over attending high school has been increasing in recent years. For example, using national average statistics, in a present discounted value calculation with a 3 % yearly rate, by age 64 the college graduate would have compiled a total of approximately $1.2 million in earnings net of tuition at age 64 as opposed to approximately $780,000 in total earnings for a high school graduate. Considering factors such as completion of college, choice of majors, and dispersion in earnings, the study concludes that overall, students do not over-borrow for university attendance. Moreover, evidence shows that some students underuse government-subsidized student loans instead of borrowing too much on credit card debts or working too much at the expense of academic performance. The study also indicates that some students at for-profit universities may borrow too much that is not worth the money (Avery and Turner 2012).

Education loan use may differ among students with different characteristics. A study investigates the determinants of taking out government-funded student loans for university study in Australia. The study finds that the probability of taking out student loans for the full cost of university is largely influenced by students' socioeconomic status. Other major influences on this decision include students' demographic and university enrollment characteristics (Birch and Miller 2008). Another researcher studies repayment behavior for college graduates who borrow under the US Federal Student Loan Program to finance higher education with US data. Findings suggest that college graduates with lower debt will lock-in interest rates, while those with higher debt will switch to an income-contingent plan (designed to help students destined for low-salary careers such as in nonprofit organizations or public services pay off their student loans) (Ionescu 2008). Using the model to quantify the effects of a reform introduced in 2006 that eliminates the possibility of locking-in interest rates for student loans, the reform leads to significant increases in default rates, which is largely accounted for by low-income borrowers (Ionescu 2008). A study quantifies the effects of alternative student loan policies on college enrollment, borrowing behavior, and default rates in a heterogeneous model of life cycle earnings and human capital accumulation. The combination of learning ability and initial stock of human capital drives the decision to enroll in college, while parental wealth has minimal effects on enrollment. Repayment flexibility increases enrollment significantly, whereas relaxation of eligibility requirements has little effect on enrollment or default rates. A policy allowing flexibility benefits low-income households, while relaxation of eligibility requirements has negligible effects on these households (Ionescu 2009).

Several studies examine student responses to student loans. A study examines college students' attitudes toward debt to determine why they are not concerned about their high debt levels. Overall, respondents are not too concerned about their debt and their financial future; optimism is greatest among sophomore/freshmen respondents; and discounting of current debt is greatest among graduate/senior/junior respondents (Wells 2007). Another study examines student workloads, debt levels, and debt perceptions of junior- and senior-level College of Business students at a Midwestern state university during the economic downturn. Overall, the students feel confident in securing employment upon graduation and in managing their debt load. Results indicate that expected salary is significantly influenced by this confidence. Additionally, students' confidence in their employment prospects and debt management abilities, and their belief that debt would impact their future lifestyles, are significantly related to student debt levels (Kuzma et al. 2010). A study explores the structure of attitudes to debt among current and prospective New

Zealand tertiary (college) students. The findings show that the structure of these attitudes is described by two dimensions, fear of debt and debt utility. On average, longitudinally, the students become less debt fearful between the end of secondary school and the end of their first year of tertiary study but their views as to the utility of debt remain unchanged (Haultain et al. 2010).

Some education loan research focuses on public policies. A theoretical research on which scholarship or student loan is better to improve student welfare in the context of moral hazard indicates that a scholarship scheme financed by a tax on graduate earnings is always at least as good as a student loan scheme. Indeed, the former will implement the first best allocation if individual effort and parental support are observable by the policy maker, and the second will be the best if they are not (Cigno and Luporini 2009). Scholars have argued that the unique nature of an investment in education results in a market failure for student loans. This market failure is said to exist despite the empirically established, attractive risk-return profile of educational investments. A review of the literature on school loan market failure argues against the market failure hypothesis and suggests that we should properly define and protect a borrower's property rights to his/her own future income. Protecting property rights and eliminating loan subsidies should result in a healthier market for educational funding (Carver 2007).

Whether educational loans should be discharged in bankruptcy is examined in the research literature. A review of government student loans in bankruptcy in Canada, Australia, England, the USA, and New Zealand suggests that all five jurisdictions are similar in that filing bankruptcy provides limited to no relief for loans funded or guaranteed by a government unit for funding post-secondary education. Two key justifications relied upon to justify this model—student abuse of the bankruptcy process and the need to protect the public interest—are unsubstantiated (Ben-Ishai 2006). Currently, the US Bankruptcy Code gives student debt the extraordinary treatment of nondischargeability, which means that, unlike all other unsecured debts, student loans are not discharged by bankruptcy proceeding. They survive a filing and continue to haunt the debtor in the post-bankruptcy life. This treatment is harsh and dramatic and some scholars recommend an income-contingent approach similar to the debt relief programs used by several high-tuition law schools in the USA (Pottow 2006). Recent decisions, however, have shown the courts' proclivities to step beyond the dictates of the Bankruptcy Code to fashion what they see to be a more equitable solution for struggling student loan debtors. For example, some courts now allow the partial discharge of student loans—discharging the portion of indebtedness that constitutes an undue hardship—as a way to mitigate the harsh outcomes produced by the undue hardship standard. Other researchers argue that partially discharging student loan debt is an ineffective and invalid option for bankruptcy courts under the Code for two reasons. The statute does not provide a definition for "undue hardship" and courts usually use the most stringent test to determine the presence of an undue hardship. Also no statutory or equitable power gives the courts the authority to pick and choose which part of student loan debt to be forgiven (Miller 2004).

10.5 Credit Card Debt

Credit card debt is an unsecured debt. Many consumers using credit cards for convenience make payments on time and do not accumulate debts. But some consumers use credit cards for the purpose of borrowing and accumulated debt that will pay an interest rate higher than that of mortgage, education, and other loans. The popularity of credit card usage is resulted from the credit market deregulation.

The deregulation of credit market in the late 1970s has made financial institutions such as credit card banks prosper. Before the deregulation, credit card divisions in banks always lost money, but after the deregulation, the credit card divisions became cash cows (Manning 2000). A researcher demonstrates that, although the structure of the credit card industry looks competitive after deregulation, its behavior is inconsistent with what conventional economic theory predicts because the credit sector in banking earned three to five times the ordinary rate of return in banking during the period 1983–1988 (Ausubel 1991). According to the economic theory, if the credit card sector is competitive, it should not earn such a high rate of return compared to other sectors in the banking industry. The profit of the credit card industry remained high in late 1990s (Ausubel 1997). Another researcher argues that the 1978 Supreme Court decision ("Marquette") fundamentally altered the market for credit card loans in a way that significantly expanded the availability of credit and increased the average risk profile of borrowers. The result is a substantial expansion in credit card availability, a reduction in average credit quality, and a secular increase in personal bankruptcies (Ellis 1998). The good news for consumers, especially low-income consumers, is that they have better access to credit than before (Bird et al. 1999; Johnson 2005; Lyons 2003). The bad news is that the probability of default among these consumers may rise too and there may be an adverse selection process occurring in the credit market. A study using market experiment data provided by a major credit card issuer presents evidence supporting this argument and find that consumers with worse credit risks are more likely to respond to and accept inferior terms of credit card solicitation. Consumers who accept inferior offers are significantly more likely to default (Ausubel 1999).

Credit market deregulation has increased consumer credit access among consumers in several special populations but they may use credit card for inappropriate purposes. A researcher estimates trends of credit access of US families. According to her findings, the ability of all households to obtain their desired debt levels increased after 1983 and more dramatically between 1992 and 1998. Those experiencing the greatest gains in credit access were black households and households with low permanent earnings (Lyons 2003). Another study using data from the 1983–1995 SCF traces the evolution of the debt position of the poor as compared to that of the population at large and finds that the fraction of poor households with a credit card more than doubled and the average balances held on these cards rose almost as rapidly as the balances of nonpoor households (Bird et al. 1999). Researchers document credit card use trends among American families in 1989–2001 and find that the proportion of households with income under $10,000 that hold credit card debts have increased by 184 %, the largest increase among all income groups, from 1989 to 2001. Black and Hispanic consumers are more likely than whites to carry credit card balances (Draut and Silva 2003). A researcher documents changes in the credit card market by using data from Surveys of Consumer Finance. Because of improvements in credit-scoring technology and risk-based pricing of credit card debt, the share of households, particularly lower income households, having a credit card has increased (Johnson 2005). A study surveys credit card use among low- and middle-income consumers nationwide and find that seven out of ten households report using their credit cards as a safety net to pay for things such as car repairs, basic living expenses, medical expenses, or house repairs. Just under half have missed or been late with a payment, with nearly a quarter of households reporting paying a late fee at least one or two times (Demos and Center for Responsible Lending 2005).

Credit card usage may be different from consumers at different life cycle stages. Researchers find that compared to young singles, older solitary households and single parents are less likely and childless middle-aged couples are more likely to keep credit card balances, while only solitary households are more likely than young singles to owe more credit card debts. Overspending is associated with both the status of keeping credit card balances and the amount of credit card debt (Baek and Hong 2004). Favorable attitude toward credit card use (i.e., approvals of using credits to make several types of purchases) is associated with credit card debts (Chien and DeVaney 2001).

For consumers at the early stage of the life cycle such as young adults, credit management is a critical developmental task in personal finance. Research on credit card behavior of college students has started in the last two decades (e.g., Grable and Joo 2006; Hayhoe et al. 1999, 2000; Joo et al. 2003; Lyons 2004, 2008; Palmer et al. 2001; Wang and Xiao 2009; Xiao et al. 1995). A survey of over 4,000 students from Arkansas, California, and Ohio indicates that as students progress through college, they acquire more credit cards and debt; furthermore, students who work 10 or more hours per week are more likely to report debt problems than those students who work less than 10 h per week (Dale and Bevill 2007). Risky credit behaviors refer to practices such as holding credit card debts, not making full payments to credit card bills, making credit card payment late, and maxing out credit card limits. These risky credit behaviors may result in negative life outcomes such as risky health behaviors (Adams and Moore 2007; Nelson et al. 2008). Credit card debts of college students have also been found to contribute to the financial stress of college students (Grable and Joo 2006). Risky use of credit card demonstrates some tendencies of compulsive buying (Roberts 1998; Roberts and Jones 2001) and materialism (Pinto et al. 2000). Additionally, credit card debts also may affect the academic performance of college students adversely (Pinto et al. 2001).

Conversely, research indicates that engaging in positive financial behaviors, including positive credit behaviors, tends to increase life satisfaction and wellbeing in other life domains (Serido et al. 2014; Shim et al. 2009, 2010; Xiao et al. 2007, 2009). College students with more financial knowledge are less likely to engage in risky credit behaviors (Xiao et al. 2011, 2014). Credit card usage among college students is less popular after the Credit Card Accountability Responsibility and Disclosure Act of 2009 has taken effect. Under this law, young adults under 21 years old need an adult cosigner to own a credit card.

10.6 Payday Loans

Borrowing from subprime debt products is an indicator of economic ill-being because subprime products are high-cost credit offered most frequently to economically disadvantaged consumers (Lander 2008). Payday loan is a typical form of subprime product and often employs a relatively standard form and lending process. Typically, a consumer will walk into a storefront location, request a loan, have their employment verified, and, if approved, walk out minutes later with the loan proceeds. In 2013, 4.2 % of American families reported taking out a payday loan (Bricker et al. 2014). The "typical" term is $15 to $30 per $100 borrowed (Stegman 2007), extremely high financial charges compared to those charged by mainstream financial institutions.

Most payday loan users are from low-income, racial and ethnic minority groups, and military families. By virtue of the product itself, customers must have checking accounts and be employed. Researchers find that these customers are disproportionately young (under age 45) and 65 % have children under age 18 living in the household. Most are from lower and middle-income households, with a moderate level of education and limited liquid assets (Lawrence and Elliehausen 2008). Fewer than half report having any savings (Elliehausen 2009). Generally, these consumers are in life stages where the demand for credit is high, and although 92 % rely on other types of credit, many have been denied credit in the past 12 months, have credit cards that are at the limit, have concerns about their ability to access credit, and are less likely to be able to tap into mortgage credit (Lawrence and Elliehausen 2008).

Risks of payday lending include paying high interest rates and, if used repeatedly, the debts will be out of control. Some research studies indicate that payday loans do not help alleviate financial distress (Melzer 2009) and are associated with poorer job performance by military borrowers (Carrell and Zinman 2008). To protect consumers in military personnel, the 2007 National Defense Authorization Act caps payday loans to service members at a 36 % APR, a regulation that industry critics support for all payday lending (CRL 2009).

However, some researchers argue that there may be reasons for the popularity of payday lending. Payday loans may be the only credits these consumers can receive. Without payday loans, these consumers may use more expensive credit forms or face worse consequences of lack of credits such as utilities being shut down or losing jobs if the car for work transportation is not fixed on time (Campbell et al. 2010).

10.7 Bankruptcy

Bankruptcy is an indicator of consumer economic ill-being because it signifies a serous sickness in a person's financial life. The current bankruptcy law allows consumers to choose between filing Chaps. 7 and 13 when facing extreme financial difficulties. Chapter 7 is the quick debt liquidation option, often referred to as straight bankruptcy, while Chap. 13 commits all of a debtor's disposable income to debt repayment for up to 5 years (Lown 2008). The number of personal bankruptcy filings in the USA rose fivefold between 1980 and 2005, from around 300,000 per year in 1980 to over 1½ million in each of the years from 2001 to 2005. By the early 2000s, more people were filing for bankruptcy each year than were graduating from college, getting divorced, or being diagnosed with cancer (White 2009). From an economic perspective, bankruptcy has two benefits for consumers, consumption insurance (to cover negative consequences of overspending) and entrepreneurship insurance (to cover failure of running own business). After reviewing relevant research, a researcher concludes that since state bankruptcy laws only differs in asset exemptions, researchers focus on effects of asset exemptions on bankruptcy and find that high-income consumers borrow more in high-exemption states and high-exemption states have more entrepreneurs (White 2009).

Researchers have attempted to identify factors associated with filing bankruptcy. Using data from the Consumer Bankruptcy Project (CBP) in the late 1970s, researchers find that debtors are commonly middle class Americans who are drowning in debt because of uncontrollable debts and increasing economic volatility (Sullivan et al. 1989). In the CBP II, they identify five sources of financial distress, job losses, skyrocketing debt levels, divorces, risking medical costs, and unaffordable homes (Sullivan et al. 2000). Some researchers believe that other factors are more important, such as gambling, credit card, and other debts besides job losses and divorces (White 2009). Examples of other sources of debt are identified in a study by Zhu (2008) with data from personal bankruptcy filings in the state of Delaware during 2003. The research shows that household expenditures on durable consumption goods, such as houses and automobiles, contribute significantly to personal bankruptcy. After reviewing several relevant studies, a researcher points out that typical bankruptcy filers are not middle class consumers but become poorer overtime. Overall, the increase in credit card and possibly mortgage debt levels since 1980 provides the most convincing explanation for the increase in bankruptcy filings in the USA (White 2007).

The Bankruptcy Abuse Prevention and Consumer Protection Act took effect in October 2005. During 2005, the highest level of individual bankruptcy filings occurred, with over two million filings. The new law has two major changes, to limit the chapter choice by imposing means tests and raising filing costs and to require pre-counseling and post-education (Lown 2008). The main purpose is to reduce the size of individual bankruptcies, a goal that seemed to be achieved in 2006 and 2007, 597,965 and 822,590 bankruptcies, respectively. However, the numbers returned to very high levels in 2008 and 2009, 1,074,225 and 1,412,838 bankruptcies (close to the level of 2001) (American Bankruptcy Institute 2010), which could be a result of the recent financial crisis that has caused high unemployment and lower income faced by many American consumers.

Researchers investigate whether the new personal bankruptcy law in 2005 plays a role in creating the mortgage crisis or making it worse. In particular, they show that there is a strong and previously unnoticed relationship between homeowners' decisions to default on their mortgages and their decisions to file for bankruptcy. In theory, bankruptcy and default could be either substitutes or complements. They show that theoretically, the bankruptcy/default relationship is complementary for most homeowners, and the relationship between foreclosure and bankruptcy is also complementary. But they find that homeowners have responded to the 2005 bankruptcy reform by treating bankruptcy as a substitute for default and foreclosure (Li and White 2009).

Researchers examine how filing for bankruptcy under Chap. 13 helps financially distressed debtors save their homes after the new bankruptcy law. Chapter 13 helps debtors save their homes by stopping foreclosure, giving debtors extra time to repay mortgage arrears, and increasing their ability to repay their mortgages by discharging some or all of their unsecured debt. They also find that nearly all debtors who use Chap. 13 are homeowners who wish to save their homes. This is despite the fact that a major bankruptcy reform adopted in 2005 was intended to force bankruptcy filers with higher incomes to repay some of their unsecured debt in Chap. 13. They also discuss how bankruptcy can be used to address the foreclosure crisis by allowing bankruptcy judges to "cram-down" (partially forgive) mortgage debt in Chap. 13 when debtors' mortgages exceed the value of their homes (White and Zhu 2010). Some researchers point out that the new bankruptcy law does not solve fundamental issues that cause bankruptcies such as improving job opportunities and tightening credit regulations (Lown 2008).

10.8 Summary

Debt helps consumers improve their economic wellbeing by allowing the consumption of goods they cannot afford such as housing, car, education, and major consumption goods if loans are not available. To measure consumer economic wellbeing, debt-related measures are better than debt-only measures. Common debt burden measures include leverage ratio, debt-to-income ratio, and payment-to-income ratio. Serious financial difficulties can also be expressed by payment-to-income ratio being 40 % or higher. Considering credit access is beneficial for consumption but heavy debt burden has negative effects on consumer economic wellbeing. Future research could examine the relationship between debt burdens and economic wellbeing and develop specific guidelines for consumers to better manage their debts in various categories.

Mortgage is the most important debt form for consumers. Without a mortgage, many Americans cannot afford to own their homes. For many consumers, fix-rate long-term mortgage may be a good choice but some consumers may use variable-rate short-term mortgage to increase their economic wellbeing if they fully understand the benefits and risks of this type of mortgage. Research indicates that many consumers are not fully informed when applying for a mortgage. Researchers have proposed a variety of ways to help better inform consumers when they are making mortgage decisions.

Vehicle loans are used by some consumers. Since many of those are short-term loans, they do not affect consumer economic wellbeing in the long run. For many consumers, buying cars without using a car loan is affordable.

An education loan is considered a good investment for human capital development. Researchers examine if students borrow too much in education loans and evidence shows that the answer is no. In fact, some students may underuse government-sponsored low-interest-rate student loans. There are some policy debates on whether or not student loans should be discharged in bankruptcy.

Borrowing credit card debt is considered an undesirable practice. Credit cards have been developed to facilitate payment efficiency. Many consumers use them for convenience purposes. Consumers use credit card for borrowing tools to smooth cash flow problems that don't hurt their economic wellbeing in a short run. However, some consumers use credit card for daily expenses that would hurt their economic wellbeing in the long run since they will never pay off their debts and can be trapped by the debt for life.

A payday loan is a form of usury employed by many low-income consumers. These consumers borrow from payday loans with extremely high interest rates because they cannot borrow money from mainstream financial institutions that offer regular, much lower interest rates. Some researchers believe that there may be some benefits for consumers to use payday loans and other usury products.

Bankruptcy is a strong indicator of consumer economic ill-being. Filing bankruptcy is to claim the serious sickness in a person's financial life. The negative record will be officially kept for 10 years compared to other negative records such as being late in payment for only 7 years by law. Consumers need to carefully manage debts to avoid bankruptcy. In the 2005 bankruptcy law, the government increased the barriers for consumers wishing to file bankruptcy. Researchers have also developed policy recommendations to help consumer bankruptcy filers reduce financial burdens.

References

Adams, T., & Moore, M. (2007). High-risk health and credit behavior among 18- to 25-year-old college students. *Journal of American College Health, 56*, 101–108.

Agarwal, S., Ambrose, B., & Chomsisengphet, S. (2008). Determinants of automobile loan default and prepayment. *Economic Perspectives, 32*(3), 17–28.

American Bankruptcy Institute. (2010). *Bankruptcy statistics*. Retrieved May 20, 2010, from http://www.abiworld.org/Content/NavigationMenu/NewsRoom/BankruptcyStatistics/Bankruptcy_Filings_1.htm

Attanasio, O., Goldberg, P., & Kyriazidou, E. (2008). Credit constraints in the market for consumer durables: Evidence from micro data on car loans. *International Economic Review, 49*(2), 401–436.

Ausubel, L. M. (1991). Failure of competition in the credit card market. *American Economic Review, 81*(1), 50–81.

Ausubel, L. M. (1997). Credit card defaults, credit card profits, and bankruptcy. *American Bankruptcy Law Journal, 71*, 249–270.

Ausubel, L. M. (1999). *Adverse selection in the credit card market. mimeo*. College Park, MD: University of Maryland.

Avery, C., & Turner, S. (2012). Student loans: Do college students borrow too much—Or not enough? *Journal of Economic Perspectives, 26*, 165–192.

Baek, E., & Hong, G. (2004). Effects of family life-cycle stages on consumer debts. *Journal of Family and Economic Issues, 25*(3), 359–385.

Ben-Ishai, S. (2006). Government student loans, government debts and bankruptcy: A comparative study. *Canadian Business Law Journal, 44*(2), 211–244.

Birch, E. R., & Miller, P. W. (2008). The impact of income-contingent provisions on students' loan-taking behaviour. *Journal of Economic Studies, 35*(1), 4–25.

Bird, E. J., Hagstrom, P. A., & Wild, R. (1999). Credit card debts of the poor: High and rising. *Journal of Policy Analysis and Management, 18*(1), 125–133.

Bricker, J., Dettling, L. J., Henriques, A., Hsu, J. W., Moore, K. B., Sabelhaus, J., et al. (2014). Changes in US family finances from 2010 to 2013: Evidence from the Survey of Consumer Finances. *Federal Reserve Bulletin, 100*(4), 1–40.

Bucks, B. K., & Pence, K. M. (2008). Do borrowers know their mortgage terms? *Journal of Urban Economics, 64*, 218–233.

Campbell, J. Y. (2006). Household finance. *Journal of Finance, 61*, 1553–1604.

Campbell, J., & Cocco, J. (2003). Household risk management and optimal mortgage choice. *Quarterly Journal of Economics, 118*, 1449–1494.

Campbell, J. Y., Giglio, S., & Pathak, P. (2009). Forced sales and house prices. *National Bureau of Economic Research Working Paper* 14866.

Campbell, J., Jackson, H., Madrian, B., & Tufano, P. (2010). *The regulation of consumer financial products: An introductory essay with four case studies. Working paper*. Cambridge, MA: Harvard University.

Carrell, S., & Zinman, J. (2008). *In harm's way? Payday loan access and military personnel performance. Working paper*. Hanover, NH: Dartmouth College.

Carver, A. (2007). The market failure for student loans. *Journal of Private Enterprise, 23*(1), 101–115.

Chien, Y., & DeVaney, S. A. (2001). The effects of credit attitude and socioeconomic factors on credit card and installment debt. *Journal of Consumer Affairs, 35*(1), 162–179.

Cigno, A., & Luporini, A. (2009). Scholarships or student loans? Subsidizing higher education in the presence of moral hazard. *Journal of Public Economic Theory, 11*(1), 55–87.

CRL. (2009). *Congress should cap interest rates. Research brief*. Durham, NC: Center for Responsible Lending.

Dale, L., & Bevill, S. (2007). An analysis of the current status of student debt: Implications for helping vulnerable students manage debt. *Academy of Educational Leadership Journal, 11*(2), 121–127.

Demos and Center for Responsible Lending. (2005). *The plastic safety net: The reality behind debt in America*. New York: Authors.

Dew, J. (2008). Debt change and marital satisfaction change in recently married couples. *Family Relations, 57*(1), 60–71.

Draut, T., & Silva, J. (2003). *Borrowing to make ends meet: The growth of credit card debt in the 90's*. New York: Demos.

Dynan, K. (2009). Changing household financial opportunities and economic security. *Journal of Economic Perspectives, 23*(4), 49–68.

Dynan, K. E., & Kohn, D. L. (2007). The rise in U.S. household indebtedness: Causes and consequences. FEDS Working Paper No. 2007-37. Retrieved from SSRN: http://ssrn.com/abstract=1019052

Elliehausen, G. (2009). An analysis of consumers' use of payday loans. In *Financial Services Research Program, Monograph No. 41*. Washington, DC: George Washington University.

Ellis, D. (1998, March). The effect of consumer interest rate deregulation on credit card volumes, charge-offs and personal bankruptcy rates. *Bank Trends, 98-05,* 1–11.

Gabaix, X., & Laibson, D. (2006). Shrouded attributes, consumer myopia, and information suppression in competitive markets. *Quarterly Journal of Economics, 121*(2), 505–540.

Grable, J. E., & Joo, S. H. (2006). Student racial differences in credit card debt and financial behaviors and stress. *College Student Journal, 40*(2), 400–408.

Green, R. K., & Wachter, S. M. (2005). The American mortgage in historical and international context. *Journal of Economic Perspectives, 19*(4), 93–114.

Haultain, S., Kemp, S., & Chernyshenko, O. (2010). The structure of attitudes to student debt. *Journal of Economic Psychology, 31*(3), 322–330.

Hayhoe, C. R., Leach, L. J., Turner, P. R., Bruin, M. J., & Lawrence, F. C. (2000). Differences in spending habits and credit card use of college students. *The Journal of Consumer Affairs, 34*(1), 113–133.

Hayhoe, C. R., Leach, L., & Turner, P. R. (1999). Discriminating the number of credit cards held by college students using credit and money attitudes. *Journal of Economic Psychology, 20,* 643–656.

Heitfield, E., & Sabarwal, T. (2004). What drives default and prepayment on subprime auto loans? *Journal of Real Estate Finance and Economics, 29*(4), 457–477.

Holmes, J., Isham, J., Petersen, R., & Sommers, P. M. (2007). Does relationship lending still matter in the consumer banking sector? Evidence from the automobile loan market. *Social Science Quarterly, 88*(2), 585–597.

Ionescu, F. (2008). Consolidation of student loan repayments and default incentives. *The B. E. Journal of Macroeconomics, 8(1),* Article 22. DOI: 10.2202/1935-1690.1682.

Ionescu, F. (2009). The Federal Student Loan Program: Quantitative implications for college enrollment and default rates. *Review of Economic Dynamics, 12*(1), 205–231.

Johnson, K. W. (2005). Recent development in the credit card market and the financial obligations ration. *Federal Reserve Bulletin (Autumn), 91,* 473–486.

Johnson, K. W., & Li, G. (2007). *Do high debt payments hinder household consumption smoothing? Finance and economics discussion series*. Washington, DC: Federal Reserve Board.

Joo, S. H., Grable, J. E., & Bagwell, D. C. (2003). Credit card attitudes and behaviors of college students. *College Student Journal, 37*(3), 405–419.

Khandani, A. E., Lo, A. W., & Merton, R. C. (2013). Systemic risk and the refinancing ratchet effect. *Journal of Financial Economics, 108*(1), 29–45.

Kuzma, A., Kuzma, J., & Thiewes, H. (2010). An examination of business students' student loan debt and total debt. *American Journal of Business Education, 3*(4), 71–77.

Lander, D. A. (2008). Regulating consumer lending. In J. J. Xiao (Ed.), *Handbook of consumer finance research* (pp. 387–410). New York: Springer.

Lawrence, E., & Elliehausen, G. (2008). A comparative analysis of payday loan customers. *Contemporary Economic Policy, 26*(2), 299–316.

Li, W., & White, M. (2009). Mortgage default, foreclosure, and bankruptcy. SSRN *Working Paper Series*.

Lown, J. M. (2008). Consumer bankruptcy. In J. J. Xiao (Ed.), *Handbook of consumer finance research* (pp. 363–374). New York: Springer.

Lyons, A. C. (2003). How credit access has changed over time for U.S. households. *Journal of Consumer Affairs, 37*(Winter), 231–255.

Lyons, A. C. (2004). A profile of financially at-risk college students. *The Journal of Consumer Affairs, 38*(1), 56–80.

Lyons, A. C. (2008). Risky credit card behavior of college students. In J. J. Xiao (Ed.), *Handbook of consumer finance research* (pp. 185–208). New York: Springer.

Manning, R. D. (2000). *Credit card nation: The consequences of America's addition to credit.* New York: Basic Books.

Mayer, C., Pence, K., & Sherlund, S. M. (2009). The rise in mortgage defaults. *Journal of Economic Perspectives, 23*(1), 27–50.

Melzer, B. T. (2009). *The real costs of credit access: Evidence from the payday lending market. Working paper*. Evanston, IL: Kellogg School of Management, Northwestern University.

Miller, L. (2004). The option that is not an option: The invalidity of the partial discharge option for the student loan debtor. *Wake Forest Law Review, 39*(4), 1053–1078.

Nelson, M. C., Lust, K., Story, M., & Ehlinger, E. (2008). Credit card debts, stress and key health risk behaviors among college students. *American Journal of Health Promotion, 22*(6), 400–412.

Palmer, T. S., Pinto, M. B., & Parente, D. H. (2001). College students' credit card debt and the role of parental involvement: Implications for public policy. *Journal of Public Policy & Marketing, 20*(1), 105–113.

Pinto, M. B., Parente, D. H., & Palmer, T. S. (2000). Materialism and credit card use by college students. *Psychological Reports, 86*, 643–652.

Pinto, M. B., Parente, D. H., & Palmer, T. S. (2001). College student performance and credit card usage. *The Journal of College Student Development, 42*(1), 49–58.

Pottow, J. A. E. (2006). The nondischargeability of student loans in personal bankruptcy proceedings: The search for a theory. *Canadian Business Law Journal, 44*(2), 245–278.

Roberts, J. A. (1998). Compulsive buying among college students: An investigation of its antecedents, consequences, and implications for policy. *The Journal of Consumer Affairs, 32*(2), 295–319.

Roberts, J. A., & Jones, E. (2001). Money attitudes, credit card use, and compulsive buying among American college students. *The Journal of Consumer Affairs, 35*(2), 213–240.

Serido, J., Shim, S., Xiao, J. J., Tang, C., & Card, N. (2014). Financial adaptation among college students: Helping students cope with financial strain. *Journal of College Student Development, 55*(3), 310–316.

Shiller, R. J. (2008). *The subprime solution: How today's global financial crisis happened, and what to do about it.* Princeton, NJ: Princeton University Press.

Shim, S., Barber, B., Card, N., Xiao, J. J., & Serido, J. (2010). Financial socialization of first-year college students: The roles of parents, work, and education. *Journal of Youth and Adolescence, 39*, 1457–1470.

Shim, S., Xiao, J. J., Barber, B., & Lyons, A. (2009). Pathways to life success: A model of financial well-being for young adults. *Journal of Applied Developmental Psychology, 30*, 708–723.

Stegman, M. A. (2007). Payday lending. *Journal of Economic Perspectives, 21*(1), 169–190.

Stephens, M. (2008). The consumption response to predictable changes in discretionary income: Evidence from the repayment of vehicle loans. *Review of Economics and Statistics, 90*(2), 241–252.

Sullivan, T., Warren, E., & Westbrook, J. L. (1989). *As we forgive our debtors*. New York: Oxford University Press.

Sullivan, T., Warren, E., & Westbrook, J. L. (2000). *The fragile middle class: Americans in debt.* New Heaven, CT: Yale University Press.

Thaler, R. H., & Sunstein, C. R. (2008). *Nudge: Improving decisions about health, wealth, and happiness*. New Haven, CT: Yale University Press.

Wang, J., & Xiao, J. J. (2009). Buying behavior, social support, and credit card indebtedness of college students. *International Journal of Consumer Studies, 33*(1), 2–10.

Wells, C. (2007). Optimism, intertemporal choice, and college student debt. *Journal of Personal Finance, 5*(4), 44–66.

White, M. J. (2007). Bankruptcy reform and credit cards. *Journal of Economic Perspectives, 21*(4), 175–199.

White, M. J. (2009). Bankruptcy: Past puzzles, recent reforms, and the mortgage crisis. *American Law and Economics Review, 11*, 1–23.

White, M. J., & Zhu, N. (2010). Saving your home in chapter 13 bankruptcy. *Journal of Legal Studies, 39*(1), 33–61.

Woodward, S. E. (2003). Consumer confusion in the mortgage market. *Sand Hill Econometrics Working Paper*. Retrieved March 31, 2010, from http://www.sandhillecon.com/pdf/consumer_confusion.pdf

Xiao, J. J., Ahn, S., Serido, J., & Shim, S. (2014). Earlier financial literacy and later financial behavior of college students. *International Journal of Consumer Studies, 38*, 593.

Xiao, J. J., Noring, F. E., & Anderson, J. G. (1995). College students' attitudes towards credit cards. *Journal of Consumer Studies and Home Economics, 19*, 155–174.

Xiao, J. J., Shim, S., Barber, B., & Lyons, A. (2007). *Academic success and well-being of college students: Financial behaviors matter.* Report. TCAI, University of Arizona. Available from http://cals.arizona.edu/fcs/tcai/research/pilotreport.pdf

Xiao, J. J., Tang, C., Serido, J., & Shim, S. (2011). Antecedents and consequences of risky credit behavior among college students: Application and extension of the Theory of Planned Behavior. *Journal of Public Policy & Marketing, 30*(2), 239–245.

Xiao, J. J., Tang, C., & Shim, S. (2009). Acting for happiness: Financial behavior and life satisfaction of college students. *Social Indicators Research, 92*, 53–68.

Xiao, J. J., & Yao, R. (2014). Consumer debt delinquency by family lifecycle categories. *International Journal of Bank Marketing, 32*(1), 43–59.

Zhu, N. (2008). *Household consumption and personal bankruptcy. Working paper*. San Diego, CA: UC Davis.

Chapter 11
Consumer Saving

Abstract This chapter summarizes the research literature on consumer savings. First an overview of consumer savings is presented. Then research on saving motives is reviewed. After that the research literature on saving for emergencies, children's education, and retirement is described. Risk tolerance, an important concept in long-term saving and investing, is then discussed. Finally, research on an institutional assistance to help low-income consumers save, Individual Development Account, is examined.

11.1 Overview of Consumer Savings

Asset is an important indicator of consumer economic wellbeing that is accumulated through saving and investing. In the last five decades, consumer economic wellbeing in the USA, measured by assets, has increased. Research indicates that the ratio of housing value to income doubled from 1962 to 2008. For retirement savings, more households own IRAs, and fewer own traditional defined benefit pension plans. Household equity holdings increased from 1989 to 2007. Low-, middle-, and high-income groups have the same pattern but different magnitudes (Dynan 2009).

About half of consumers are saving as reported by themselves but self-reported saving rates are diverse among families with different demographic characteristics. Based on the 2013 Survey of Consumer Finance, 53.0 % of families report having saved. Income is positively associated with self-reported saving (Bricker et al. 2014, Box 4).

Net worth (total assets minus total debts) is another important indicator of consumer economic wellbeing. Net worth amounts are also diverse among families with various demographic characteristics. In 2013, the median net worth of American families was $81,200. Family net worth is positively associated with family income. The median net worth of the bottom 20 % income families was $6,400 while that of the top 10 % income families was $1,125,900. The age is also positively associated with net worth until the second oldest age group. In 2014, consumers aged 65–74 had the highest median $232,100. The youngest group (under 35) had the lowest median, $10,400 (Bricker et al. 2014, Table 2).

Asset can be categorized as financial asset and nonfinancial asset. In 2013, 94.5 % of American families held some form of financial assets. Most commonly

J.J. Xiao, *Consumer Economic Wellbeing*, International Series on Consumer Science, DOI 10.1007/978-1-4939-2821-7_11

held financial assets are transaction accounts (checking and savings accounts) (93.2 %) and retirement accounts (49.2 %). Other commonly held financial assets were cash value life insurance (19.2 %), stocks (13.8 %), savings bonds (10.0 %), pooled investments (8.2 %), and certificates of deposit (7.8 %). Among American families in 2013, 91.0 % held nonfinancial assets. Most commonly held nonfinancial assets were vehicles (86.3 %) and the primary residence (65.2 %). Family holding rates of other nonfinancial assets include other residential property (13.2 %), business equity (11.7 %), equity in nonresidential property (7.2 %), and other (7.3 %) (Bricker et al. 2014, Table 3).

Research shows patterns of household financial asset ownership. Based on data from the 1989 Survey of Consumer Finance, in terms of ownership associations between two assets, 22 pairs (61 %) of assets showed positive effects on each other. For instance, owning a savings accounts increases the chance of owning checking accounts, and vice versa. Eight pairs (22 %) did not affect each other in terms of ownership. Four pairs (11 %) negatively influenced the ownership on each other. The remaining two pairs (6 %) showed asymmetrical effects (Xiao 1995). Another study examines the effects of income and life cycle variables on the ownership of 11 household-held financial assets, using the 1989 Survey of Consumer Finance. The results show that life cycle variables, such as household head's age, marital status, employment status, and child's presence, influenced ownership of 11 financial assets. The results can be used to construct various family life cycle scenarios to improve educational and business programs in financial planning and counseling (Xiao 1996).

Researchers examine determinants of household holdings of bonds and stocks and find that households having a planning horizon of at least 10 years have higher amounts of bonds and stocks. Reporting a saving motive of "growth" is associated with higher stock holdings. Controlling for income and other variables, stock and bond holdings increase with education and are higher for whites than nonwhites (Zhong and Xiao 1995). Another study examines the trend of checking accounts during a period of significant deregulation of depository institutions (1983–1989) and finds that low-income households are worse off in terms of owning various checking accounts and balances of primary checking accounts (Xiao et al. 1997).

11.2 Saving Motives

Saving motives can be considered saving goals to help improve consumer economic wellbeing. Eight saving motives are first mentioned by Keynes (1936) that include the precautionary ("to build up a reserve against unforeseen contingencies"), life cycle ("to provide for an anticipated future relationship between the income and the needs of the individual"), intertemporal substitution ("to enjoy interest and appreciation"), improvement ("to enjoy a gradually increasing expenditure"), independence ("to enjoy a sense of independence and the power to do things, though without a clear idea or definite intention of specific action"), enterprise ("to secure a masse de manoeuvre to carry out speculative or business projects"), bequest ("to bequeath a fortune"), and avarice ("to satisfy pure miserliness, i.e., unreasonable but insistent inhibitions against acts of expenditure as such") (pp. 107–108). Some of these motives are developed into formal theories such as the life cycle hypothesis by economists (see Chap. 9 for a discussion of these theories). A review of saving theory and evidence finds that many motives mentioned by Keynes are still valid after 60 years (Browning and Lusardi 1996).

Many economic theories imply saving motives with indirect evidence. For example, the life cycle hypothesis conceptualizes the existence of a retirement savings motive. This concept encompasses the assumption that workers save in their work years and draw savings when they retire from work, implying a retirement saving motive (Ando and Modigliani 1963). The precautionary saving motive assumes that people are uncertain about their future income and expenses so that they save for emergencies (Carroll 1997, 2001). Somewhat related is the theory of intergenerational transfer, which suggests that people save to accumulate wealth for their children (Barro 1974; Kurz 1984).

In reality, it is possible to identify multiple saving motives (Browning and Lusardi 1996). Most commonly reported saving reasons, according to the 2010 Survey of Consumer Finance, are retirement (30.1 %) and liquidity (emergency) (35.2 %). Other saving reasons are for future purchases (11.5 %), educational cost (8.2 %), for the family (5.7 %), buying a home (3.2 %), and investment (1.2 %) (Bricker et al. 2012, Table 3). A study based on data from a national survey in China shows that emergency, retirement, and education are major saving reasons for Chinese urban consumers (Yao et al. 2014).

Research on self-reported saving motives suggests that saving motives have a hierarchical pattern, in which saving motives reflecting financial needs move up when economic resources increase. For example, low-income consumers are more likely to save for daily expenses, middle-income consumers for emergency, while higher income consumers save for retirement (Xiao and Noring 1994). Hierarchical saving motives may be related to mental accounting (Xiao and Olson 1993). These multilevel saving motives are reflected to consumer financial asset shares (Xiao and Anderson 1997). The hierarchy of saving motives is also found in other studies (DeVaney et al. 2007; Canova et al. 2005). Consumers in different countries may value different saving motives. For example, compared to Americans (all races), Chinese are more likely to report saving for their children (Xiao and Fan 2002).

11.3 Savings for Emergencies

Transaction accounts are usually considered important emergency funds for families. In 2010, the median amount of transaction accounts among American families was $3,500. Amounts in transaction accounts are different by demographic groups. Families in the bottom 20 % income category had a median value of $700 while families in the top 10 % income category possessed a medium value of $35,000 for these accounts in 2010. Age shows a positive association with the transaction account. In 2010, the oldest age group (75 or older) had the highest median value of $7,200, while the youngest group (under 35) had the lowest value of $2,100. Family structures show diverse patterns. Couple families without children had the highest value of $7,100, while singles with children had the lowest median values of $1,000 (Bricker et al. 2012, Table 6).

A number of studies have examined factors associated with family emergency fund holdings and the effects of emergency fund holdings on family financial well-being (Harness et al. 2008). Emergency funds are defined as savings available to cover household expenses in the event of significant income disruption (Johnson and Widdows 1985). Based on the degree of liquidity, emergency funds are categorized as quick, intermediate, and comprehensive funds. Varying across studies, an adequate emergency fund level is defined as a resource intended to cover 3–6-month expenses of a family. Emergency fund-related ratios have been used to study the financial wellbeing of older women (Hong and Swanson 1995) and newly married households (Godwin 1996). Studies also compared emergency fund holdings among households in two time periods (Chang and Huston 1995) and with different emergency fund guidelines (Bhargava and Lown 2006). Research also examines emergency fund holding among Asian American households (Hong and Kao 1997) and among households with various employment statuses (Rodriquez-Flores and DeVaney 2007) and family types (Huston and Chang 1997). The amounts of emergency funds saved by households are more a function of their ability to save than their actual need (Bi and Montalto 2004). Based on expected utility theory, households should have different ratios of emergency funds based on income uncertainties (Chang et al. 1997). Emergency fund levels may also be associated with financial behavior. A study finds that the perceived emergency fund level of consumers is associated with several financial behaviors such as saving regularly, paying credit card bills in full, and having a written financial plan (Joo and Grable 2006).

11.4 Saving for Children's Education

Saving for children's college education indicates parental contributions to children's human capital investment that would enhance children's economic wellbeing when they become financially independent. Many parents report saving for children's education as a saving goal. Based on the 1992 Survey of Consumer Finance data, researchers find that more educated parents are more likely to have college saving as a goal than otherwise similar less educated parents. Asian and Hispanic parents are more likely to have college saving as a goal than similar White non-Hispanic parents. Parents with a retirement account are more likely to have college saving as a goal, but no other financial variables were significant (Lee et al. 1997).

Saving for children's education may be consistent with the life cycle hypothesis, which stresses the importance of consumption smoothness. Using the actual amount of parents' financial support reported in the Survey of Consumer Finances, a researcher estimates the expected expenditures on children's college education and investigates the effect of expected expenditures on parents' savings. The results show that parents' support for each of their children's college expenses decreases with the number of children. The results are consistent with the predictions of the life cycle theory of saving and consumption that households save in advance for expected expenses to smooth their consumption (Yilmazer 2008). Another researcher examines households' standard of living as they pay for college. Using the Consumer Expenditure Survey, he finds that households appear to do a relatively good job smoothing their consumption into the academic year, despite large expenses, which is consistent with the life cycle hypothesis. Some evidence shows a delayed decline in consumption and a decline for households with children first beginning college, but the magnitudes of these declines are quite small (Souleles 2000).

Parental contributions to children's college education vary by family types. Using parent interview data from a subsample of the National Postsecondary Student Aid Study, researchers compare the financial contributions of married, divorced, and remarried parents toward their children's college education and find that although divorced parents contribute significantly less than married parents, remarried parents contribute amounts similar to those of divorced parents, despite having incomes similar to those of married parents. They also investigate the financial contributions of divorced and remarried parents who lived in states that permit courts to extend child support beyond the age of 18 for college expenses (postmajority states) and find that living in a postmajority state is not associated with increased parent contributions (Turley and Desmond 2010).

Some parents even use their retirement funds to help children's college education. Research based on a survey of a sample of parents shows that parents with two children in college are more likely to use retirement savings to pay for college costs. When the first child has contributed less to college, parents are more likely to use retirement savings. Upper income parents are less likely to use retirement savings for college expenses (Todd and DeVaney 1997).

Many parents use 529 plans to save for children's higher education because these plans allow parents to save state taxes when the funds are used for children's college education. Research of effects of 529 plans on consumer economic wellbeing is limited. One study examines the 529 college savings plan markets and finds a positive relationship between state tax benefits and 529 plan fees. A $100 increase in potential taxable income benefit from investing in a 529 plan is associated with a 3–6 basis point increase in investment management fees for direct-sold 529 college savings plans, suggesting that government policies designed to make college more affordable could enable investment firms to charge excess fees (Bogan 2014).

Child Development Account (CDA) is another government policy to encourage parents to save for their children's higher education. In Maine, a statewide CDA program has been established using the state's 529 plan platform and offering a $500 financial incentive for postsecondary education to every newborn in the state. This program is designed to increase access to higher education by encouraging college savings at the beginning of a child's life. Early evidence shows that the overall enrollment rate is 21 % among all eligible children. Data from a survey of 437 eligible parents suggest that the $500 incentive is attractive and that financially sophisticated parents are more likely to enroll their child (Huang et al. 2013).

11.5 Saving for Retirement

Saving for retirement is an active saving goal for many consumers. Adequate retirement savings is an important indicator of consumer economic wellbeing. However, many consumers have inadequate retirement savings and many even do not have retirement saving accounts. Based on the 2010 Survey of Consumer Finance data, only about half (50.4 %) of American families had retirement saving accounts. Holding rates of retirement accounts vary by family characteristics. The rate is positively associated with income; only 11.2 % of families in the bottom 20 % held retirement accounts, while 90.1 % of top 10 % income families did so. Age shows another inverse U-pattern. The middle age group (45–54) had the highest holding rate of 60.0 %, while the youngest group (under 35) had the lowest holding rate, only 41.1 %. Family structures show diverse patterns too. Couples without children had the highest holding rate (61.6 %) while singles without children and aged 55 or older had the lowest rate of 33.7 % (Bricker et al. 2012, Table 6).

Retirement account median values are moderate too, which was $44,000 in 2010. It is positively associated with income. Families in the bottom 20 % income levels had a median value of $8,000 while the top 10 % income families had a median value of $277,000. Two age groups (aged 55–64, 65–74) had the highest value ($100,000), while the youngest group (under 35) had the lowest value ($10,500). Families with different structures have diverse median values of retirement accounts. Couples without children had the highest retirement account value of $77,000, while singles with children had the lowest value of $17,800 (Bricker et al. 2012, Table 6). Work-related retirement plans are voluntary and many consumers decide not to participate. Income is strongly related to nonparticipation, with the nonparticipation rate among the bottom 20 % income families being 54.6 % while that of the top 10 % families being only 5.5 % (Bricker et al. 2012, Table 6.7).

In the USA, major retirement sources are social security, employer-sponsored defined benefits, defined contribution retirement plans (401k type plans), and private savings (Hanna and Chen 2008). In recent years, retirement income adequacy has become a major issue because of the uncertainty of the social security system and the trends moving from defined benefit plans to defined contribution plans. The trend started because of the Employee Retirement Income and Security Act of 1974. In 1978, a section 401(k) was added to the Internal Revenue Code. Then in 1981 a clarification allowed employers to exclude employer and employee 401(k) contributions from taxable income (Campbell et al. 2010). In 1975, defined benefit (DB) plan participants outnumbered defined contribution (DC) plan participants by 2.4 to 1 while by 2007, DC plan participants outnumbered DB plan participants by 3.4 by

1 (US Department of Labor 2010). Many factors associated with work-related retirement plan participation and contributions. For example, employer matching, ability to withdraw or borrow from the plan, risk tolerance, labor income, and years of working for the current employer are positively related to 401k plan contributions (Xiao 1997).

In the last decades, behavioral economists find evidence that workers cannot behave rationally to participate in, contribute to, and manage their retirement plans effectively. For example, plan participation, contribution rates, and asset allocation outcomes are heavily influenced by employer defaults (Carroll et al. 2009; Choi et al. 2004a, 2005; Madrian and Shea 2001; Thaler and Benartzi 2004); participants chase past returns in both their asset allocation and contribution rate choices (Benartzi 2001; Choi et al. 2004b, 2009); they fail to rebalance (Ameriks and Zeldes 2004; Mitchell et al. 2006), they believe that their own company stocks have higher than the market return (Lai and Xiao 2010); and their asset allocation choices are sensitive to the structure of the investment menu (Benartzi and Thaler 2001; Brown et al. 2007; for a review, see Benartzi and Thaler 2007). These findings suggest that there are cognitive limitations of workers when they save for retirement.

These concerns have motivated several key provisions in the Pension Protection Act of 2006. This law allows employers to structure their saving plans to incorporate automatic enrollment, automatic contribution escalation, and a diversified default asset allocation (Campbell et al. 2010). New evidence shows that sponsors offering automatic enrollment and target date funds as default investment options for workers are increasing. Researchers suggest further government regulation opportunities such as promoting access, promoting annuitization of retirement wealth, and assisting with workers' investment decisions (Campbell et al. 2010).

A number of studies examine retirement saving adequacy. Perceived retirement income adequacy may be associated with age, gender, income, self-employment status, and planning horizon (Malroutu and Xiao 1995). Based on different assumptions for major parameters such as rate of return on investment and consumption needs at retirements, estimated actual adequacy rates vary (Hanna and Chen 2008). The most pessimistic estimate is that only 31 % of households have a high enough savings rate, assuming a retirement at age 62 (Moore and Mitchell 1997). The most optimistic estimate is that 80 % of households would achieve an optional consumption level in a retirement (Scholz et al. 2006). Other estimates are in between, from 52 % (Yuh et al. 1998a, b), 56 % (Ameriks 2000, 2001; Yao et al. 2003), 57 % (Hanna et al. 2003), to 65 % (Butrica et al. 2003).

Researchers examine sources of inequality among American households with a retired elderly head with decomposition of Gini coefficients. Results show that inequality of investment and labor income contributes most to overall income inequality. Income inequality of three types of households—couples with one retiree, retired couples, and retired singles—is studied in terms of sources of income inequality. Inequality of investment income contributes most to income inequality for retired singles and for retired couples (Xiao et al. 1999).

11.6 Risk Tolerance

In long-term investing such as saving for retirement at young age, consumers need to consider the financial risk of return on their financial assets. Risk tolerance is an important concept in economic research and financial planning. Risk tolerance is labeled variously and defined differently in diverse fields.

Grable (2008) provides a comprehensive review of risk tolerance in the literature of economics and behavior science. The conceptual frameworks of risk tolerance can be divided into two broad categories, the neoclassic and descriptive frameworks. The neoclassic framework refers to the expected utility theory (EUT), originated by Von Neumann and Morgenstern (1947). Under this framework, consumers know the options and probabilities of these options and select the option with the highest expected value. Consumers make rational choices that result in the highest expected value. Under this framework, consumers are assumed to be risk averse and constant relative risk aversion is generally represented graphically so that as wealth increases marginal utility slowly increases, at an ever-slowing rate (Deaton and Muellbauer 1980). As an extension of EUT, the modern portfolio theory is developed to analyze investment portfolios. This theory predicts that investors should only be willing to take additional risk if the return associated with the risk is high (Markowitz 1952). The neoclassical model has limitations and more rigorous normative analyses with computer assistance can be developed (Hanna 1989). For example, Hanna et al. (1995) use the computer expert system and the EUT theory to predict optimal retirement savings, assuming different levels of risk tolerance that result in different life cycle retirement savings. Modern economic treatments use the normative approach in which researchers compare actual behavior to optimal (normative) behavior to ascertain which households are more likely to be making mistakes (Yuh and Hanna 2010).

The descriptive framework refers to a set of frameworks that describe actual consumer behavior. The expected utility theory has advantages to specify the research question with mathematical functions that render specific predictions with certain assumptions. However, some fundamental assumptions of the utility function are challenged by researchers. Friedman and Savage (1948) were the first to challenge the assumption of utility function that consumers have a constant risk aversion throughout the entire domain of wealth. Allais (1953) provided contradictory evidences to show that consumers do not make rational decisions. Based on these and other studies that show violation of assumptions of the expected utility theory, Kahneman and Tversky (1979) developed the prospect theory. The prospect theory is revolutionary that has inspired the development of new fields of behavioral economics and finance. Kahneman, a psychology professor at Princeton University, won Nobel economics prize in 2002 because of this and other contributions to economics.

The prospect theory has developed its own language to substitute for corresponding concepts in EUT. For example, in prospect theory, utility is called value, probabilities are called decision weights, and options are called prospects. Unlike EUT that asserts consumers have the same risk aversion tendency in financial decisions, prospect theory explains that consumer risk tolerance tendencies are different depending on context. Specifically, in the context of gain, consumers are risk averse, where in the context of loss, consumers are risk tolerant (Kahneman and Tversky 1979). In the advanced prospect theory (Tversky and Kahneman 1992), consumer risk tolerance is described in high and low probability contexts. Based on two principles, diminishing sensitivity and loss aversion, this cumulative prospect theory asserts a fourfold pattern of risk-taking attitude: risk aversion for gains and risk seeking for losses of high probability, and risk seeking for gains and risk aversion for losses of low probability.

Both EUT and prospect theory assume that consumers make decisions based on assessment of consequences. However, consumer decisions on risky options may be influenced by emotions. Loewenstein et al. (2001) have proposed "risk-as-feeling" as an alternative conceptual perspective in the literature of risk tolerance. Under this framework, emotional responses influence decision making. For example, people in good moods tend to view risky situations as less threatening than those in bad mood.

Measures of risk tolerance can be divided into six methods: personal or professional judgment, heuristics, objectively, single-item questions, risk scales, and mixed measures (Grable 2008). Research shows that personal and professional judgment is not accurate (Roszkowski and Grable 2005). A heuristic is a simplified rule that applies to investment decisions. Many heuristics are not reliable (Grable 2000). The objective measure is to use outcome measures of investments. Examples include the ownership of stocks (Fan and Xiao 2006) or the share of risky assets to wealth (Riley and Chow 1992; Xiao et al. 2001). Because investment outcomes may be influenced by many factors and human attitudes and behaviors are only part of the factors, this measure may also not be accurate.

A commonly used single-item measure is in the Survey of Consumer Finance. The item asked the risk-taking question related to financial returns. The single-item measure is easy to use and used in many risk-taking studies. However, it is criticized as most consumers responded as zero risk tolerance, which may not be accurate (Hanna and Lindamood 2004) and does not represent the spectrum of financial risk tolerance (Grable and Lytton 2001).

Several multiple-item risk scales have been developed in the last two decades. After comprehensive literature review, Grable and Lytton (1999) conclude that risk tolerance includes three core dimensions, investment risk, comfort and experience, and speculation. Based on these factors, they have developed a 13-item risk scale. Another financial risk scale is developed for American College by Roszkowski (1999). These scales are based on the need of financial planning industry. Other scales are developed under the framework of EUT. These scales asked hypothetical questions based on percentage changes in income such as one developed by Barsky et al. (1997) and an improved version by Hanna and Lindamood (2004).

Risk tolerance may be associated with consumer economic wellbeing in an indirect way. Appropriate risk tolerances matched with appropriate asset allocation and investment strategies would achieve desirable financial goals that contribute to economic wellbeing. Future research is needed to examine the association between risk tolerance and economic wellbeing and relevant mediation and moderation factors.

11.7 Individual Development Account

Consumer savings can be considered an accumulation of financial resources for future consumption. Can low-income consumers save for long-term goals when they worry about their daily survival? Michael Sherraden, a professor of social policy at Washington University, argued yes. In a keynote speech at the annual conference of American Council on Consumer Interests, Sherraden (2000) discussed how Individual Development Account (IDA) emerged as an idea from an academic and transformed into popular policy initiatives. The IDA idea was first proposed in academic papers (e.g., Sherraden 1988) and then in books (e.g., Sherraden 1991). With help of several influential Senators, foundations, and nonprofit organizations, IDA is developed to a popular policy initiative that has programs in over 40 states. Specifically, the USA has implemented matched savings for millions of low-income families, and an experimental test of IDAs has generated policy impacts in the USA and abroad (Center for Social Development 2011).

IDAs are a strategy for the inclusive asset-building policy. The key assumption is that assets change thinking and behavior. IDAs have been introduced as a matched saving strategy to show that the poor can accumulate assets if they, like the middle and upper classes, have incentives and opportunities. IDAs are special savings accounts, started as early as birth, with savings matched for qualified families, to be used for education, job training, home ownership, small business, or other development purposes. IDAs can have multiple sources of matching deposits, including governments, corporations, foundations, community groups, and individual donors. The purpose of IDAs is to lay the groundwork for a large-scale, progressive, asset-based policy, which is likely to take decades (Sherraden 2000).

According to the theory of IDA, low-income consumers can save if appropriate institutional factors are created and effective. Sherraden and his colleagues identify six institutional factors that are critical to encourage the poor to save (Beverly and Sherraden 1999; Sherraden et al. 2003): (1) *access* institutionalized mechanisms of saving; (2) *information* that helps individuals understand the process and benefits of asset accumulation; (3) *incentives* that should be attractive to promote saving; (4) *facilitation* that involves making available mechanisms of contractual saving or precommitment constraints and techniques that make it difficult to choose current pleasure at the expense of future pleasure; (5) *expectations* that are, in IDA, embodied in the monthly saving target and the social pressure of staff and peers; and (6) *limits* that refer to fixed policy and program boundaries or constraints, such as match caps and withdrawal restrictions.

Evaluation research conducted for IDAs suggests some impacts of the initiative. For example, a longitudinal study suggests that IDA participants have significant variations in saving patterns. Participants with highly positive attitudes at both 18 and 48 months had significantly more savings than participants without highly positive attitudes, suggesting that attitudes may influence saving outcomes in IDAs (Han and Sherraden 2009). More importantly, the IDA project has broad impacts on social welfare policies in the USA and beyond. First, IDAs facilitated direct public resource allocation. IDAs were included as a state option in the 1996 "Welfare Reform Act." The federal Assets for Independence Act, the first public IDA demonstration, became law in 1998. Other bills to extend IDAs are regularly before the US Congress. Over 40 US states have adopted some type of IDA policy. Second, IDA changed public mindset about saving by the poor. Today encouraging the poor to save is almost a mainstream idea in the USA and received bipartisan political support. Third, research on IDAs provided informative support for economic policy making in the USA and several other countries. Finally, IDAs stimulated financial innovations by financial institutions to better serve low-income consumers (Sherraden 2008).

IDAs are considered a policy innovation, described as "putting in place a decidedly new way of doing things that is defined in law and regulation, is funded and operational, affects real people at a meaningful scale, and is sustainable" (Sherraden 2000, p. 160). Professor Sherraden can be considered an academic policy entrepreneur. According to him, academic policy entrepreneurship requires the purposeful development of an idea along two fronts, the academic and applied front. Information for researchers and practitioners on IDA and relevant topics can be found on the website of the Center for Social Development at Washington University at St. Louis, Missouri, USA (http://csd.wustl.edu/Pages/default.aspx).

11.8 Summary

Consumer savings can be measured by assets that are an important indicator of consumer economic wellbeing. Another important measure is net worth. Based on research, consumer economic wellbeing measured by assets and net worth has been increased in the last five decades because of many financial innovations in the financial markets. Consumers in all income groups have increased their savings but disparities between income groups also grow wider than before.

Saving motives encourage consumers to accumulate financial resources for short- or long-term goals. Common saving motives include saving for emergency, children's education, and retirement. Unlike economic theories imply, multiple saving motives coexist. Saving goals may be hierarchical along with consumer financial resource levels. Consumers with higher financial resource levels have longer term saving goals.

Saving for emergencies can be considered a short-term saving goal. Most consumers in the USA do not save adequately for emergency funds. Many of them may be rational because they have stable jobs and are confident about the economy regarding labor income. However, consumers with unstable income need to put 3–6 months of income to emergency funds in case of job loss.

Saving for children's education is important for consumers who have children or plan to have children. Because supporting children to attend college is a major expenditure, saving early is important to smooth consumption for families with children in college. Some consumers start early to save for children's education by taking advantage of 529 plans with tax advantages. Some consumers even use retirement accounts to support their children's college education that is undesirable.

Saving for retirement is important for most consumers in the USA because the Social Security system is insecure and most companies now move from offering defined benefit pensions to defined contribution retirement plans (401k or similar plans). Based on national statistics, many consumers have not started work-related retirement plans or do not contribute enough to the current plan. Another issue faced by many consumers is the use of less than rational and optimal approaches to manage retirement investments, which may hurt their long-term return and economic wellbeing.

Risk tolerance is a critical concept in financial planning and economic theory. Many theories and methods are developed to measure this concept. Based on the modern portfolio theory, high risk is associated with high return. To seek high return, consumers need to bear high risk. Risk tolerance can be measured both objectively and subjectively. It may affect consumer economic wellbeing indirectly through some mediator factors.

To encourage low-income consumers to save, IDA has been implemented in many states in the USA. Theoretically assumed, low-income consumers are able to save if appropriate institutions are created and effectively functioned to support this behavior. Also, consumers starting with a certain level of assets may change behavior and be more self-sufficient than before. Evaluation research on this social policy provides some evidence to support these arguments.

References

Allais, M. (1953). Le comportement de l'homme rationel devant le risqué: Critique des potulats et axioms de le'ecole Americaine. *Econometrica, 21*, 503–546.

Ameriks, J. (2000). Using retirement planning software to assess Americans' preparedness for retirement: An update. *Benefits Quarterly, 16*(4), 37–51.

Ameriks, J. (2001). Assessing retirement preparedness with planning software: *1998* update. *Benefit Quarterly, 17*(4), 44–53.

Ameriks, J., & Zeldes, S. P. (2004). *How do household portfolio shares vary with age? Working paper*. New York: Columbia University.

Ando, A., & Modigliani, F. (1963). The life cycle hypothesis of saving: Aggregate implications and tests. *American Economic Review, 53*(March), 55–84.

Barro, R. J. (1974). Are government bonds net wealth? *Journal of Political Economy, 82*(November/December), 1095–1117.

Barsky, R. B., Juster, F. T., Kimball, M. S., & Shapiro, M. D. (1997). Preference parameters and behavioral heterogeneity: An experimental approach in the health and retirement study. *Quarterly Journal of Economics, 5*, 537–579.

Benartzi, S. (2001). Excessive extrapolation and the allocation of 401(k) accounts to company stock? *Journal of Finance, 56*(5), 1747–1764.

Benartzi, S., & Thaler, R. H. (2001). Naive diversification strategies in retirement saving plans. *American Economic Review, 91*(1), 79–98.

Benartzi, S., & Thaler, R. H. (2007). Heuristics and biases in retirement savings behavior. *The Journal of Economic Perspectives, 21*(3), 81–104.

Beverly, S., & Sherraden, M. (1999). Institutional determinants of saving: Implications for low-income households and public policy. *Journal of Socio-Economics, 28*, 457–473.

Bhargava, V., & Lown, J. M. (2006). Preparedness for financial emergencies: Evidence from the Survey of Consumer Finances. *Financial Counseling and Planning, 17*(2), 17–26.

Bi, L., & Montalto, C. P. (2004). Emergency funds and alternative forms of saving. *Financial Services Review, 13*(2), 93–109.

Bogan, V. L. (2014). Savings Incentives and Investment Management Fees: A Study of the 529 College Savings Plan Market. *Contemporary Economic Policy*, 32(4), 826–842.

Bricker, J., Dettling, L. J., Henriques, A., Hsu, J. W., Moore, K. B., Sabelhaus, J., et al. (2014). Changes in US family finances from 2010 to 2013: Evidence from the Survey of Consumer Finances. *Federal Reserve Bulletin, 100*(4), 1–40.

Bricker, J., Kennickell, A. B., Moore, K. B., & Sabelhaus, J. (2012). Changes in US family finances from 2007 to 2010: Evidence from the Survey of Consumer Finances. *Federal Reserve Bulletin*, (June), 1–80.

Brown, J. R., Liang, N., & Weisbenner, S. (2007). Individual account investment options and portfolio choice: Behavioral lessons from 401(k) plans. *Journal of Public Economics, 91*(10), 1992–2013.

Browning, M., & Lusardi, A. (1996). Household saving: Micro theories and micro facts. *Journal of Economic Literature, 34*(December), 1797–1855.

Butrica, B. A., Iams, H. M., & Smith, K. E. (2003). *It's all relative: Understanding the retirement prospects of baby-boomers*. Center for Retirement Research at Boston College, WRP 2003-21.

Campbell, J., Jackson, H., Madrian, B., & Tufano, P. (2010). *The regulation of consumer financial products: An introductory essay with four case studies. Working paper*. Cambridge, MA: Harvard University.

Canova, L., Rattazzi, A. M. M., & Webley, P. (2005). The hierarchical structure of saving motives. *Journal of Economic Psychology, 26*(February), 21–34.

Carroll, C. D. (1997). Buffer-stock saving and the life cycle/permanent income hypothesis. *The Quarterly Journal of Economics, 112*(February), 1–55.

Carroll, C. D. (2001). A theory of the consumption function, with and without liquidity constraints. *The Journal of Economic Perspectives, 15*(3), 23–45.

Carroll, G. D., Choi, J. J., Laibson, D., Metrick, A., & Madrian, B. C. (2009). Optimal defaults and active decisions. *Quarterly Journal of Economics, 124*(4), 1639–1674.

Chang, Y. R., Hanna, S., & Fan, J. X. (1997). Emergency fund levels: Is household behavior rational. *Financial Counseling and Planning, 8*(1), 47–55.

Chang, Y. R., & Huston, S. J. (1995). Patterns of adequate household emergency fund holdings: A comparison of households in 1983 and 1986. *Financial Counseling and Planning, 6*, 119–128.

Center for Social Development. (2011). Inquiry, innovation, & impact: Report to the community. St. Louis, MO: Author.

Choi, J. J., Laibson, D., Madrian, B. C., & Metrick, A. (2004a). For better or for worse: Default effects and 401(k) savings behavior. In D. A. Wise (Ed.), *Perspectives in the economics of aging*. Chicago: University of Chicago Press.

Choi, J. J., Laibson, D., Madrian, B. C., & Metrick, A. (2004b). Employees' investment decisions about company stock. In O. S. Mitchell & S. P. Utkus (Eds.), *Pension design and structure: New lessons from behavioral finance* (pp. 121–136). New York: Oxford University Press.

Choi, J. J., Laibson, D., Madrian, B. C., & Metrick, A. (2009). Reinforcement learning and savings behavior. *Journal of Finance, 44*(6), 2515–2534.

Choi, J. J., Laibson, D., & Madrian, B. C. (2005). Are empowerment and education enough? Underdiversification in 401(k) plans. *Brookings Papers on Economic Activity, 2005*(2), 151–198.

Deaton, A., & Muellbauer, J. (1980). *Economics and consumer behavior*. Cambridge: Cambridge University Press.

DeVaney, S. A., Anong, S. T., & Whirl, S. E. (2007). Household savings motives. *Journal of Consumer Affairs, 41*(Summer), 174–186.
Dynan, K. (2009). Changing household financial opportunities and economic security. *Journal of Economic Perspectives, 23*(4), 49–68.
Fan, J. X., & Xiao, J. J. (2006). Cross-cultural differences in risk tolerance: A comparison between Americans and Chinese. *Journal of Personal Finance, 5*(3), 54–75.
Friedman, M., & Savage, L. J. (1948). The utility analysis of choices involving risk. *Journal of Political Economy, 56*, 279–304.
Godwin, D. D. (1996). Newlywed couples' debt portfolios: Are all debts created equally? *Financial Counseling and Planning, 7*, 57–69.
Grable, J. E. (2000). Financial risk tolerance and additional factors which affect risk taking in everyday money matters. *Journal of Business and Psychology, 14*(4), 625–630.
Grable, J. E. (2008). Risk tolerance. In J. J. Xiao (Ed.), *Handbook of consumer finance research* (pp. 3–34). New York: Springer.
Grable, J. E., & Lytton, R. H. (1999). Financial risk tolerance revisited: The development of a risk assessment instrument. *Financial Services Review, 8*(3), 163–181.
Grable, J. E., & Lytton, R. H. (2001). Assessing the concurrent validity of the SCF risk assessment item. *Financial Counseling and Planning, 12*(2), 43–52.
Han, C., & Sherraden, M. (2009). Attitudes and saving in individual development accounts: Latent class analyses. *Journal of Family and Economic Issues, 30*, 226–236.
Hanna, S. (1989). Optimization for family resource management. *Proceedings of the Southeastern Regional Association for Family Economics-Home Management Conference*, 4–16.
Hanna, S. D., & Chen, S. C. (2008). Retirement savings. In J. J. Xiao (Ed.), *Handbook of consumer finance research* (pp. 35–46). New York: Springer.
Hanna, S., Fan, J. X., & Chang, Y. R. (1995). Optimal life cycle savings. *Financial Counseling and Planning, 6*, 1–15.
Hanna, S., Garman, E. T., & Yao, R. (2003). Projected retirement adequacy of workers Age 50 to 61: Changes between 1998 and 2001. *Profit Sharing*. 1–40.
Hanna, S. D., & Lindamood, S. (2004). An improved measure of risk aversion. *Financial Counseling and Planning, 15*(2), 27–38.
Harness, N., Chatterjee, S., & Finke, M. (2008). Household financial ratios: A review of literature. *Journal of Personal Finance, 6*(4), 77–97.
Hong, G. S., & Kao, Y. E. (1997). Emergency fund adequacy of Asian Americans. *Journal of Family and Economic Issues, 18*(2), 127–145.
Hong, G. S., & Swanson, P. M. (1995). Comparison of financial well-being of older women: 1977 and 1989. *Financial Counseling and Planning, 6*, 129–138.
Huang, J., Beverly, S., Clancy, M., Lassar, T., & Sherraden, M. (2013). Early program enrollment in a statewide Child Development Account program. *Journal of Policy Practice, 12*(1), 62–81.
Huston, S. J., & Chang, Y. R. (1997). Adequate emergency fund holdings and household type. *Financial Counseling and Planning, 8*(1), 37–46.
Johnson, D. P., & Widdows, R. (1985). Emergency fund levels of households. *The Proceedings of the American Council on Consumer Interests 31th Annual Conference*, 235–241.
Joo, S., & Grable, J. E. (2006). Using predicted perceived emergency fund adequacy to segment prospective financial consulting clients. *Financial Services Review, 15*(4), 297–313.
Kahneman, D., & Tversky, A. (1979). Prospect theory: An analysis of decision under risk. *Econometrica, 47*, 263–291.
Keynes, J. M. (1936). *The general theory of employment, interest, and money*. New York: Harcourt Brace.
Kurz, M. (1984). Capital accumulation and the characteristics of private inter-generational transfers. *Economica, 51*(February), 1–22.
Lai, C. W., & Xiao, J. J. (2010). Consumer biases and competences in company stock holdings. *Journal of Consumer Affairs, 44*(1), 179–212.
Lee, S., Hanna, S., & Siregar, M. (1997). Children's college as a saving goal. *Financial Counseling and Planning, 8*(1), 33–36.

Loewenstein, G. F., Weber, E. U., Hsee, C. K., & Welch, N. (2001). Risk as feelings. *Psychological Bulletin, 127*, 267–286.

Madrian, B. C., & Shea, D. (2001). The power of suggestion: Inertia in 401(k) participation and savings behavior. *Quarterly Journal of Economics, 116*(4), 1149–1187.

Malroutu, L., & Xiao, J. J. (1995). Perceived retirement income adequacy. *Financial Counseling and Planning, 6*, 17–23.

Markowitz, H. (1952). Portfolio selection. *Journal of Finance, 7*(1), 77–91.

Mitchell, O. S., Mottola, G., Utkus, S., & Yamaguchi, T. (2006). *The inattentive participant: Trading behavior in 401(k) plans. Working paper*. Philadelphia, PA: Pension Research Council, University of Pennsylvania.

Moore, J. F., & Mitchell, O. S. (1997). Projected retirement wealth and savings adequacy in the Health and Retirement Study. *NBER Working Paper 6240.*

Riley, W. B., & Chow, K. V. (1992). Asset allocation and individual risk aversion. *Financial Analysts Journal, 48*(6), 32–37.

Rodriquez Flores, A., & DeVaney, S. A. (2007). The effect of employment status on households' emergency funds. *Journal of Personal Finance, 5*(4), 67–84.

Roszkowski, M. J. (1999). Risk tolerance in financial decisions. In D. M. Cordell (Ed.), *Fundamentals of financial planning* (pp. 179–248). Bryn Mawr, PA: The American College.

Roszkowski, M. J., & Grable, J. (2005). Estimating risk tolerance: The degree of accuracy and the paramorphic representations of the estimate. *Financial Counseling and Planning, 16*(2), 29–47.

Scholz, J., Seshadri, A., & Khitatrakun, S. (2006). Are Americans saving "optimally" for retirement? *Journal of Political Economy, 114*, 607–643.

Sherraden, M. (1988). Rethinking social welfare: Toward assets. *Social Policy, 18*(3), 37–43.

Sherraden, M. W. (1991). *Assets and the poor: A new American welfare policy*. Armonk, NY: M.E. Sharpe.

Sherraden, M. (2000). From research to policy: Lessons from individual development accounts. *Journal of Consumer Affairs, 34*(2), 159–181.

Sherraden, M. (2008). IDAs and asset-building policy: Lessons and directions. *Center for Social Development working paper*, (08-12).

Sherraden, M., Schreiner, M., & Beverly, S. (2003). Income, institutions, and saving performance in Individual Development Accounts. *Economic Development Quarterly, 17*(1), 95–112.

Souleles, N. S. (2000). College tuition and household savings and consumption. *Journal of Public Economics, 77*(2), 185–207.

Thaler, R. H., & Benartzi, S. (2004). Save more tomorrow: Using behavioral economics to increase employee savings. *Journal of Political Economy, 112*(1, Part 2), S164–S187.

Todd, K. J., & DeVaney, S. A. (1997). Financial planning for retirement by parents of college students. *Financial Counseling and Planning, 8*(1), 25–32.

Turley, R. N. L., & Desmond, M. (2010). Contributions to college costs by married, divorced, and remarried parents. *Journal of Family Issues, 32*(6), 767–790.

Tversky, A., & Kahneman, D. (1992). Advances in prospect theory: Cumulative representation of uncertainty. *Journal of Risk and Uncertainty, 5*(4), 297–323.

U.S. Department of Labor, Employee Benefit Security Administration. (2010). *Private Pension Plan Bulletin: Abstract of 2007 Form 5500 Annual Reports*. Retrieved from http://www.dol.gov/ebsa/pdf/2007pensionplanbulletin.pdf

Von Neumann, J., & Morgenstern, O. (1947). *Theory of games and economic behavior*. Princeton, NJ: Princeton University Press.

Xiao, J. J. (1995). Patterns of household asset ownership. *Financial Counseling and Planning, 6*, 99–106.

Xiao, J. J. (1996). Effects of family income and life cycle stages on household financial asset ownership. *Financial Counseling and Planning, 7*, 21–30.

Xiao, J. J. (1997). Saving motives and 401(k) contributions. *Financial Counseling and Planning, 8*(2), 65–74.

Xiao, J. J., Alhabeeb, M. J., Hong, G.-S., & Haynes, G. W. (2001). Attitudes toward risks and risk-taking behavior of business owning families. *Journal of Consumer Affairs, 35*, 307–325.
Xiao, J. J., & Anderson, J. G. (1997). Hierarchical financial needs reflected by household financial asset shares. *Journal of Family and Economic Issues, 18*(4), 333–356.
Xiao, J. J., & Fan, J. X. (2002). A comparison of saving motives of urban Chinese and American workers. *Family and Consumer Sciences Research Journal, 30*(4), 463–495.
Xiao, J. J., Malroutu, L., & Olson, G. I. (1997). Family cheque accounts and banking deregulation in the US. *Journal of Consumer Studies and Home Economics, 21*, 25–39.
Xiao, J. J., Malroutu, Y. L. & Yuh, Y. (1999). Sources of income inequality among the elderly. *Financial Counseling and Planning, 10*(2), 49–59.
Xiao, J. J., & Noring, F. E. (1994). Perceived saving motives and hierarchical financial needs. *Financial Counseling and Planning, 5*, 25–44.
Xiao, J. J., & Olson, G. I. (1993). Mental accounting and saving behavior. *Home Economics Research Journal, 22*(1), 92–109.
Yao, R., Hanna, S. D., & Montalto, C. P. (2003). The capital accumulation ratio as an indicator of retirement adequacy. *Financial Counseling and Planning, 14*(2), 1–11.
Yao, R., Xiao, J. J., & Liao, L. (2014). Effects of age on saving motives of Chinese Urban consumers. *Journal of Family and Economic Issues*. Online First.
Yilmazer, T. (2008). Saving for children's college education: An empirical analysis of the trade-off between the quality and quantity of children. *Journal of Family and Economic Issues, 29*(2), 307–324.
Yuh, Y., & Hanna, S. D. (2010). Which households think they save? *Journal of Consumer Affairs, 44*(1), 70–97.
Yuh, Y., Hanna, S. D., & Montalto, C. P. (1998a). Mean and pessimistic projections of retirement adequacy. *Financial Services Review, 9*(3), 175–193.
Yuh, Y., Montalto, C. P., & Hanna, S. D. (1998b). Are Americans prepared for retirement? *Financial Counseling and Planning, 9*(1), 1–12.
Zhong, L. X., & Xiao, J. J. (1995). Determinants of family bond and stock holdings. *Financial Counseling and Planning, 6*, 107–114.

Index

J.J. Xiao, *Consumer Economic Wellbeing*, International Series on Consumer Science, DOI 10.1007/978-1-4939-2821-7

CPI Antony Rowe
Eastbourne, UK
February 21, 2020